PENGUIN BOOKS

A BEGINNER'S GUIDE TO REALITY

JIM BAGGOTT

A Beginner's Guide
to Reality

PENGUIN BOOKS

PENGUIN BOOKS

Published by the Penguin Group
Penguin Books Ltd, 80 Strand, London WC2R ORL, England
Penguin Group (USA) Inc., 375 Hudson Street, New York, New York 10014, USA
Penguin Group (Canada), 90 Eglinton Avenue East, Suite 700, Toronto, Ontario, Canada M4P 2Y3
(a division of Pearson Penguin Canada Inc.)
Penguin Ireland, 25 St Stephen's Green, Dublin 2, Ireland (a division of Penguin Books Ltd)
Penguin Group (Australia), 250 Camberwell Road, Camberwell, Victoria 3124, Australia
(a division of Pearson Australia Group Pty Ltd)
Penguin Books India Pvt Ltd, 11 Community Centre, Panchsheel Park, New Delhi – 110 017, India
Penguin Group (NZ), cnr Airborne and Rosedale Roads, Albany, Auckland 1310, New Zealand
(a division of Pearson New Zealand Ltd)
Penguin Books (South Africa) (Pty) Ltd, 24 Sturdee Avenue, Rosebank, Johannesburg 2196, South Africa

Penguin Books Ltd, Registered Offices: 80 Strand, London WC2R ORL, England

www.penguin.com

First published 2005
4

The author and publisher are grateful to the following for
permission to reproduce material: 'Money', words and
music by George Roger Waters. Copyright © 1973 Roger
Waters Music Overseas Ltd, Warner/Chappell Artemis
Music Ltd, London W6 8BS. Lyrics reproduced by
permission of IMP Ltd. All rights reserved.
Every attempt has been made to contact
copyright-holders. The author and publisher will
be glad to make good in future editions
any omissions brought to their attention.

Set in Sabon 9.5/12.5 pt by
Palimpsest Book Production Limited, Polmont, Stirlingshire
Printed in England by Clays Ltd, St Ives plc

ISBN-13: 978–0–141–01930–7
ISBN-10: 0–141–01930–1

To Mum,
in memory of Dad

Contents

Preface

Where are you right now?

Maybe you're standing in a bookstore, flicking idly through the pages of this book. Maybe you're sitting on a train, or in an airport lounge, killing time. Maybe you're sitting up in bed, reading this as a way of shutting out the mental clamour of your day prior to shutting down.

How do you know any of this is real?

We take the reality of our world very much for granted. And why not? Reality does have this habit of always being there when we wake up in the morning. It remains pretty consistently predictable through the day, and is still with us at night when we drift off to sleep.

This reality has a social dimension – we live and work alongside other people; we make money, we spend money (in bookstores, for example). We get married. We vote in elections.

This reality also has a physical dimension – we live in a world that contains physical objects, such as books, houses, cars, trains, mountains, rivers and trees. These objects give us sensations, of sight, taste, smell, hearing and touch. Underpinning all this is supposed to be a long list of tiny unobservable physical objects that scientists tell us make up the larger objects that we see and interact with. These tiny physical things are molecules, atoms, protons, neutrons, electrons, photons, and many more things besides, all dancing on the stage of three-dimensional space, to the tune of one-dimensional time.

This book is an exploration of reality from the social to the perceptual to the physical level. My aim is to lead you down through these levels in search of something we can point to, hang our hats on and say *this is real*. Organized into three parts, it asks three basic questions. Is money real? Are colours real? Are photons real?

Surprisingly, the answers aren't at all obvious, and many are quite disturbing. At each step the book examines some of the things that have been said about reality by a few of the world's greatest thinkers, from the philosophers of ancient Greece to modern scientists and social theorists, all kept firmly within the bounds of common comprehension.

This is basically a philosophy book. It starts with aspects of social theory and the philosophy of society, takes in classical, classical modern and contemporary philosophy, and ends with what I have always preferred to call natural philosophy, what others might call physics. If you have no background in social studies, or philosophy, or science, do not be alarmed, for you will not need it.

Philosophy is a perfectly natural human activity. We engage in philosophical speculation about the nature of our reality virtually every day. With a little effort, we can analyse and interpret these speculations in ways that help us first to recognize the nature of the problems that might exist with our common-sense conceptions of reality, and secondly to appreciate where some solutions might come from. Most importantly of all, if we can gain enough understanding of the problems and their possible solutions then we can form opinions of our own. So, this is a book for anyone who has ever wondered what is real, and how we know.

My thanks go to those with whom I have discussed both the idea of this book and its content; specifically Peter Atkins, John Blackman, Marsha Filion, Les Naylor and Marga Vega. I'd also like to thank the following for permission to reproduce extended direct quotes from their works or song lyrics: Andy and Larry Wachowski, Peter Gabriel, Roger Waters, Macmillan Ltd, the University of Michigan Press and Warner Brothers. Special thanks go to Jon Turney, my editor at Penguin Books, for asking the question. As usual, any errors and misconceptions found herein are all my fault.

It goes without saying that this book would not have been possible without the love and support of my family.

JEB, Reading, July 2004

PROLOGUE

Follow the White Rabbit

> *. . . Alice started to her feet, for it flashed across her mind that she had never before seen a rabbit with either a waistcoat-pocket, or a watch to take out of it, and burning with curiosity, she ran across the field after it, and fortunately was just in time to see it pop down a large rabbit-hole under the hedge.*
>
> *In another moment down went Alice after it, never once considering how in the world she was to get out again.*
>
> Lewis Carroll, *Alice in Wonderland*

All long journeys, as they say, start with the first step. Our starting point is provided by our common-sense view of what constitutes our everyday reality. Take a moment to stop and think. If you had to note down the key features of your reality, and describe them to a friend or a colleague, what would you say?

Think of green grass, a gentle stream, a blue sky and a bright yellow sun rising above a distant horizon. Think about a typical day in your life. Think of rising in the morning, going to work, striving to earn enough money to pay for the things that make life worth living: a nice home environment, a car, entertainment, a holiday.[1]

You might be mildly troubled. Perhaps there is a sense in which you feel bound by unwritten laws, constrained by invisible conventions that are quite real to you but which, like liquid mercury, you

---

1. Just remember that money can't buy you happiness (although it might make misery more tolerable).

can't quite put your finger on. Perhaps you feel that you have tended in the past to take reality at face value. Maybe you feel that this is a reality not of your making and not of your design, in which you try to exercise what free will you can.

Perhaps the first thing we would want to admit is that reality should be independent of human beings. Reality should surely be independent of our ability to conceive it and form theories about it. The fact that humankind has developed to the point where we can construct elaborate theories about reality should have no bearing on the very existence of this reality. How could reality depend on having someone around clever enough to conceive of it? Did the reality that we know have to wait for some suitably qualified smart alec to come along? With a Ph.D.?

The sun rises, and you get out of bed. You make your way to work, a place full of people which obviously exists independently of your ability to go there. You work all day and return home. You watch the television news, which shows you images of events that have happened in different parts of the world, places that you believe to exist though you have never been there and will probably never go.[2] The sun sets, and you go to bed, confident in your belief that the sun will rise again tomorrow. It seems fairly obvious that people and objects continue to exist 'in reality' when you're not looking at them or thinking about them.

Secondly, we might agree that, whatever reality is, it does seem to be predictable, within recognized limits. Reality appears to be logically consistent. It is hard to conceive a world without rules, a world where anything goes, where things happen for no reason, where the sun might not rise tomorrow.

After several centuries of philosophy and science we have uncovered a large number of 'natural' laws, and we can understand and explain these laws using theories of varying complexity. You will have heard of Newton's laws of motion, and of Einstein's laws of relativity. One of the principal concepts underpinning this consistency is that of *cause and effect*. The sun will rise tomorrow because the earth rotates

2. Kabul, anyone?

on its axis as it moves around the sun. The earth rotates on its axis because . . . and so on and on.

It might also be reasonable to suppose that science has been so successful in the last few hundred years because scientific theories take us *progressively closer to the truth* about reality as it 'really is'. Scientific theories are imperfect in many ways, but can be thought to possess a verisimilitude, a truth-likeness, which increases with each successive generation of scientific development. Perhaps scientific theories can never be the absolute truth but they can have varying levels of truth-likeness that, over time, progressively get closer to the absolute.

Scientists are constantly refining and improving their theories and, as it makes no sense to develop new theories that are less useful than their predecessors, we might be tempted to conclude that these theories develop closer and closer to the 'truth', however this is defined. So, we no longer believe that the sun and stars revolve around a stationary earth, as the ancient Greeks did, because we have found this to be not true. We believe it is more true to say that the earth goes around the sun, as this provides a better description of reality.

Finally, we have to work out what to do about the fact that reality is made up of things we can't see, such as molecules and atoms. But this really isn't so difficult. It is very hard to imagine how our world would work at all were it not for the unseen microstructures at the heart of all matter (including ourselves), and all light. Modern technology would be impossible if we did not first acknowledge the existence of these microstructures. We cannot be easily persuaded that just because we can't see them, they aren't real. No, these tiny bits of matter are there, all right. Unobservable objects really exist and do have real effects. These things feature in scientific theories because they explain aspects of our reality and are as real as trees, bananas or grains of sand.

Now look back over these common-sense conclusions regarding reality. Draw on experiences from your own life. Our starting point is that reality is independent of us, our ability to conceive it and form theories about it. Reality is filled with regularities derived from natural cause-and-effect relationships. Science takes us progressively closer to the truth about reality as it really is and unobservable objects such as molecules and atoms really do exist and have real effects even though we can't see them. Do you agree?

If you have not spent a lot of time poring over the prognostications of philosophers, the chances are that you find all this not only very reasonable, but also rather obvious. You are certainly not alone in this view. If you have already delved into the murky depths of philosophy texts or have read about some of the more bizarre conclusions of quantum physics, be patient. I'll get to you.

Before we can really get started, there are a couple of housekeeping items we need to look at. Roughly two-thirds of this book will deal with levels of reality that are deeply entwined with the workings of the human mind. Sometimes, it may appear that the book has wandered off into the world of mental processes and mental states and has lost sight of its subject. I won't try to make excuses for any unnecessary authorial meanderings, but reality and mind are very closely interconnected, and it will help to spend a little time here on the philosophy of mind by way of preparation.

Theories of the mind come in two basic flavours. There is *dualism*, the theory that mind is very distinct from physical substances, such as water and stone, bodies and brains. There are also various forms of *materialism*, which hold that our mental states (such as thoughts, images or memories) are derived from the physical and chemical processes which occur in our brains. I will make no bones about the fact that I consider myself to be a materialist.

Dualist theories date back to the seventeenth century and are today considered by professional philosophers to be largely discredited (though there are some modern-day advocates). The problem with dualism is that it leaves us with a rather mysterious non-physical 'mind stuff', similar in many ways to the theological concept of the soul, or spirit. In this view, your mind is a 'ghost' in the physical machine that you call your body. The problem is that this ghost must somehow interact with the physical world if minds are to be responsible for making things happen.

If you're not sure why this might present a problem, try the following quick experiment. Place this book down on a table in front of you. Now, without touching it, pick it up using only your mind.

Having trouble?

Now if you pick up the book in your fingers, we can trace this physical act all the way back through your hand, muscles, nervous system and spinal cord to specific signals from a part of your brain called the motor cortex. All this activity takes place in the physical world, involving bits of matter and electrical signals. But now we need to explain how a thought, occurring in a non-physical mind, triggers the signals in a physical brain that lead to action, to bodily movement. This cannot be an interaction describable by any physics that we currently understand. Just how this happens – how the non-physical ghostly mind stuff causes things to happen in the physical world – remains very mysterious in dualist theories of the mind. This is why the philosopher Daniel Dennett has said that accepting dualism is giving up.

Recall the story of the 1990 film *Ghost*, starring Patrick Swayze, Demi Moore and Whoopi Goldberg. The story is briefly this: Sam Wheat (Swayze) is murdered during a robbery. Initially drawn to the white light that signals his path to ascension, he chooses instead to remain on earth as a ghost, to protect his young girlfriend (Moore) from an evil he doesn't yet understand. He has to come to terms with the fact that, as a ghost, he can pass unseen through walls and doors,[3] but cannot interact physically with his environment and therefore cannot communicate directly with his partner. He eventually learns the trick from another ghost: by channelling his emotions and focusing his disembodied, ghostly mind on physical objects he manages to interact with them. Now, whatever it is that he has learned (the film doesn't say) is exactly what is required in dualist theories for a mind to exert direct influence in the physical world.

It would be a mistake to think that dualism is easily dismissed, however. In fact, dualism is insidious. Any theory of mind that tries to bring the act of thinking into some kind of central control room, where perceptions are interpreted, decisions are made and mechanical

---

3. We'll leave aside just how exactly he manages to walk on floors.

levers are pulled, is guilty of a creeping form of dualism. In such a central screening room of the mind, just who is meant to be doing the watching?

Materialists hold the view that mental states are the direct result of physical and chemical events unfolding in the brain and the consequent development of specific brain states. Nerve cells (neurons) fire in different parts of the brain corresponding to vision, hearing, smelling, tasting, feeling, the processing of these sensory inputs in working memory, the retrieval of content from long-term memory, the triggering of both rational and emotional responses and the co-ordination of bodily movement. The relationship between brain chemistry and mental states appears to be very strong. Imbalances in the delicate chemical composition of the brain can result in a variety of mental disorders, such as Parkinson's, Huntingdon's and Alzheimer's diseases, schizophrenia, anxiety, depression and mania.

But there is considerable mystery here, too. We could suppose that the physics and chemistry is all there is, that mental states don't actually exist (no thoughts, no beliefs, no desires, no memories) and there are only brain states – various combinations of neuronal interaction that we interpret for ourselves as mental activity. This is a form of materialism generally known as *eliminative materialism*. A thought, then, does not exist except as a specific pattern of neuronal activity and we invent the idea of mental states as a way of explaining behaviour (ours and others).

An alternative is to take mental states to be the result of some emergent properties of highly complex activity in the brain. A pattern of neuronal activity is in itself not enough to constitute a thought; rather, a thought is a higher-order property of patterns of activity, a little like the properties of water (freezes to form a clear solid at zero Celsius, boils to a vapour at one hundred Celsius) can be thought of as higher-order properties of the sub-atomic particles – protons, neutrons and electrons – that make up the structures of hydrogen and oxygen atoms. Just as it might be very difficult to predict the bulk properties of water using only our knowledge of the properties of protons, neutrons and electrons, so it might be very difficult to predict the properties of mental states from the patterns of firing of individual neurons in the brain.

In this view, if we were able to build a structure with the brain's function and complexity (100 billion neurons, connected together and packed in grey matter with the consistency of cold porridge and weighing about three pounds), then we *might* expect consciousness, self-awareness and mind to emerge naturally.[4]

The fact is that we have various views but as yet no fully functioning scientific theory of the mind. You might worry that this will impair our ability to explore reality properly. Be reassured. It won't.

The second item of housekeeping concerns one particular Hollywood blockbuster movie. This is *The Matrix*, of course; the mother of all reality movies. It starred Keanu Reeves, Lawrence Fishburne and Carrie-Anne Moss and was first released in America on 31 March 1999 – Easter weekend. It cost $65 million to make, grossed a little over $450 million at the box office worldwide, and became a world-wide phenomenon on DVD, a technology that could have been developed for movies such as this. It was followed in 2003 by two further films, *The Matrix Reloaded* and *The Matrix Revolutions*. I will have a little more to say about these sequels later, but for now I want to concentrate on the 1999 original.

There are already several good books about the philosophy and interpretation of the main themes of *The Matrix*, and these are included in the bibliography on pp 241–5. This is not another such book. Rather, this is a more complete exploration of reality and our knowledge of it which draws on some of the themes of *The Matrix* for illustration, at least from the perspective of reality at the social and perceptual levels. The film has little to say about our more scientific understanding of physical reality.

It is not necessary to have seen it to appreciate what I have written here. But it does help to be familiar with the story. Here, then, is the

---

4. This seems to suggest that if we could ever build an artificial brain constructed to mimic entirely the operation of a human brain, then it would become conscious and self-aware all by itself. I think this is fallacious. Human minds do not enter the world fully formed. Exposure to a lifetime's experience of physical and emotional conditions is necessary both to shape the patterns of neuronal connections in the brain and to define the self.

very briefest of outlines. Thomas Anderson works as a software engineer for a respectable company. By day, that is. By night he is a computer hacker with the alias Neo. He is approached by other famous hackers, Morpheus and Trinity, he 'follows the white rabbit' and meets Trinity in a nightclub. We have already seen Trinity in some earlier scenes performing some impossible kung-fu (and wearing some impossibly skin-tight PVC). She offers to help Neo understand the one question that drives him: *what is the matrix*?

Before anything else can be done, Neo is arrested and interrogated by what appear to be FBI agents. Of these, Agent Smith commands our attention. Smith reveals that they (whoever they are) know all about Neo's nefarious activities, and offers him a deal: they will wipe his record clean if he will lead them to Morpheus, whom they brand a computer terrorist. Neo refuses, and some things then happen to him that just can't happen in the real world. He wakes, and imagines he has been the victim of a rather compelling nightmare.

The next day he is contacted again by Trinity, some more impossible things happen to him and she takes him to see Morpheus. Morpheus offers him a choice of two coloured pills:

This is your last chance. After this, there is no turning back. You take the blue pill, the story ends, you wake up in your bed and believe what you want to believe. You take the red pill, you stay in wonderland. And I show you how deep the rabbit hole goes.

Neo takes the red pill, and discovers that his entire life and the lives of everyone he has ever known have been an illusion. In reality, his body is trapped in a capsule of viscous pink nutrient. A cable feeds electrical signals to the base of his skull, and thence to his brain. Everything he has ever experienced in his life has been a virtual reality simulation called the matrix,[5] fed to his mind by a belligerent machine intelligence which, though originally created by humans, has now turned on them and is using human bodies as sources of energy. The matrix is used to keep passive the minds and hence the bodies of virtually the entire human race.

5. This term was first applied to virtual reality by the author William Gibson who, with his 1984 novel *Neuromancer*, helped to found the 'cyberpunk' genre. Many of the themes explored in *The Matrix* can be found in Gibson's novel.

Because he has woken from the matrix, Neo is no longer useful as an energy source and is flushed from the capsule by the machines, down a waste pipe into the sewers. In a very real sense, Neo is born. Here, he is picked up by the real Morpheus and Trinity and taken on board their hovercraft, the *Nebuchadnezzar*. In the real world they are members of the last remnants of human resistance, with its base at the core of the earth. These resistance fighters routinely hack into the matrix, where they have learned to bend its programming rules – hence the 'impossible' kung-fu.[6] The Agents are, in fact, sentient programmes developed by the machines to track down and destroy the resistance movement.

It turns out that Neo is potentially very important. Morpheus believes he is 'The One' – a Christ-figure[7] who can completely break the rules of the matrix and bend it to his will, and ultimately deliver victory in the war against the machines. Neo is sceptical. Back in the matrix he visits the Oracle, a kindly woman with the gift of foresight who has predicted the return of The One, but before anything further can be discovered the entire crew is betrayed to the Agents by a Judas-figure, fellow crew member Cypher.

Cypher has grown weary of life in the real world, and wants to have his mind returned to the matrix, as '. . . someone important. Like an actor'. Morpheus is captured. As commander of the *Nebuchadnezzar* he holds in his mind the access codes to the resistance movement's mainframe computer. With these codes the machines can completely destroy the last vestiges of human resistance. Neo and Trinity rescue Morpheus from a secure government building in the matrix, in one long cinematic adrenalin-rush, and Neo realizes that he is indeed 'The One'.

If you've seen the movie you will know that I've eliminated numerous embellishments, sub-plots and references to Buddhist philosophy. But for the purposes of this book, the key elements are all here.

The Wachowski brothers set out to make an 'intellectual action movie'. Whether or not they achieved this, the film certainly achieved

6. And, alas, we learn that Trinity's impossibly skin-tight PVC clothing isn't real either.
7. Actually, Buddha-figure would be a better description.

cult status and got people talking. This is not something the average Hollywood blockbuster product tends to do.

The interpretation of the sequels, *The Matrix Reloaded* and *The Matrix Revolutions*, is being actively debated by several internet communities. These sequels are much less concerned with our understanding of the nature of reality, however. Rather, they address other philosophical issues such as free will and the nature of human love, and evolve a storyline that continues to fuse together Western and Eastern religious mythologies. A complete interpretation of the entire trilogy is the subject of another book.[8] For now, let's think of *The Matrix* in the context of the original.

Now, where did that rabbit go?

---

8. Matt Lawrence's *Like a Splinter in Your Mind*, published by Blackwell in 2004, is an excellent example.

PART ONE

Social Reality
or
Is Money Real?

I

Hyperreal

*It used to be said that we are what we eat. And then people,
maybe a little more fashion-conscious, would say: No, you
are what you wear. Or, you are what you read. But we
would say, in this millennium, you are what you watch.*

Peter Gabriel, *Growing Up Live*

Are you living in a dreamworld?

No, you respond, perhaps rather indignantly. You are certain in your conviction that you can tell dreams from reality. You are not in any doubt. You are not a dreamer.

And yet, there is a compelling argument that you're not living in a real world at all. You are living in a world created almost entirely by the modern consumer society of which you are a part. You work hard and earn money just so that you can pursue a dream in a world fabricated almost entirely from your fertile imagination, aided by a relentless barrage of images from the media, in which it has become impossible to distinguish image from reality, style from substance. Some would argue that this is a world that has become a simulation, one in which all contact with or reference to the 'real' reality beneath has been lost. A world where, according to the postmodern social theorist Jean Baudrillard, the images and the style and the substitutes have become more real to us than reality itself. This is *hyper-reality*.

It is the first stop on our journey in pursuit of the rabbit.

*

For sure, this is still a world of physical things, of houses and cars and planes and credit cards. But these physical things have become much less important than the images they create, or the messages they send. So, we no longer drive a car, we drive the ultimate driving machine, one with *Vorsprung durch Technik*, hand-built by robots. We board a plane and fly the friendly skies, with the world's favourite airline. We use a credit card because it's everywhere you want to be, your flexible friend, and you don't leave home without it. We buy consumer goods that are designed for living, made with us in mind, through the appliance of science. We talk to our friends on the phone because it's good to talk, and the future's bright. We drink probably the best lager in the world, because it's reassuringly expensive, because it's what your right arm's for and we couldn't give a XXXX for anything else. We try harder. We just do it, because we're worth it and we know where we want to go today.

You will insist that you can tell the difference between reality and the images woven by the marketers, the public relations executives, the government spin doctors, or the news media. But you can't.[1] In every case what you receive is an imperfect representation or a simulation of reality that will be more or less distorted, depending on what's being sold, or the size of the lie. Baudrillard insists that in hyperreality, the representation no longer bears any resemblance to anything that we might otherwise accept to be real.

Modern consumer society runs on a simple principle. We are fed an illusion of what we would want our world to be: a world in which we are more handsome or beautiful, slimmer, more successful, more respected, cleverer, richer, happier. We allow ourselves to become convinced that we can achieve this world if only we buy this car, own this home, this stereo, this mobile phone, read this book, eat this food, drink this beer, use this credit card, fly this airline.

Aspiring to this world keeps us in wage slavery, functioning as

---

1. Here's an interesting fact, courtesy of John Stauber and Sheldon Rampton's *Toxic Sludge is Good for You!*, first published in 1995. There are more people employed in the US advertising and public relations businesses than there are journalists. In itself not a particularly important statistic, you might think, until you realize that a large (and growing) proportion of news reports are unedited and undiluted PR releases.

perfect consumer units, to the point where it is no longer necessary to feed us the illusion: we *are* the illusion. Not for nothing is it called the American dream. In the twenty-first century, the dream has become our reality. We are living in a dreamworld.

I'm reminded of a joke.

A senior partner of a global management consultancy company suffering from overwork, stress and nervous exhaustion decides to take an extended holiday. He stays at a tiny Mexican fishing village, a long way off the tourist map. Late one afternoon he finds himself in conversation with a local fisherman. He asks the fisherman about his life.

'Well,' the fisherman replies in halting English, 'I sleep late. Take the boat out in the early afternoon and catch enough fish for my family and some more to sell so that I have money to buy other kinds of food and a little wine. When the sun goes down I join my friends at the local bar and we drink and we talk. Then I go to bed.'

The consultant is intrigued. 'Why don't you get up earlier, go out in your boat a little longer, and catch even more fish to sell?' he asks.

'Why would I want to do that?' the fisherman responds.

'Well, with the extra money you could save up and buy another boat, and employ another fisherman and catch even more fish.'

'So, what would I do then?'

'Well, with the extra money you could continue to buy more boats – maybe a trawler or two – and recruit more fishermen, and before long you would have your own fishing fleet.'

'What then?'

'Then you would have a healthy balance sheet that you could take to a bank or investment company, and you could get financing to buy up other fleets. You could take your company public and trade shares on the New York stock exchange. You could build a fishing empire and then think about diversifying, maybe into the wider agricultural sector or maybe the leisure industry or anything you like. You could become a Fortune 500 company, with your picture on the front of *Forbes* magazine.'

'What then?'

'Well, hey, then you could sell up. You would have a personal fortune. You could live the life of your dreams, with no more stress and worry. You could settle in some little village, sleep late in the morning, maybe take a little boat out to do some fishing and spend the evenings with your friends at the local bar . . .'

The joke highlights the absurdity of some aspects of our modern consumer culture. We struggle to make our way through the reality of our complex social existence, striving to earn enough to buy things we don't need, pay off the mortgage, pay the bills, the school fees, the expensive holidays, and so achieve our world of the imagination, our dream of a simpler existence. In our complex lives, simplicity is bought only at a high price, it seems.

Why? What is it about us and the society we live in that creates this kind of reality?

Let's go right back and start at the beginning.

Evolution through natural selection can be crudely interpreted as 'survival of the fittest', which we take to mean that living organisms best adapted to their environment are more likely to live long enough to procreate and pass their genes to successive generations. In the presence of selection pressures, chance adaptations resulting from random mutations in genetic material can give rise to better-adapted organisms which may then come to dominate a particular ecological niche.

One view has it that *Homo sapiens* is the most successful higher-order species on the planet. Whether you agree with this or not, if nothing else the spread of humankind from its origins on the plains of Africa to virtually every habitable part of the globe signals highly successful adaptation. All of this success is down to the capacities of our brains and, however it is done, the brain's ability to generate an extraordinarily complex mental life.

I like to think that, whatever initial evolutionary advantage was created by the chance adaptations that led to a larger brain, this was more than superseded by the sheer scope and agility of the mind that emerged. Our minds do not need to have anywhere near the sophistication that they possess for us as humans to survive in or even dominate our environment. We do not need such highly developed minds in order to survive. In this view, the richness of our mental life may well be an unintended by-product. All evolution is accident, but our minds may be the biggest accident of them all.

Much of this mental richness is gained from the external world, both the world as we find it and the world that we create for ourselves. Reality in all its variety impresses itself upon our minds: high, snow-capped mountains, gently trickling streams, tall trees, soft, brown earth. But there is obviously more to our mental lives than the passive impression of an external reality resulting from an ability to observe. Here lies the secret. With our highly developed minds we can also have *imagination*.

With imagination we can see things that do not yet exist. We can anticipate things we haven't yet experienced. We can envisage a future yet to come. We can plan.

Our ability to think about how things could be rather than just how things are feeds right back into our external reality. For about 1.4 million years humans have used this feedback to hunt animals, catch fish, gather wild roots, berries and vegetation and build nomadic communities of no more than about fifty people. The transition from hunter-gathering to agriculture led to the establishment of larger societies, and marginalized those small communities that preferred to stick with the older methods.

Humans are social animals, perhaps with an innate biological drive for social interaction. We do not just live in society: we invent society in order to live.[2] The first towns started to appear about ten thousand years ago. With the rise of science, technology and industry in the last few hundred years came the possibility of establishing societies on a vast scale, and our external reality is now filled with cities nestling close to the mountains, bridges over the streams, and carefully tended parks filled with tall trees and soft, brown earth.

Within these physical structures there exist breathtakingly complex social structures. These social structures are founded on a broad array

2. This is a quotation adapted from Maurice Godelier, *The Mental and the Material*, Verso, 1986.

of institutions which purport to provide ready-made solutions to the kinds of everyday problems that most ordinary people face. Humans develop society and society develops an infrastructure to provide education, healthcare, economic management, a system of law, organized religion, defence against other societies, governance and personal support for individuals and families. This infrastructure operates through a cascade of social institutions, such as money, marriage, politics and war, woven into a near-invisible fabric.

It has been estimated that a hunter-gatherer typically needs to expend about one calorie of human energy in pursuit of three calories of food-energy. In a hunter-gatherer society, you are what you eat. With the emergence of food production on an industrial scale, expending one calorie of human energy provides something of the order of five thousand calories of food-energy. With the external environment largely conquered, and where it is no longer necessary to devote great time and effort in pursuit of the things needed to sustain life, the human mind with all its extraordinary sophistication turns its attention to other needs. In a very different but very real sense, we are still what we eat, as the irresistible rise in obesity in America and Britain signifies. But this is not eating to survive, it is eating to feed emotional needs, or eating as a lifestyle choice.

Imagination allied to emotion fosters desire. This can be a biologically driven desire for things: to assuage hunger, to quench thirst, to have sex. It can also be a socially driven desire: to belong, to gain greater self-esteem, to acquire greater status and prestige, to be respected by others.[3] Furthermore, we use our imagination to fend off that most insidious form of torture for the developed mind, boredom. We no longer desire nourishment for our bodies, but for our minds. We demand stimulation and entertainment to provide us with

3. In his book *Status Anxiety*, Alain de Botton defines this as 'A worry, so pernicious as to be capable of ruining extended stretches of our lives, that we are in danger of failing to conform to the ideals of success laid down by our society and that we may as a result be stripped of dignity and respect; a worry that we are currently occupying too modest a rung or are about to fall to a lower one . . . And from failure will flow humiliation: a corroding awareness that we have been unable to convince the world of our value and are henceforth condemned to consider the successful with bitterness and ourselves with shame.'

distraction. We become what we wear, or what we read, or what we watch.

This ability to have emotional and socially driven desires kindled to the intensity of a furnace by a hugely fertile imagination has led to the creation of our consumer society. We now live within a reality that has become a complete invention of our postmodern urban, industrial society and media culture. To some it has become a dreamworld, a hyperreality, no longer based on anything identifiably real.

Think back to the American society of the 1950s. This was a period and a place that witnessed a tremendous acceleration in the development of our consumer culture. Selling goods and services to increasingly sophisticated consumers in a vast American market became so lucrative that companies committed considerable effort and expense to the task of understanding how it works. The disciplines of professional marketing and consumer advertising came into their own.

These companies learned that consumers bring all their rationality *and* their emotional needs to bear on their purchase decisions. Yes, consumer products had to fulfil their physical functions, but so long as these functional requirements were satisfied then there were a whole raft of emotional requirements to be satisfied, too. If these emotional needs could be met successfully and in a manner that could be sustained over time, then extremely valuable brands could be created that were next to impossible for competitors to copy. This was an age that also saw the rise of super-brands, such as Levi jeans, Marlboro cigarettes and Coca-Cola.

These brands could help make consumers feel better about themselves, or create the impression of status and prestige, or earn them greater respect. Recall the styling of the huge American cars from this period, the 'gas-guzzlers'. Many had elaborate tail fins that were an aerodynamic nonsense. Functionally, these fins created more drag and actually slowed the vehicle down. But they gave the illusion of speed, or spoke to consumers of a speed that was more pure or absolute because it was not contaminated or constrained by any physics of the real world, and this was more important to them. Style triumphed over substance.

Any doubts about the power of a super-brand were dispelled in the 1980s, when the Coca-Cola company, one of the most successful of the global consumer marketers,[4] made a near-catastrophic mistake. Faced with declining sales, and unnerved by the results of blind taste tests which showed their archrival Pepsi-Cola to have the better product (the 'Pepsi Challenge'), the Coca-Cola company decided that the time had come to change a product formula that had remained unchanged and locked in a vault for over eighty years. They developed a new, slightly sweeter formula and launched the product in America amidst a blaze of publicity, as New Coke. It was a disaster.

They had lost sight of the fact that most consumers had long ceased to buy their product solely for the taste. They were buying it because it had become an intrinsic part of American cultural identity, with deep emotional links to the American psyche. Changing the product was just plain anti-American. Within weeks of the launch of New Coke, a campaign was begun by consumers to force the company to give them back the original Coca-Cola, to give them back the 'real thing'. They won.

Although the campaigners remarked negatively about the taste of New Coke, this was not, after all, a campaign about taste. The company had not been misled by the results of its blind taste tests. When deprived of knowledge about the brand, consumers chose Pepsi because it had the better taste. What the company had failed to understand was that consumers bought Coca-Cola not because of the taste but because it was Coca-Cola, a total package of physical taste, imagery and emotional satisfaction. Change any one of these and you no longer had Coca-Cola. Changing the taste was tantamount to taking the brand away from consumers.

Acknowledging their mistake, the company backed down and re-launched the original as Classic Coke (and, incidentally, succeeded in not only restoring but increasing their market share).

---

4. Here's another interesting fact. Anyone who cherishes the traditional imagery of Father Christmas – the jolly, fat Santa with the flowing white beard and the red-and-white garb – might like to know that this is a 'tradition' that goes back no further than the 1930s, and a Coca-Cola advertising campaign (red and white being very much part of the company's corporate identity).

With our attention drawn ever more compellingly to brands, the complexity of mass production means that we have completely lost sight of how modern consumer goods relate to the real world. We buy the package of physical functionality and emotional satisfaction without ever stopping to wonder where the physical product has come from, what it is made of, or how it has been put together. We have largely ceased to buy products because we value the use to which we can put them; we buy products because of what they say about us, to ourselves and to others.

Witness the collection of incredibly useful labour-saving modern gadgets you own that are so incredibly useful that you rarely, if ever, use them. We buy the style, not the substance; the brand, not the product. We construct a reality based on models of how we would like that reality to be, not on reality itself.

The rise of the consumer society triggered an explosion of mass communications media. Getting your message across in an ever-more crowded 'information space' was fundamental, not just to consumer marketers, but to anyone who wanted to grab the consumers' attention, including politicians, charities and pressure groups. It has been estimated that today each of us is on the receiving end of a staggering 1,500 marketing messages every day. And we have surely not reached the end of human inventiveness when it comes to ways of channelling messages directly at consumers. In Steven Spielberg's film *Minority Report*, set fifty years into the future, people entering a shopping mall are first recognized individually by their retinal images and then constantly bombarded with marketing messages aimed directly at them, by name, as they walk around.

The basis for exploiting mass media had already been established in the 1930s by, among others, Austrian-born Edward Bernays, the 'father of public relations' or the 'father of spin', a nephew of Sigmund Freud. Bernays was a highly successful publicist, the first to use theories of human psychology and social science to develop persuasive publicity campaigns in what he referred to as the 'engineering of consent'. He was also among the first to use the endorsement of leading opinion-formers and experts in support of his campaigns – often without their knowledge. Exploiting the pact between celebrities hungry for lucrative advertising revenue and the 'oxygen of publicity' and marketers or PR executives seeking celebrity endorsement of their products remains extremely significant in modern marketing.[5]

In his most influential work, *Propaganda,* first published in 1928, Bernays wrote:

The conscious and intelligent manipulation of the organized habits and opinions of the masses is an important element in democratic society. Those who manipulate this unseen mechanism of society constitute an invisible government which is the true ruling power of our country . . . We are governed, our minds are molded, our tastes formed, our ideas suggested, largely by men we have never heard of.

Bernays certainly practised what he preached. In 1929, a group of debutantes marched down New York's Fifth Avenue, openly defying the social conventions of the day by smoking cigarettes in public. They were dubbed the 'torches of liberty contingent'. We might today applaud this early expression of female emancipation, this bold action against a male-dominated society which imposed insidious inequalities through exactly this kind of social taboo. Until, that is, we learn that the march was organized (and paid for) by Bernays, on behalf of the American Tobacco Company. After this stunt, smoking in public rapidly became an acceptable form of social behaviour for women, and sales of Lucky Strike rocketed.

Of course, manipulation of the public mind can be an instrument of evil as much as it is an instrument of publicists and marketers, as Bernays himself discovered in the late 1930s on learning that his own work was being used by Joseph Goebbels to wage a propaganda war against German Jews.[6]

If the principles of manipulation of organized societies were estab-

---

5. It seems that even Bob Dylan, the archetypal anti-establishment singer/songwriter and once the consciousness of his generation, now lends his name to the advertising of Victoria's Secret underwear.
6. Propaganda didn't originate with Bernays. In fact the word 'propaganda' originates with a committee of cardinals set up in 1622 to oversee the propagation of the Roman Catholic faith in non-Christian countries.

lished by Bernays and his contemporaries, then it was the Canadian Marshall McLuhan who some thirty years later established the nature and influences of the mass media. McLuhan argued that each communications medium has its own intrinsic impact which is its unique message, independent of whatever content the medium may be carrying. The message of any medium (or any technology) is the change of scale or pattern of society that results from its use. The introduction of new forms of transportation such as railways or motor cars did not just increase the speed and volume of human traffic, it transformed societies and the ways people live and work in them. So too, McLuhan argued, the introduction of print, radio, film and terrestrial television (and we would now add satellite and digital television, mobile phones, video and DVDs, electronic mail and the internet) has been similarly transforming. McLuhan wrote that it is the 'medium that shapes and controls the scale and form of human association and action.' The medium *is* the message.[7]

We can see this played out in the compelling rise of reality television. Thursday, 11 January 1973 witnessed an event that was to change our relationship with the medium of television, probably forever. The first episode of a new series entitled *An American Family* was broadcast. The series chronicled the day-to-day lives of Bill and Pat Loud and their five children, a typical middle-class American family living in Santa Barbara, California. It was the first 'fly-on-the-wall' documentary (soon followed in Britain by *The Family* and in Australia by *Sylvania Waters*).

The Louds' marriage disintegrated live on television and headed towards divorce. Their eldest son announced his homosexuality. An appetite developed for the voyeuristic examination of the lives of ordinary people, where we could 'get up close and personal' but maintain a detached, clinical distance. Television was the perfect medium for this.

This appetite has given us the *Jerry Springer Show* and *Big Brother* and the genre's many spin-offs. We are now invited to watch a group

7. This is one of many famous 'McLuhanisms'. Among my favourites are: 'Money is the poor man's credit card', 'Mud sometimes gives the illusion of depth', and 'I may be wrong, but I'm never in doubt'.

of 'real' people (sometimes celebrities) attempt to negotiate their way through absurd challenges, internal rivalry and social tensions much as we would watch laboratory rats attempt to negotiate a maze. Television it is, reality it's not.

Whilst reality television is intended as light entertainment, a kind of chewing gum for the mind, Michael Moore's film *Bowling for Columbine* is (at least in parts) a more thoughtful and thought-provoking examination of the darker influence of the medium of television. The film is an investigation of American gun laws and gun culture and their relationship with the Columbine high school massacre. The film targets prevailing gun laws and the American constitutional right to bear arms, but these appear strikingly less important in determining the incidence of firearms-related deaths in America than a culture of fear and prejudice, fed relentlessly by news media obsessed with violent crime: 'if it bleeds, it leads'. Against a background of falling rates of violent crime in Britain, the public perception is nevertheless that society is a more dangerous place than ever. When asked to justify their perception, many will refer to things they have seen on television, forgetting that they were watching fictional drama. They have lost sight of the difference between reality and invention.

Does the media hold up a mirror to modern society and its culture, and passively reflect it back to us? Or does the media hold up a lens so distorting that it contributes to and reinforces the invention of a hyperreality, a virtual reality with no foundation in the real world?

In *The Matrix*, we first meet Neo late one night alone in his apartment. It is the apartment of a computer geek, filled with the junk of modern information technology. He has fallen asleep in front of his computer, oblivious to the music blaring in his ears from a pair of headphones. He is woken when his computer starts to write messages to him. He tries to stop the messages but it becomes clear that he is no longer in control of his computer.

The screen tells him to 'Follow the white rabbit', then: 'Knock, knock, Neo.' There comes a knock at the door, and the screen goes blank. Not sure if this experience was real or part of a dream, Neo opens the door to Choi, and some of Choi's friends. Choi has come to buy some illegal software. Neo reaches for a book, *Simulacra and Simulation*, by Jean Baudrillard. The book is indeed a simulation, being nothing more than a hollow fake. Inside Neo keeps a collection of computer disks, all of which we assume hold illegal programmes. He picks one out and hands it to Choi.

Few who saw *The Matrix* will have heard of Baudrillard or post-modernism. The book itself appears so briefly on screen that it is hardly possible to identify it.[8] And yet Andy and Larry Wachowski, the scriptwriters and directors, were obviously seeking to make some subtle point. In addition to many months of kung-fu training, Keanu Reeves was also asked to study *Simulacra and Simulation* in preparation for the part of Neo. When Morpheus finally introduces Neo to the 'real' world, a charred relic of an otherwise familiar late twentieth-century cityscape huddled beneath a blackened sky, Morpheus refers to it as the 'desert of the real', a Baudrillard phrase.

Specific reference to Baudrillard is made in the shooting script of the original movie. At one point Morpheus says: 'You have been living inside a dreamworld, Neo. As in Baudrillard's vision, your whole life has been spent inside the map, not the territory.' This reference did not make it from the shooting script into the movie's cinema or DVD release.

So, who is Baudrillard? What does he have to say about reality that the Wachowski brothers wanted to acknowledge through these references?

We measure the success of a simulation in terms of the extent to which it resembles the reality it is simulating, the extent to which we can tell the difference between reality and simulation. According to Baudrillard, a first-order simulation is one in which an imperfect representation is

8. One of the pleasures of DVD technology is the ability to freeze a specific frame. When Neo opens the book in the middle to retrieve the disk, the hollow section appears in a chapter 'On Nihilism'. The real book is much shorter than the fake (and does not therefore have the capacity for such a large hidden compartment) and the chapter appears at the end, not in the middle.

rendered. Examples might include a novel which attempts to create a mental world for the reader that represents or reflects the real world but leaves much still open to interpretation, or imagination. It could be a painting which, no matter how artistically accomplished, is still a two-dimensional representation of a real three-dimensional scene. Or it could be a map which shows us where everything is in relation to everything else but still suffers from the fact that it is a two-dimensional representation (drawn to scale) of the surface of a sphere.

A second-order simulation is one that so perfectly resembles reality that it could be mistaken for reality itself. The starting point for Baudrillard's essay 'The Precession of Simulacra', which is included as the first chapter in *Simulacra and Simulation*, is a fable told by the Argentine poet and philosopher Jorge Luis Borges. This fable, *On Exactitude in Science*, concerns an Empire whose map-makers strive for perfection:

In time, those Unconscionable Maps no longer satisfied, and the Cartographers Guilds struck a Map of the Empire whose size was that of the Empire, and which coincided point for point with it.

The cartographers produced a full-scale map of the territory of the Empire so accurate that it was no longer possible to tell the difference between the territory and the map, between the real and the simulation. The fable continues to tell of further generations of cartographers who rejected the usefulness of this map. They cast it aside and left it to rot in the 'Deserts of the West', where it remained, in tattered ruins.

A third-order simulation, then, is one that *no longer has a basis in anything real*. This is hyperreality. It is a virtual reality without reference to reality, a map for which there is no territory. And, Baudrillard asserts, this is what has become of the modern consumer society within which we live out our lives. Society is an abstraction, a virtual reality without reference, a hyperreality, with no basis in anything we can discern to be real.

It is the generation by models of a real without origin or reality: a hyper-real. The territory no longer precedes the map, nor does it survive it. It is nevertheless the map that precedes the territory . . . that engenders the territory . . . It is the real, and not the map, whose vestiges persist here and there in the deserts that are no longer those of the Empire, but ours. *The desert of the real itself.*

Baudrillard uses two examples from American culture and modern American political history to highlight the nature of hyperreality. These are Disneyland and the Watergate scandal.

Disneyland in California (or Disneyland in Paris or Tokyo or Walt Disney World in Florida) is an enclosed world of childlike imagination. It is fantasy theme-park entertainment on a grand scale, the 'happiest place on earth', derived in part from the themes and characters of children's fairy tales, as interpreted and adapted to suit modern tastes. It is a place to take children, though many adults visit without the excuse of children in tow.

Disneyland is not real in a multiplicity of ways. Most obviously the buildings – such as the fairy-tale castle – are clearly exaggerations of real buildings that will never be found in this form in the real world. Most adults who visit the attraction speak of Disneyland's dream-like quality and its marvellous attention to detail. The image is not spoiled by the intrusion of real-world practicalities. A dead light bulb, for example, is just never seen. Either bulbs are replaced before they expire or they are instantly replaced so as to create the illusion of a perfect world. There is no litter. Should any customer drop litter, it is removed almost immediately by a seeming army of Disneyland employees armed with long-handled dustpans. The levels of personal service inside Disneyland are extraordinary, and most adult visitors will have some tale to tell of the experience of excellent service.

The unreality of Disneyland is not Baudrillard's point, however. The real point about Disneyland is that the purpose of its picture-book unreality is to disguise the fact that it is America itself that is hyperreal.[9]

9. Of course, Disneyland theme parks are now also established in Europe and Japan, with another to come in Hong Kong. But (as most French citizens of a certain intellectual persuasion will tell you) these reflect American cultural hegemony as much as anything.

Disneyland exists in order to hide that it is the 'real' country, all of 'real' America that is Disneyland . . . Disneyland is presented as imaginary in order to make us believe that the rest is real, whereas all of Los Angeles and the America that surrounds it are no longer real, but belong to the hyperreal order and to the order of simulation.

Baudrillard uses the example of Watergate in a similar argument. During the 1972 presidential election campaign, officials of the Committee to Re-elect the President were involved in a break-in at the offices of the Democratic National Committee, at the Watergate building in Washington, DC. A number of administration officials resigned, some were later convicted of offences related to an attempted cover-up. The incumbent, President Richard M. Nixon, denied involvement, but was subsequently caught on tape actively seeking to derail the investigation. Nixon resigned in August 1974 to avoid almost certain impeachment.

This undeniable evidence of corruption in the Nixon administration was not, Baudrillard says, the real scandal of Watergate. The scandal is that government is fundamentally unprincipled and immoral. The purpose of Watergate was to provide an instance in which rare and aberrant wrong-doing by an elected government is uncovered, and the guilty punished, in order to sustain the illusion that wrong-doing by an elected government is rare and aberrant. Nixon's resignation 'to begin a process of healing' allowed the American public to draw a line under the scandal and re-establish faith in the moral principles of democratically elected officials (and, in turn, the moral principles of the society that such officials represent). Like Disneyland, the purpose of the obvious 'unreality' of Watergate is to disguise the fact that in hyperreality no such moral principles exist. With no territory to relate to, the map establishes its own landmarks.

This, then, is one sub-text of *The Matrix* and of Cypher's betrayal. The virtual reality simulation of the matrix is a metaphor for the hyperreality of modern American society (and, more widely, of modern consumer society everywhere). Our perceived reality of existence in society is based on models, or maps, not the real world itself.

Neo takes the red pill and is 'liberated' from his previously unconscious existence within this prison for his mind. He is woken from the
American dream. It is no coincidence that life in the real world
aboard the *Nebuchadnezzar* is cold, harsh and brutal. It has a gritty
realness.

This interpretation of the matrix should not, in my opinion, be
taken too literally, which is why I prefer to think of it as a sub-text.
Remember, in Baudrillard's definition, a third-order simulation has no
basis in *any* reality. Waking from hyperreality does not entail waking
into anything that can be considered to be more real, as there is no
reality. There can be no red pill to free us from Baudrillard's vision.
However, in *The Matrix*, the division between the real world and the
virtual reality simulation of the matrix is made clear both in the script
and cinematographically, through the use of different lighting effects
and filters. Waking from the matrix does imply waking into the real
world.

Some have argued that the close identification of the matrix with
hyperreality breaks down owing to the fact that, consciously or not,
society creates hyperreality for itself, whereas the humans imprisoned
in the matrix have virtual reality forced upon them. This is resolved in
The Matrix Reloaded, when it becomes apparent that humans have
indeed been given a choice at the 'near-unconscious level'.

A much stronger criticism is that the Wachowski brothers have
tried to raise awareness of Baudrillard's rather pessimistic postmodern critique of consumer society using the very vehicle – a
money-spinning Hollywood blockbuster full of violent action
spectacle and computer-driven special effects – that appears to be
such an integral part of modern consumer society. The live action
films (and the computer games, and the animated movie, and the
book spin-offs) form a package directly targeted at young, thrill-
seeking consumers.

But still, if you wish to raise awareness of some interesting ideas
concerning modern society and the nature of our social reality,
where better to place them than in a movie franchise destined to
reach millions? The message is channelled through a favoured

medium of popular culture because that's where the people are.[10]

Perhaps the Wachowski brothers want to do no more than challenge our thinking. When Cypher cuts a deal with Agent Smith, he requests that his body be re-inserted into a capsule in the power plant, that his memory be erased and that his mind be returned to the matrix, as someone important, such as an actor. Trinity reminds him that the matrix isn't real, but Cypher disagrees. He believes that the matrix can be more real than the real world: 'I'll go back to sleep and when I wake up, I'll be fat and rich and I won't remember a goddamned thing. It's the American dream.'[11] Cypher has concluded that what matters to him is not the physical world, but the mental world. He will happily sacrifice his body to the machines in order to live what he considers to be a more fulfilling mental life.

Cypher's actions have sparked numerous philosophy class debates about the blissfulness of ignorance. Given a free choice, what would *you* do? Live in the cold, harsh artificial light of the real world, 'eating the same goddamn goop every day'? Or, like Cypher, would you prefer to go back to sleep, all memory of the real world erased, be rich and famous and live out the celebrity lifestyle of your dreams?

Think carefully before answering.

On the one hand, Baudrillard's rather pessimistic vision is a dead end. We may have no difficulty recognizing hyperreality as this, after all, is where many of us live and work. Spend even a small amount of time working within the culture of a large company, or an academic institution or in the presence of celebrities and you will get a very strong sense of what a truly hyperreal existence might be like.

On the other hand, Baudrillard is a postmodern critic, not a philosopher in the traditional sense. His task is to bring to our attention and criticize aspects of modern society, and seek to make us think differently about some of the things we take for granted.

10. With acknowledgements to William Irwin, editor of *The Matrix and Philosophy*, Open Court, 2002.
11. This quote is taken from the shooting script. There is no reference to the American dream in Cypher's dialogue with Trinity in the cinema or DVD release.

Hyperreality is a kind of social conditioning that leaves us unable to perceive anything beyond the models and the maps. It is not necessarily concerned with what does, or does not, exist. We might conclude that there is still a physical world, of mountains and streams and trees and earth. We might also conclude that there is still a social world, of people, cities, money, marriage, politics and war. There is nothing in Baudrillard's writings to shake our initial conviction that there does exist a reality independent of our ability to conceive it or form theories about it.

Think again about your own life. About how sometimes, particularly when you're feeling a bit low, it might sometimes seem as though you're trapped. Society is a structure that supports but it also imprisons. You may be a fully paid-up, card-carrying member of society but you might also feel that there is so much of your life that you do not control. Not so much in the sense of the big things, like politics or the law. Most ordinary citizens do not feel so passionately about government policy or perceived injustice that they take a more active role in these things (and nor should they). You may have never been a 'joiner', of a political party or protest group. You may have never marched or attended a rally. No, this sense of not being in control is in some way much more about the little things, the mundane, the everyday. Perhaps you can't quite put your finger on it.

Think about the social microstructure that makes a day in your life possible. Without the idea and the rules of driving perhaps you would not be able to get to work. Without the idea of buying and selling, there would be no company and no office for you to go to, or factory for you to work in. Without the idea of money there would be no purpose in you going to work, anyway. None of these ideas could work unless very large numbers of people agreed with them or believed in them. They require an astonishing level of co-operation. Yet, at no time in your life have you ever been asked if you agree with the idea of money, or if you believe in it or are prepared to co-operate in its use.

There are endless debates in Britain about currency, about whether the government should forsake the pound in favour of the euro, but this is different. This is all about economic policy and the form that money should take, not the very idea of money itself. How, then, can there be consensus in society for social institutions such as money without anyone ever giving consent? It just seems to happen all by itself.

But *how* does it happen? What is the nature of these social institutions and how do they work?

2

Living in a Material World

Money, so they say, is the root of all evil today.
But if you ask for a rise it's no surprise that they're giving
none away . . .   Pink Floyd, *Dark Side of the Moon*

There is a scene in *The Matrix* which opens with Agent Smith staring out of an office window. He asks the imprisoned Morpheus to marvel at the beauty and the genius of the matrix: 'Billions of people just living out their lives . . . oblivious.'

The city outside the window is Sydney[1] but most of the location references in the film are to Chicago, the Wachowski brothers' home town. It doesn't matter. Stand in contemplation in the midst of the rush-hour in any large city – London, Paris, New York, Rio de Janeiro, Kuala Lumpur – and observe the press of people hurrying to get to work, the steady crawl of traffic. Absorb the sights, sounds and smells and, as Agent Smith suggests, marvel at the beauty and complexity of our human social structures. We go to work. We earn money. We spend this money on life's necessities and on life's distractions. We get married. We have children. We elect politicians to represent us in government. Elected governments make laws. The laws are enforced by the police and judicial system. Governments declare wars. And so on, and on.

If you imagine a world in which you have never existed (and you are a reader who, like me, has not to date had a particularly significant

1. It is actually a huge photograph of Sydney, called a translite, with giveaway landmarks such as the Harbour bridge obscured by additional buildings.

influence on world events) then you might be able to convince your-self that these social structures continue to function without you pretty much the same way they function with you. If you did not exist, people would still go to work. People would still get married. Governments would still be elected. Alas, governments would still declare wars. This lends credence to the idea that these elements of social reality are indeed part of something that is independent of you, or me. Societies are formed from millions or billions of individuals, just living out their lives as Agent Smith observed. Remove one indi-vidual and little appears to change.

Or does it? Whatever they may be, societies are constructed from individuals. These individuals are not inanimate objects conforming to brute statistical laws.[2] Individuals have minds and, by their very nature, these minds are intensely private, personal places. On the surface, my mind would appear to be principally about me. My thoughts are mine alone. All these impressions of the city and its wider social structures might indeed be marvellous, but they are all still impressions created in my mind and without my mind there is a sense in which they cease to exist.

In his book *The Construction of Social Reality*, the American philo-sopher John Searle sets out a theory of social institutions based on three fundamental building blocks. The first of these is the use by society of physical objects (natural or man-made) to serve social func-tions. We take whatever physical object we can find or make and assign it a social function. A river becomes a boundary between territories. A band of precious metal becomes a wedding ring. A rectangular piece of paper made from cotton fibre becomes money (a twenty-dollar bill, perhaps).[3] As a result of being assigned a social function, these physical objects gain a certain *status* in society.

2. Science fiction fans might recall Isaac Asimov's *Foundation* trilogy, based on the idea that the behaviour of a future galactic-scale society is predictable in much the same way that the behaviour of bulk materials can be predicted from the statistical properties of their component atoms or molecules. The idea of a 'physics of society' is actually taken quite seriously: see, for example, Philip Ball's *Critical Mass*, published in 2004.
3. Actually, dollar bills are about three parts cotton fibre and one part linen, with a security thread of polyester. I tell you this just in case you were interested.

Searle is careful to distinguish between objects that are assigned certain status functions which are not immediately obvious from their physical constitution and appearance and other objects (such as a screwdriver or a chair), whose social functions are more immediately apparent. We will return to this point later.

The second building block is the development and use of a system of rules that make possible what Searle calls institutional 'facts' derived from these status functions. The river counts as a boundary between territories when the geographies of the territories are defined, drawn on a map and formal border controls are established. A band of precious metal counts as a wedding ring in a marriage ceremony when the ceremony is presided over by someone recognized in society as qualified to perform marriage ceremonies, and when the appropriate words are uttered: 'With this ring . . .' So long as it carries the appropriate printed marks and is issued under the authority of the United States Treasury, the rectangular piece of paper counts as a twenty-dollar bill when purchasing your morning coffee and newspaper.

The third building block is the mechanism by which collective recognition and acceptance of the status function and its rules are derived. The river counts as a boundary when the people on either side recognize it and accept it as a boundary and observe the rules pertaining to the relevant border controls. The band of precious metal counts as a wedding ring when you, your spouse and the rest of society recognize that you are married and accept your observance of the rules of marriage. The piece of interestingly decorated paper counts as a twenty-dollar bill when you and the guy working the Starbucks counter recognize it and accept it to be legal tender.

Choose any social institution from the bewildering complexity of our everyday lives and, Searle argues, you will find the assignment of a status function, rules that constitute the institutional facts that are derived from the status function and collective recognition and acceptance of the status function and the rules of its use.

Are all social functions underpinned by physical objects? It's hard to think of one that isn't. Money is signified by interestingly decorated pieces of paper. Marriage is signified by bands of precious metal and patterns of ink on a piece of paper that we call a marriage certificate. Of course, there is much more to the social institution of marriage than simply the physical objects and their assigned functions. Marriage also requires the performance of certain acts: we need to say 'I do', and to observe the rules of marriage. But even a speech act has a physical result, in terms of compressions and rarefactions – sound waves – in the air. I might like to run through a marriage service in my mind and to think that I'm married to Jennifer Aniston, but the truth is that I'm not. Beneath every assigned function, no matter of what kind, we expect to find physics in some form or another.

It is fairly obvious that some physical objects fulfil their social functions principally by virtue of their physical nature. They function as we need them to because of what they are. The river that functions as a boundary might be wide, deep and turbulent, making unregulated passage across the boundary very difficult. But the boundary could also be a narrow stream, affording very easy passage from one territory to the next. Or it could be just be a series of markers. Its function as a boundary then depends firmly on the existence of rules governing the boundary (perhaps people are not allowed to pass either way except through recognized border points) and on the recognition and acceptance of it as a boundary.

Many social functions are fulfilled using objects that have no physical relation to the function being fulfilled. I'm not sure what the actual value of a rectangular piece of paper made from cotton fibre is, but I can guarantee you that it is worth a lot less than twenty dollars. How, then, do we come to accept that it *is* worth twenty dollars?

The historical development of money amply illustrates the assignment of a status function in virtually all the different ways this is possible.[4] Barter emerged as a natural and essential form of trade as soon as humankind developed primitive social skills and people realized that they could get things they wanted from others by giving them things they themselves didn't want, or need, in a fair exchange. More sophis-

4. This brief history of money is drawn largely from Jack Weatherford's excellent book *The History of Money*, published by Three Rivers Press in 1997.

ticated forms of trade emerged with the growth of the first civilizations and the first merchants. Our present-day language is littered with references to this kind of trade. The word *salary* comes from the Latin word for salt. *Impecunious* (meaning an habitual state of having very little or no money) can be traced to a Latin word meaning 'wealth in cattle'. The American slang word *buck* derives from trade in the skins of North American deer.

Whilst barter proceeded very successfully, it also had its drawbacks. We might sympathize with the nineteenth-century French opera singer whose payment for a performance on some tiny islands in French Polynesia was three pigs, twenty-three turkeys, forty-four chickens, five thousand coconuts and lots and lots of fruit.

The real problem faced by anyone trading goods is that, when all the haggling has been done, different commodities don't always command value in integral multiples of each other. I might judge that my beautifully crafted bow is worth a bit more than your three pigs, and you're not prepared to cut the leg off a fourth in order to make up the difference. One solution developed by the Aztecs was to use cacao beans as a way of equalizing the value of an exchange. These beans were a form of primitive commodity money. Other examples include amber, beads, cowrie shells, drums, eggs, feathers, gongs, hoes, ivory, jade, kettles, leather, mats, nails, oxen, pigs, quartz, rice, salt, thimbles, umiaks, vodka, wampum, yarns and zappozats.[5] It would be a mistake to think that we no longer use this kind of commodity money in 'civilized' society. In times of great political and economic uncertainty commodity money returns, as revealed in the early 1990s by the use of Levi jeans and Marlboro cigarettes in the Soviet Union.

Commodity money has obvious advantages and disadvantages. If amassing a lot of commodity money didn't make you happy, you could always use it for something else, or eat it. But the units of commodity money were not uniform and were not always durable. When Croesus, the king of Lydia in what is now Turkey, minted coins of silver and gold in around 640 BC, he revolutionized commerce, paved the way for the first retail market, amassed an immense fortune and so

5. Look it up, like I had to. This list is taken from *A History of Money*, by Glyn Davies.

discovered the possibility of highly conspicuous consumption. Money became *the* medium and *the* message. It completely transformed the societies of the early Mediterranean world, first in Greece and then in Rome. Silver coins minted in 269 BC by the Romans bore the image and the name of the goddess Juno Moneta, from which the word money is derived.

It was not to last. Nero not only fiddled while Rome burned, he fiddled with the size of his coins and their silver content, in an attempt to stave off a monetary crisis brought about by a massive trade imbalance. With the collapse of the Roman Empire around AD 476, Europe descended into feudalism and coins became much less important. Society reverted to a more primitive form, in what we now call the Middle Ages. The stability required for the re-emergence of coins was established by the formation of the first major banking systems, first by the Knights Templar in the twelfth century, then by families from northern Italy in the fourteenth. Seeking to avoid the appearance of profiting from lending money (still very much frowned upon by the Church authorities), the Italian banks introduced bills of exchange, which became a kind of paper money. Instead of trading with large and unwieldy bags of gold coins, merchants could deposit the coins at the bank and use the bills of exchange in their place. In this way the banks also increased a supply of money that was otherwise limited by the supply of silver and gold.

Paper money was used in China from the first or second century AD, but this was abandoned in the fourteenth century. Various attempts to issue paper money in Europe and America in the eighteenth century, often in attempts to finance either foreign adventures or the resolution of significant domestic problems, were confounded by greed and mismanagement. More paper money would be issued than could be backed by a reserve of precious metals, ultimately making the money worthless.

The establishment of paper money had to await the relative stability of the British Empire during the reign of Queen Victoria. Money issued by the Bank of England was backed by a 'gold standard', first adopted in 1717. The notes issued by the Bank of England since 1883 carry a promise to pay the bearer the value of the note. Payment would originally have been in gold.[6] In effect, gold was the world currency.

But this was not to last, either. The predilection of the rulers of European nations for foreign adventures led eventually to World War I.[7] It was impossible for the European nations to finance war on this kind of scale based on the amounts of gold they had in their reserves. They simply printed more money, declared its value by fiat, and removed their currency from the gold standard. Franklin Roosevelt applied the same solution but to a different problem. He removed the US dollar from the gold standard in 1933 in an attempt to stimulate the economy after the Wall Street crash four years earlier. By 1937, the gold standard was history. Inflation, virtually unknown under the gold standard, was set to become an economic disease of late twentieth-century society.

The legacy of Germany's defeat at the end of World War I and the punitive reparations demanded of it fostered the social climate that made World War II possible, only twenty-one years later. Shortly after D-Day in June 1944 the representatives of forty-four nations gathered in New Hampshire to debate the financial systems of a post-war world. The Bretton Woods agreement,[8] ratified in 1946, bound their currencies to the US dollar and thence to the value of gold, and at the same time created the World Bank and International Monetary Fund. Exchange rates were not permanently fixed under this agreement: occasional devaluations were allowed so that individual nations could fix their balance of payments problems.

6. The wording 'I promise to pay the bearer on demand the sum of . . .' first appeared on English banknotes in 1855 and remains unchanged to this day. However, if you try to return a note to the Bank of England all you will get in exchange is more banknotes. I actually phoned the Bank of England to confirm this.

7. Serbian nationalists assassinated Archduke Franz Ferdinand, heir to the throne of the Austro-Hungarian empire, in Sarajevo on 28 June 1914. Although Emperor Franz Josef was not overly fond of his heir, Austria-Hungary chose to implicate the Serbian government in the assassination and use the episode as an opportunity to strengthen their influence in the Balkans. A veritable spider's web of treaties and alliances between European nations and Japan meant that what might have been a limited war between neighbouring countries became a global conflagration. The United States entered the war in 1917.

8. Bretton Woods was the name of the hotel in which the meeting took place. I guess the delegates thought better of naming the agreement after their location, near Mount Deception.

The resulting stability enabled unprecedented economic growth through the 1950s and 1960s. But then in 1971, facing a funding crisis for America's own foreign adventure in Vietnam, Richard Nixon finally cut the tie with gold and allowed the US dollar to float freely relative to gold and other currencies. Attempts were made to restrict exchange rate fluctuations within a narrow range but a second devaluation of the dollar in 1973 triggered the demise of any attempt at management. Currencies were left to float freely.

Money entered a new level of abstraction, with exchange rates determined as much by emotional factors as on rational economic facts. Democratically elected governments could keep their citizens happy by creating more money to finance trade imbalances, just as Emperor Nero had done, usually at a cost to the value of their currency. Today the market in currency is the largest market in the world.

Still further abstraction was to come. Diners Club introduced a charge card in 1950, American Express followed in 1958. At around the same time the Bank of America introduced a credit card (which became Visa in 1977). Barclaycard followed in 1966 and in 1967 the City Bank of New York introduced a credit card that eventually became MasterCard. Plastic credit cards enabled a fantastic growth in the money supply. In effect, people could borrow money from the future to pay for the things they wanted today. This both unleashed and fed an enormous appetite for consumer goods. It also facilitated the building of unprecedented levels of personal debt, particularly in America and latterly in Britain.

The introduction of electronic payments systems in the mid-1970s has fostered a virtually cashless society. Aside from small change required for small transactions (such as buying my morning coffee and newspaper from the guy on the Starbucks counter), money is nothing more than the records of the numbers of dollars that I either own or owe. Baudrillard might say that money has become hyperreal.

Increasing demands for secure methods of making payments via the internet may yet create a new kind of money that exists only in cyberspace.

*

This rather potted history of money is actually a history of the use of physical objects to serve a status function. The transition from cowrie shells and zappozats to gold and silver was simply a matter of consistency and convenience in the choice of tokens. Gold served as a basis for money, as money itself or as the ultimate reference for its value, for over two and a half thousand years. It might be tempting to think that, with the introduction of fiat money (or money by government decree), the rise of plastic and the spread of electronic transactions, there are forms of money that no longer depend on the physical world for their existence.

But this is not so. There are still magnetic imprints on the rectangular pieces of plastic, or patterns of phosphorescence on the computer screen, or patterns of ink on the pieces of paper sent to you by your bank and your credit card company. If it were not for this physical realization or expression of money, there would be nothing to prevent me from simply thinking that I'm not only married to Jennifer Aniston, but I'm also as rich as Croesus (or Bill Gates). Alas, no amount of thinking on my part will change the social fact of my account balance.

If we take the view that the physical world exists independently of us, then this dependence on some kind of physical object, realization or expression might then lead us to think that the assigned functions also have an existence independent of our minds. But this is also obviously false. Money ceases to be money when there are no minds to think of it as money. All we have are interestingly decorated pieces of paper, or meaningless magnetic imprints on rectangular pieces of plastic.

Think about *un-earth*. This is what the world would be like if there had been no accident of evolution leading to human beings capable of conscious thought, self-awareness and complex social interaction. It is at once beautiful, a totally natural world unsullied by human interference, excess or wastefulness. But at the same time it is not beautiful, as there are no creatures on the planet to be conscious of its beauty. This is truly a world of high snow-capped mountains, gentle streams, tall trees and soft earth. It is a world of rivers and of rock and of metal (but not precious metal, for there is nobody to value the metal as such). Without people with minds, however, there are no boundaries, no wedding rings, and no money.

We become aware of a significant difference between objects in the physical world, of mountains, streams, rivers, trees and earth, and objects to which we have assigned a status function. With no minds on un-earth to observe it or have thoughts about it, a mountain is still a mountain. There is nobody to call it a mountain, of course, but this would seem to make no difference to the physical fact of its existence and constitution. However, a twenty-dollar bill is no more than a piece of interestingly decorated paper without minds to think of it as a twenty-dollar bill in the context of buying and selling or storing value.

We tend to assign function and purpose to objects almost unconsciously. This goes for many objects in the natural world as well as both natural and man-made objects that we use to serve social functions. We might not expect to find purpose in many natural objects such as a mountain, a tree, or a stone, but we are so compelled by the idea that we sometimes mistakenly look for purpose where it clearly cannot exist.

Modern science is founded on the principle that there exist some fundamental, causal relationships in nature that we can begin to understand in terms of natural laws. When this kind of thing happens then this other kind of thing tends to happen immediately afterwards, and we say that this thing causes that thing. But there is no function or purpose to be discovered here.

For example, gravity is a physical force of attraction between bodies of material substance and, as such, it has no purpose. This might not cause you much pause for thought, so let's bring the point closer to home. Your heart consists of two upper chambers (atria) and two lower chambers (ventricles) and four valves, the tricuspid, pulmonary, mitral and aortic. The muscles contract and relax, the valves open and close, thereby pumping blood around your body.

But your heart has no function or purpose. It is a mechanical construction of living tissue that causes blood to flow in a regulated manner. When we start to ascribe a function or purpose to gravity (useful for keeping your feet on the ground and for indicating which way is up) or your heart (good for keeping you alive), we start to impose our own specifically human sense of values on the natural world in order to make judgements of usefulness or goodness. We slip into teleology, the idea that these natural objects conform to some kind of original design principles, perhaps drawn up by nature's grand architect. In principle, science needs no such assumption.

According to Searle, in assigning function to natural objects in this sense, what we are really doing is nothing more than identifying causal relationships. But our sense of function and purpose is so ingrained in our perception, thinking and language that it is enormously hard to resist conclusions such as 'the function of a heart is to pump blood'. As soon as we draw such a conclusion it brings with it a whole raft of consequences. In *The Construction of Social Reality,* Searle writes:

This is shown by the fact that a whole vocabulary of success and failure is now appropriate that is not appropriate to simple brute facts of nature. Thus we can speak of 'malfunction', 'heart disease', and better and worse hearts. We do not speak of better and worse stones, unless of course we have assigned a function to the stone.

The point that Searle is making is that the assignment of all function, whether natural or social, depends on the existence of conscious minds with the ability to judge the relative value of an object in relation to some activity – minds that can judge success or failure, goodness or badness. *Take the minds away and all function disappears.*

Though fraught with difficulty and frustrated by a number of false starts, the emergence and acceptance of paper money nicely illustrates Searle's second building block of social reality. The rules that allow a social act to be performed based on a status function (such as paying for something with money) actually constitute the institution. In terms of its purely physical constitution, a twenty-dollar bill is just not worth twenty dollars. Assigning to it the status of representing twenty-dollars' worth of value requires that it first be printed in a very specific way on a very specific kind of paper by the 'money factory', the American Bureau of Engraving and Printing. However, a piece of a specific kind of paper printed in a specific kind of way by the money factory is not in itself enough to constitute money. To be money with a certain value it must be endorsed by the American government, backed by the strength of the American economy and collectively recognized and accepted by all who seek to use it as money. In other words, it must count as legal tender and be recognized as holding a certain value in an exchange.

The rules are constitutive rather than just conventions. In fact, the conventional design of American currency is undergoing changes. A new twenty-dollar bill was introduced in October 2003 as part of a programme entitled 'the new colour of money', and features background colours different from the old green and black.[9] A new fifty-dollar note was issued in September 2004, and a new ten-dollar note is due in 2005. The appearance of the notes is just a convention, but the assignment of their status as money is based on rules. Searle uses an analogy from chess to make this clear. The rules of chess dictate how the pieces can be moved, and anybody not moving the pieces according to the rules is not playing chess; but the design and appearance of the chess pieces is a matter of convention.

Rules, as they say, are made to be broken, and the fact that these are social rules rather than social conventions is signified by the fact that they can be broken.[10] The changes to the design of American currency are being made primarily to combat the escalating use of digital technology in counterfeiting. The new designs have a watermark and security thread and make use of ink that changes colour as the note is tilted under the light.

There is a further important point that Searle makes about constitutive rules. To apply them requires abstract symbolism, almost entirely in the form of language. Some objects that have been assigned a social function exhibit this function directly in their physical constitution and appearance. Take the example of a chair. If you had never seen a chair before and there was nobody around to tell you what it is or what it does, it would nevertheless be possible for you to figure out its function without recourse to language. Play long enough with a chair and there's a chance that you'll eventually work out that it is for sitting on. But if you had no concept of money there is no way you

9. The old designs will continue as legal tender.
10. In contrast to what we acknowledge to be physical cause-and-effect rules expressed through natural laws, which we take to be unbreakable until such evidence has accumulated that may force a revision of these rules.

would be able to tell the status and function in society of a twenty-dollar bill. Play all you like with a twenty-dollar bill and a tall skinny latte, but you'll never figure it out. Searle writes:

Suppose I train my dog to chase dollar bills and bring them back to me in return for food. He still is not buying the food and the bills are not money to him. Why not? Because he cannot represent to himself the relevant [relationships to certain expectations and obligations]. He might be able to think 'If I give him this he will give me that food.' But he can't think, for example, now I have the *right to buy things* . . .

Think back to the river that serves as a boundary. Let's assume it is easy to cross. The people on either side might come to accept that they can never cross it as a result of some form of conditioning, resulting perhaps from a long tradition passed down the generations. They would not necessarily know why they must never cross it, they just never do because their fathers never did, and their fathers before them never did, and so on. But the river is now functioning as a very different kind of boundary. It has become almost a physical boundary, one that it has become impossible to cross because the people just don't do that, they don't behave in that way. It functions as a boundary in the social sense when people understand that crossing the boundary is a matter of rights and obligations established by mutual recognition and agreement with their neighbours. This requires language of some kind.

Any doubt about this last point should be dispelled by reference to another joke.

Three monkeys are kept in a cage. One day, the monkeys awake to discover that a small platform has been placed inside their cage, and a banana has been suspended a few feet above the platform. One of the monkeys quickly figures out that he can reach the banana if he climbs on the platform. As he does so, the other two are sprayed with ice-cold water. It becomes apparent to them that when any one of them attempts to reach for the banana, the others are subjected to some very unpleasant treatment. By mutual acceptance or by force, the monkeys collectively learn not to reach for the banana.

When is it clear that the monkeys have understood this new rule about reaching for the banana, one of them is replaced by a new monkey. The new arrival has no appreciation of the rule, and immediately attempts to reach for the banana. Much to his surprise, he is attacked by his fellows in the cage. Without understanding why and without ever directly experiencing the icy water treatment, the new monkey quickly comes to understand that he must not reach for the banana.

One by one, all three of the original monkeys are replaced. Now none of the monkeys have ever experienced the icy water, yet they all understand that they should not reach for the banana. The joke is intended to illustrate how the culture of a large company works.

By the time all three monkeys have been replaced by new ones, the rule about reaching for the banana has been acquired by socially impressed conditioning. Acquiring this rule has not required language and does not involve any sense of understanding of rights and obligations towards the banana.

The conclusion is, perhaps, rather obvious. A social institution such as money is a creation of a society of people. It is based on objects found or manufactured in the physical world but it works by virtue of people assigning to these objects the status of money, by the development of (language-based) rules by which these objects are understood to be money, and through a mechanism for establishing collective recognition and acceptance that these objects are indeed money (we will come to this last building block in the next chapter).

On un-earth, without people or society, there are no status functions (no functions at all, in fact), no language and no constitutive rules and so there can be no money. Without minds, money isn't real, at least in the way we defined our common-sense reality at the beginning of the book.

So what? The obvious fact that money does not exist when there are no people around doesn't alter the conviction you might have that money still continues to exist independently of you. Perhaps we are having to dilute our first assumption, that reality is independent of all human beings capable of conceiving it and forming theories about it, but then we didn't really mean this to apply to social institutions such as money. Did we?

You might prefer to conclude that you believe in the reality of money because we all believe in it, and your belief is contingent on everybody else's. If tomorrow everyone you met was to refuse to accept your twenty-dollar bill because, for whatever reason, they no longer believed it to be money, then you might wonder what on earth had happened but after a while it would be pointless for you to resist. You would come to believe that it wasn't money either.

It takes many individuals, you might argue, all with minds of their own, to make a society. And yes, individuals think their own private thoughts that are primarily about 'me, myself, I'. But society is about 'we'. Surely, social institutions such as money, marriage, politics and war are derived from the interaction of many individual minds and can't all just be in your head?

Oh, but they can. And they are.

3

Me, Myself, . . . We

Great minds think alike.   Anonymous

The third building block of social reality is the collective recognition and acceptance of the use of objects to serve status functions and the rules of their use. The trouble is, it is not at all clear how such collective recognition and acceptance is established. Yet it happens routinely, unconsciously and without effort. Understanding how this can happen will ultimately allow us to appreciate how it is possible for social reality to be constructed such that it exists only in your head.

To see why there might be a problem, picture the following scene, which could take place in an any office in any city, on any business day.

Alice paused for the first time in about twenty minutes. She had come to the end of the summary she had worked on into the depths of the previous night. She had nothing left to say.

Bob shifted uncomfortably in his seat.

He had sat quietly throughout. Alice had been quick to note that he had not given his usual pensive nods of agreement, as he had always done before. He wouldn't meet her eyes.

'Look,' said Alice, 'I know what you're thinking . . .'

Now this is, of course, palpably untrue. This might be a familiar scene, and even a familiar statement, but of course there are no circumstances under which Alice could know what Bob was really thinking.

There are no real life Nick Marshalls or Miles Muldoons.[1] Professional 'mind readers' can no more read minds than professional magicians can do real magic.

Yet even though we don't know what any of this is about, we can quickly backfill the story. Whatever it is, Alice is proposing something that Bob doesn't like. She appears to have known beforehand that he wouldn't like it and this is now confirmed through his reticence and in his body language. They have obviously worked closely together in the past, and she is prepared for Bob's objections. She probably rehearsed her responses to them as she drafted the summary. Although she can't have true knowledge of what is going on in Bob's mind, in a very real sense she *does* know what he's thinking.

This kind of social interaction is a fundamental part of our everyday lives – our 'lived reality' – and an essential building block of social institutions such as money and marriage. My ability to ascribe value and social function to a piece of interestingly decorated paper (such as a twenty-dollar bill) would appear to create an association in my mind and my mind alone. Clearly, this same association must be created in the minds of everyone in society if the concept of paper money is going to work, if money is to be an element of social reality. The fact that I believe this piece of paper to be worth twenty dollars gains me nothing whatsoever unless you too believe it to be worth twenty dollars. It is obvious that this not only happens but it happens apparently without our noticing.

How? If I have no access to anybody else's mind, and nobody has access to my mind, then how does 'me' become 'we'?

Here, at least, there is one saving grace. Social reality is built on mental content, not mental processes *per se*, so our ability to understand how this reality is created in our minds does not depend on having to

---

1. Nick Marshall is the character played by Mel Gibson in Nancy Meyers' film *What Women Want*. Marshall is involved in a fluke accident which gives him the ability to read women's minds. Miles Muldoon is the central character of Jonathan Karp and Seth Weinstein's musical comedy *I Know What You're Thinking*. Muldoon is a phobic tour guide at the United Nations who, after being rendered unconscious by being pelted with Guatemalan melons, develops an ability to read people's minds.

hand a fully worked out theory of mind. We need to focus our attention more on what we think about, not so much on how the thinking is done.

If you do stop to think about it, then you will quickly come to the conclusion that thinking is always thinking about *something*. From your first waking moment to the moment you drift into the unconsciousness of deep sleep, your mind is busy with thoughts that are always about things. These things might be objects in the physical world: mountains, streams, lakes, trees, houses, cars. They might be people: your wife, husband, children, work colleagues, boss, subordinates, the prime minister, the president, the dictator, the terrorist. They might be entirely imaginary: wizards, elves, dwarves, hobbits, unicorns, terminators, replicants, Agents. They might be states of affairs: the house is mine, the car is cheap, the boss is stupid, Gandalf is great. Try to imagine having a thought that is not about something.

This aspect of mental content, this 'aboutness', is referred to by philosophers as *intentionality*. We can extend this notion beyond the straightforward activity of having passive thoughts to include much more active states of believing and desiring. I have beliefs about things. I have desires for things. I also have emotions – love, joy, happiness, hope, sorrow, anger, fear, despair – about or directed at things.[2]

Intentionality means more than just intending things, such as I intend to buy a house or you intend to steal a car. Intentionality is the ability of a conscious mind to represent to itself physical objects, people and states of affairs (real or imaginary).

But it is still only about me and my thoughts. This might be a good starting point, but we are still far from understanding how to get from 'me' to 'we': how individual intentionality becomes the collective intentionality required to construct social reality. This is an essential bridge from things that go on only inside my head to a commonality of things that go on inside our heads whenever we participate in a

2. Although it is thought to be possible to possess some emotional states that are not directed in this way, such as a general feeling of anxiety, for example.

social act, such as buying a newspaper or getting married. Without this bridge, there can be no society.

One possible solution is to reduce everything to individual intentionality. As there are no real mind readers, it seems reasonable to accept that my beliefs and desires are mine alone. I can never know your beliefs or desires, since I can't read your mind. But, of course, I can form beliefs of my own about your beliefs and desires.

Time to return to Alice and Bob.

Remember, Alice believes that Bob doesn't like what she has written in her summary, even though Bob hasn't actually said anything. Bob's mental states are private to Bob and therefore unobservable and unknowable to anyone but Bob, so where does she get these beliefs from? From a cursory analysis of their situation, we would say that Alice derives these beliefs from her *empathy* for Bob, her ability to represent Bob's mind to herself based on a kind of 'folk psychology'. There are two ways in which this empathy can arise. Either she has formed a theory of her own about how Bob's mind works based on long observation of his behaviour as they have worked together, or she has used her own innate mental processes to 'put herself in Bob's shoes' and 'see the world through Bob's eyes'.

The first of these possibilities generally goes by the name of the *theory theory*. The theory that Alice forms about Bob's mind is not a complete scientific theory, as we learned earlier that no such theory is available yet. But it is nevertheless a theory with a pseudo-scientific rationale.

The theory theory suggests that Alice develops her own theory about the circumstances that have in the past caused Bob to have certain mental states – joy, happiness, sadness, anger. These mental states have been expressed by Bob through certain types of external physical behaviour: perhaps he whoops with joy, smiles when he is happy, hangs his head when he is sad and goes red in the face when he is angry. Alice uses her theory to connect circumstances with behaviour and Bob's unobservable mental states bridge the gap between the two. When *this* happens, Bob tends to do *that*. Like a conventional scientific theory, her theory has been developed and refined following a long series of observations of Bob, and this enables her to predict how he will react to new circumstances in the future.

The second possibility is called the *simulation theory*. In this theory, Alice calls upon her understanding of her own self in simulating the states likely to be developing in Bob's mind. She literally pretends to be him, putting herself into the set of circumstances that he faces, generating a set of beliefs and desires that she believes Bob possesses and then running all this through her own mental processes in order to understand how he is likely to react. She can then interpret why certain circumstances make Bob whoop with joy or grow red-faced with anger, because she herself knows how she would react in these different circumstances and she knows what it is to be joyful and angry. When *this* happens to her, she tends to do *that*, and assumes (perhaps with suitable modification) that Bob would do much the same.

Not sure? Try the following test.

Suppose that Alice and Bob have left the office to head for the airport. They are setting out on journeys to different final destinations but have discovered that their planes leave at about the same time. They have therefore agreed to share a taxi. It is early evening. The taxi gets stuck in heavy traffic, and they arrive at the airport thirty minutes late. On arrival, Alice learns that her flight departed on time and she has therefore missed it by a sizeable margin. Bob learns that his flight was, in fact, delayed, but the gate has just this minute closed and he is unable to board. Who is more upset – Alice or Bob?

If, like the 96 per cent of experimental subjects exposed to this test, you think that Bob is more upset, then ask yourself why. Chances are you think that Bob would be more upset because you know that you would be the more upset if you were in his place.

The theory theory is detached and rational and appears to depend for its successful application on a long acquaintance with the target subject, in this case Bob. Obviously, the more exposure Alice has had to Bob's behaviour under as wide a variety of circumstances as possible, the more accurate her theory is likely to be and so the more accurate her predictions of his future behaviour. In contrast, the simulation theory appears more instinctive. It is not necessary for you to have had a long acquaintance with Bob to guess that he is likely to be the most upset on learning that he has just missed his plane. All you need is the ability to imagine yourself in the same position, and perhaps even call on your own direct experience if you have ever narrowly missed a flight.

In the simulation theory, all you need is the history of your own experiences and individual intentionality, combined with the assumption that Bob's mind works in many ways like yours. You can apply the simulation to someone you've never met. In fact, you can apply it to fictional characters that don't even exist. You do this every time you read a novel.

Until relatively recently, it has not been possible to say which of these theories of human empathy is right. Indeed, your initial reaction might be to assume that it will never be possible to understand what really goes on. But in the late 1990s, a team of Italian neuroscientists obtained evidence for the existence of what have become known as *mirror neurons* in the brains of macaque monkeys. It was subsequently established that humans have these mirror neurons as well. These neurons are active when we observe someone performing an activity, and they literally mirror the neuronal activity in the target subject's brain.

For example, in some of the most recently reported experiments, seven men and four women were exposed to pictures of human faces expressing different emotions – happiness, sadness, anger, surprise, disgust and fear – whilst simultaneously undergoing brain scans. Their scans revealed that their emotion centres were far more active when asked to generate internal representations of the pictured emotions than if they were asked simply to observe them. Representing to ourselves the happiness of another involves triggering neurons that mirror those active in the brain of the happy person.

Through empathy we mimic an observed activity subconsciously in our brains without actually performing the activity itself. The test subjects in the above experiment were not asked to reproduce the facial expressions on their own faces; they were asked merely to represent these expressions to themselves in their minds. A mechanism has been identified which inhibits the neurons responsible for bodily movement, so we don't end up comically aping our observed subject (although I defy anyone to watch the dental torture scene in John Schlesinger's *Marathon Man* without physically wincing). Our ability to put ourselves in an observed subject's position is hard-wired in our brains. This is seemingly unassailable evidence in favour of the simulation theory.

The origin and development of mirror neurons can be argued from an evolutionary perspective. There can be little doubting the survival advantages of a brain system that allows a species to anticipate the reactions of fellow species members. The more accurately we can represent to ourselves the mental states we see visibly portrayed in the behaviour of others the more we are able to adjust our own responses in relation to others' likely future behaviour. This might lead us to share another's joy or happiness, offer deeply-felt consolation for another's sadness, or even prepare to defend ourselves from another's wrath.

This is not an entirely uncontrollable biological activity. By recognizing how others might empathize with us, we can deliberately seek to create desired mental states in others by manipulating the way we interact with them. Perhaps one of the best examples of this was Bill Clinton's use of his own characteristic body language, his 'body tells', to create the impression of genuine acceptance of wrongdoing and deep regret over the Monica Lewinsky affair.[3] The impact was so powerful it even had some members of his audience in tears. This is not to say that his regret was not genuine, although our judgement should, perhaps, be informed by the knowledge that Clinton is a past master of this kind of non-verbal communication and emotional manipulation.

The possibility of empathy based on a simulation of other minds provides an important first step in the process of getting from 'me' to 'we', from individual intentionality to collective intentionality. But is this enough?

Empathy can certainly help us to align our mental states, such that we are 'thinking alike' or 'thinking with one mind', but what we are really trying to do is build collective intentionality from individual intentionality. This would seem to commit us to an endless stacking of

3. See, for example, *The Book of Tells*, published in 2003 by the UK's *Big Brother* resident psychologist Peter Collett.

beliefs on top of beliefs. I start with my beliefs. It then becomes necessary for me to form beliefs about your beliefs. You start with your beliefs. You then form beliefs about my beliefs. In order to get anything done it would seem that I now have to form beliefs about the beliefs you have about my beliefs, and so on and on, *ad nauseam*. This is a bit like those comic episodes involving bluff and double-bluff: 'But he doesn't know that I know that he knows that I know . . .'

This is sometimes referred to as higher-order intentionality, but in his theory of social institutions Searle rejects the idea that collective intentionality can be reduced to individual intentionality plus beliefs about other beliefs. He regards collective intentionality to be biologically primitive and a characteristic of higher-order species, humans and animals. The existence of mirror neurons might be taken to indicate just such a biologically primitive capability, but if mirror neurons do no more than help us to form beliefs about what's going on in other minds then they do not fit Searle's bill.

What Searle is saying is that intentional states that are about 'we' are just as much a feature of our minds as intentional states that are about 'me'. We are social animals. The fact that the content of my mental processes is mine alone does not necessarily imply that it can only ever be about me and me alone. I can have intentional states that are about *us*: 'we-intentions' that are about us doing things, as well as 'me-intentions' that are just about me doing things.

Searle points to pack hunting among hyenas as one among many possible examples of co-operative behaviour resulting from biologically primitive collective intentionality.[4] The pack brings down prey that may have been very difficult for one hyena to bring down by acting alone. Each hyena knows what it must do as part of a team focused on a collective intention and this intentionality is instinctive: a hyena does not stop to ponder on the beliefs of the other hyenas in the pack before committing itself to action and fulfilling its role in going for the kill.

---

4. There is a difference between pack hunting and co-operative hunting. Pack hunting involves multiple members of the pack working together as a team to bring down prey, whereas co-operative hunting may involve relatively few animals, typically with one making the kill. Hyenas do occasionally pack hunt, but wolves may have provided a better example.

If collective intentionality cannot be derived from individual intentionality plus beliefs about another's beliefs, and we want to avoid the idea that somehow our minds are all connected in some kind of collective consciousness or 'world spirit' (a nice idea perhaps but one for which we have no evidence), then arguing that individuals have we-intentions still leaves us asking questions about how this happens.

There are at least two further essential ingredients. These are intimately linked, but for clarity I will try to treat them separately. The first is that, even if collective intentionality is regarded as biologically innate, precisely how it is developed and used is derived entirely from learning and experience. The second ingredient is that minds connect within a social network of collective intentions forged through communication.

It seems clear that empathy and the development of a capability for collective intentionality have to be developed and refined when young. Arctic wolf pups are oblivious to the intricacies of pack hunting and often spoil the hunt completely by running directly for the prey. In their first summer, at about eight weeks old, they will join the hunt and learn the ropes, eventually taking their place in the pack when they are sufficiently mature. The desire to have 'we'-intentions may be primitive to the young pup, but the precise form of these intentions must be developed in order for the pup to take its proper place in the social order of the pack.

Similarly, any parent knows that small children have a tendency to perceive a universe organized entirely for their own benefit, with themselves firmly at the centre. Children begin life as instinctive pre-Copernicans. Their world is predominantly 'me, myself, I'. This is doubtless a survival instinct in an otherwise entirely helpless being. At around two years, this selfishness knows virtually no bounds. This is a time of temper tantrums and immense frustration as children gradually learn to accept that they can't have everything they want. It is tempting to think that a young child's mind is almost completely filled with 'me'-intentional states, the only thing that matters to the child is how all those objects out there relate to them, their needs and desires.

The influential Swiss psychologist Jean Piaget concluded that young children are incapable of empathy, based on their inability to imagine a scene from a perspective completely different from the one that confronts them.[5] Nevertheless empathy, perhaps of a primitive kind, appears to be innate even in very young children. This empathy may be expressed only in terms of responses to the overt happiness or the pain of a child's caregivers. It develops as the child becomes more self-aware and socially aware, and it develops under the instruction of caregivers who teach the child to feel guilt when they inflict pain or suffering on others, and to avoid such guilt by becoming more aware of other people's feelings. Empathy is not the same as collective intentionality, but may be a necessary prerequisite for it.

Note that having these mental states does not require that they first be put into words, as intentionality precedes language. A child will rely on the parents (and especially the mother) for the empathy and precise form of collective intentionality that the child lacks. In time, with the right kinds of development opportunities, the child learns to take account of the feelings, needs, desires and beliefs of others, develops the ability to have fully formed collective intentional states and enters society as a fully rounded individual. This is no place to have a debate about nature vs. nurture in bringing up children, but few will deny the importance of nurture in the development of a young mind ready to take its place in society.[6]

This transition is aptly summarized in an episode of the American sitcom *Friends* by the character Phoebe Buffay:[7]

5. This is Piaget's 'three mountains' experiment. A child is shown a picture of a mountain range and asked to describe the view from the perspective of a doll, positioned on the opposite side. Piaget took the child's inability to put themselves in the doll's position as evidence for the absence of empathy. Such experiments have subsequently been shown to be flawed. When challenged to respond to different hypothetical social rather than spatial situations, evidence for empathy in young children does emerge.

6. Nature – interpreted to mean what a child brings into the world in the form of genetic inheritance – cannot be ignored, however. It has been suggested that a lack of functional capability associated with mirror neurons might account for the socially isolating psychiatric disease known as autism.

7. *Friends* series 8, episode 6: the one with the Halloween party.

I love the second grade. It's so much better than first grade, where you don't know what's going on, and definitely better than third grade, you know, with all the politics and the mind games.

By the third grade (if we take the writers of *Friends* literally) children have learned enough folk psychology, they have refined their subconscious simulation techniques and have developed a capability for collective intentionality sufficient to participate fully in the mental world of their society. Let's not get too hung up on precisely when this happens, let's just acknowledge that it does.

A child can obviously learn about social reality by passively observing the things that take place in it. Better still, the child can gain considerably more insight by physically interacting with reality. Young children learn by picking things up and putting them in their mouths, for example. Or they drop things to see what breaks or bounces (and hence what makes their parents angry). But as the child starts to talk, the possibilities for learning through communication become virtually limitless. Children go through a phase in which they ask seemingly endless questions about the world around them.

The human instinct for communication is truly remarkable, and precedes a spoken or written language. Communication is possible without these. In the last chapter of his book *Life on Earth*, David Attenborough describes an encounter between an expedition to an unexplored territory in New Guinea and the previously unencountered tribespeople living there. He writes:

Then one morning, we awoke to find seven men standing in the bush within a few yards of our tent . . . The river men spoke to them, but the Biami understood nothing. We had to rely on such gestures as we had in common, and it turned out that there were many of them.

Relying on gestures alone, particularly facial expressions, the two groups succeeded in conveying welcome and pleasure, and they even began to trade.

The social instinct and the desire to communicate are deep rooted in human psychology. Think of Chuck Noland, the Federal Express systems engineer played by Tom Hanks in Robert Zemeckis's *Cast*

Away. In an effort to maintain his sanity whilst marooned alone on a remote island, he creates for himself a friend by painting a face on a volleyball. He calls it Wilson. He talks to it, and on a cave wall he tells his own story in pictures, much as his prehistoric ancestors felt compelled to do.

With learning, experience and the development of language and communication comes what Searle has called the *background*. This is an enormously wide and varied backdrop against which we interact with reality. It is everything we learn from experience and come to take for granted, social and physical, as we live out our daily lives. The background is where we find all the regularities and the continuity, the expectation that the sun will rise tomorrow, that things will be found where they are left, that cars won't turn into trees, that friends today will remain friends tomorrow, that this twenty-dollar bill is worth twenty dollars, and that when you turn the next page it will be covered by profoundly interesting text, not pictures of sausages.

We usually don't stop to think about the content of the background. Our presumptions about it precede thought (and are said therefore to be pre-intentional). Without the background, we would not be able to make sense of the world. Much of our humour is derived from rules drawn from the background (linguistic or physical), that we have long ceased to think about, juxtaposed with either a literal interpretation or an inappropriate context. The American cartoonist Gary Larson is famously good at this.

The background is also the repository of our human culture, defined through language and speech, traditions, habits, history, morality, standards of behaviour, sense of humour, politics, and much more besides. If you had entertained the notion that the background is one single independently real backdrop against which we try to organize our affairs, just think of the extraordinary diversity of human cultures.

So, where does the background exist? It exists only in our minds. As children learn they construct the background in their minds piece by piece and develop a set of capabilities that allows them to navigate their way through life. There was a time in my childhood when I didn't know of the regularities and idiosyncrasies of social reality. Some I learned quickly, some took a little more time. Some I'm still learning.

The mechanism by which our brains learn and form memories was identified by the Canadian psychologist Donald Hebb in 1949. This mechanism involves the strengthening of connections between neurons to form distinctive pathways in the brain's neuronal network. All our years of experience of reality results in the formation of neural highways which make our brains and hence our minds individually unique. Reality is impressed upon our minds both in childhood and in maturity like some kind of cookie cutter in soft dough.

What makes social reality possible, then, is the similarity of these mental impressions, derived from a broad set of common experiences, the ability to simulate the mental states of others as we interact with them, a common body of knowledge and commonly accessible forms of communication. The backgrounds that exist individually in our minds are often similar and this makes interaction possible.

Similar, but not the same. Within my mind is the social reality with which I have learned to interact. You have no access to this reality, because you have no access to my mind. Within your mind is the social reality with which you have learned to interact. I have no access to this reality, because I have no access to your mind. My reality is not your reality. But these individual realities possess many common features, such as the recognition that a twenty-dollar bill is money. Through the extraordinary complexity of everyday social interaction, through body language, gestures, spoken and written language, through use of mirror neurons and a combination of individual 'me'-intentional and 'we'-intentional states, we perceive these separate realities as one.

Money, then, as with all other elements of social reality, continues to exist only for as long as we collectively believe it to exist. The pieces of interestingly decorated paper in my wallet and the lists of numbers that appear on my monthly bank and credit card statements represent money only if everyone agrees that it is money. If everyone stopped believing it is money then I would be in big trouble (though it might be nice if you could all selectively disbelieve the numbers that appear on my credit card statements). This is a remarkable conclusion for something that casts such a wide-ranging and often insidious spell on most aspects of modern life.[8]

This belief is not all-or-nothing. Whilst it is perhaps rare to encounter members of society who do not believe in money, it is certainly possible to find others who do not believe in other social institutions, such as marriage, the prevailing political process or war. The fact that dissidence is possible means that it is not necessary for all members of a society to embrace and accept all of society's institutions. Even advocates of an institution (such as members of a political party) may not accept everything that the institution stands for. The way we interpret and assign meaning to an institution can also change over time as our social perspectives change. Examples in the Western world include marriage and organized religion, which do not hold the same meaning for society as they did perhaps fifty years ago.[9] The wholesale abandonment of one set of institutions and its replacement with another is often associated with political revolution.

Societies are made up of individuals with 'we'-intentional mental states. But the 'me'-intentional states have not disappeared. Each of us achieves something of an individual balance between these states, between co-operative behaviour and self-interest. Some people, as we well know, are generally more co-operative and 'socially minded' than others. Even the establishment of rational motives for certain kinds of co-operative behaviour in society does not necessarily mean that co-operative behaviour will automatically result. This is admirably

8. I'm reminded of an early passage in Douglas Adams' *The Hitch Hiker's Guide to the Galaxy*: 'The planet has – or rather had – a problem, which was this: most of the people living on it were unhappy for pretty much all of the time. Many solutions were suggested for this problem, but most of these were largely concerned with the movements of small green pieces of paper, which is odd because on the whole it wasn't the small green pieces of paper that were unhappy.'

9. For some couples in France, for example, marriage has been replaced by a Pacte Civil de Solidarité (PaCS), a legal alternative to marriage which is recognized also for same-sex couples.

illustrated by an early and rather famous discovery in game theory by RAND[10] scientists Merrill Flood and Melvin Drescher.

Suppose you and I rob a bank. We almost get away with ten million dollars, but instead of escaping to Barbados we are picked up by the police on suspicion of having committed the crime and we are imprisoned in separate cells. We are each offered a deal. If we both separately confess to the crime, then we will both receive a prison term of seven years (it was an armed robbery). If I confess but you stay silent, you receive a ten-year sentence and I go free. If you confess but I stay silent, I receive a ten-year sentence and you go free. If we both stay silent, we both receive a maximum one-year term for a lesser offence. This is the *prisoner's dilemma*.

What do you do? The rational choice would be for us to co-operate and stay silent. However, the chances are that you will confess. Even if we had prior knowledge of the deal and were able to agree that we should co-operate and stay silent before being separately imprisoned, you will draw on your background understanding of basic human motivation and you will probably decide to confess. If you know for sure that I will stay silent, then you have an opportunity to go free by confessing. If you're unsure that I will stay silent, or if you figure that your commitment to stay silent might tempt me to confess, then you better confess or you will face a ten-year sentence. Either way, you confess.

The consequences in this example for society at large are minimal, perhaps, but the dilemma applies equally to nation states embroiled in disarmament talks. The prisoner's dilemma featured extensively in cold war nuclear weapons policy-making, where the equivalent of confession was to order a pre-emptive nuclear strike. The only safeguard against a pre-emptive strike was mutual assured destruction.

Happy days.

Our conclusion that social institutions such as money continue to exist only for as long as we collectively believe them to exist does suggest a

10. A non-profit organization formed in the US in late 1945 to maintain close relationships between top scientists and the military.

circularity of definition. If we distinguish between money as a concept (or as a type) and the different forms money can take (different instances of the type, or tokens), then it seems we are concluding that *our belief in money as a type of thing is founded on the simple fact that we believe this type of thing is money.*

It is important to distinguish here between types and tokens as there are many examples we could invent in which the tokens are never used as money (think of a twenty-dollar bill encased in clear, heavy plastic and used as a paperweight). There will also be instances where we mistakenly believe something to be money that is not money (a counterfeit twenty-dollar bill, for example). We can expand the definition of money as a type in an attempt to avoid the circularity, by talking in terms of buying things, selling things and storing value. But in doing so all we have done is widen the net of social concepts we are using to define money. There is no getting around the fact that money as a type is *self-referential*, and contributes to an intricate network of similarly self-referential interdependent concepts that form part of the background to social reality.

In *The Construction of Social Reality,* Searle makes this point rather tellingly:

If, for example, we give a big cocktail party, and invite everyone in Paris, and if things get out of hand, and it turns out that the casualty rate is greater than the battle of Austerlitz – all the same, it is not war; it is just one amazing cocktail party. Part of being a cocktail party is being thought to be a cocktail party; part of being a war is being thought to be a war.

M. C. Escher's 1948 lithograph *Tekenen*, or 'Drawing Hands', provides a visual analogy. On the left of the drawing is a right hand sketching a shirt cuff. From this cuff there emerges a left hand. The drawing of the cuff is not complete, but the left hand is sufficiently detailed for it to rise from the plane of the paper. It is sketching a shirt cuff for the right hand. This cuff is incomplete. Escher's drawing is the essence of self-referentiality. The left hand exists because the right hand has sketched it. The right hand exists because the left hand has sketched it. The reality of either hand depends on the other.

*

After the confusion of hyperreality we tried to reach out for the basic elements of social reality – the social institutions that indisputably do so much to shape our everyday lives – such as money, marriage, politics and war. But what before seemed so real has now become a tortuous net of interlinking and interdependent strands, all ultimately dependent for their existence on our sustained collective belief in them and all existing only in our minds. This is a reality that is just in my head, and something very similar is in your head.

This all seems rather ephemeral, and hardly a strong foundation on which to build a completely independent reality. We are standing at the edge of a precipice. Time to take a step back before we end up doing something that we'll regret.

It is clear that social reality cannot meet the requirements of our first assumption regarding reality, that it be independent of us, our ability to conceive it and form theories about it. We also can't get away with a more dilute version of this assumption, one that says reality is at least independent of me, or you, because we all carry our own social reality around with us in our heads. This reality is impressed on our minds from childhood. Removing me removes my reality completely, and can therefore hardly be considered to be independent of me. Removing you removes your reality completely.

It might be fair to say that without either of us the world is still left with lots of people all carrying their own social realities around with them in their own heads, and we would speculate that there is a great deal of commonality between these realities, such that we have an illusion of unity. But this can hardly justify hanging on to our first assumption, even in its dilute form.

We appear to have no real choice but to accept that the assumed independence of reality does not apply at the social level. Our problems stem from the fact that society is a creation of the human mind, and cannot therefore exist without the human mind. But what binds our otherwise individual mental lives together and makes society possible is the use of physical objects to carry social functions and the need for some form of physical realization or expression of these functions. If we are to agree that this piece of interestingly decorated paper is money, then we rely on physical manifestations of some form or another in order to arrive at this agreement, even if this involves no more than the transmission of a pattern of high-speed electrons down my broadband internet connection. We can't have society by just thinking. We also have to do things that have physical consequences, and so the social world is underpinned by the physical.

Time, then, to turn our attention to the reality of the physical world itself.

PART TWO

The Doors of Perception
or
Are Colours Real?

4

The Prisoner

*Like everyone else, you were born into bondage, kept inside
a prison that you cannot smell, taste, or touch. A prison for
your mind.*   Morpheus, *The Matrix*

Here we seem to be on firmer ground.[1] Mountains continue to be
mountains even if there is nobody looking at them. Streams continue
to be streams. Houses continue to be houses. Trees continue to be
trees.

As we stand peacefully observing the static objects in our environment, we might imagine that they have a certain unchanging character.
There is certainly a sense of permanence about mountains, streams
and trees and even, perhaps, about some of the older buildings in our
immediate environment, such as an Oxford college or the White
House. But of course we are not so foolish as to think that this sense
of permanence implies the absence of change. In fact, the one thing
that we can be certain of in our modern consumer world is that
nothing is permanent, everything changes.

Change has become a byword for modern society. There are business consultants and journals that specialize in change management.
There are any one of a number of sources of advice on how each of us
can cope with a changing business environment, a change of career, a
changing workplace, changing relationships or life partner, changing
technology, all happening at an accelerating pace. James Gleick's

---

1. No pun intended.

Faster, first published in 1999, is a darkly humorous dissection of our modern condition in which we work longer, commute longer, shop longer and sleep 20 per cent less than we did a century ago. In our modern world the elevator button most worn down by constantly repeated pushing says 'door close'.

Modern film special effects can give us an impression of what it might be like to have freedom of movement in a world that has stopped, a world that no longer changes. There is a scene in *The Matrix* where Morpheus and Neo are together in another training simulation. Morpheus is warning Neo of the dangers of the Agents who, as sentient programs 'can move in and out of any software still hardwired to their system'. Anyone represented in the matrix who is still 'in reality' lying oblivious in their pod of nutrients in the power plant is potentially an Agent. Morpheus calls for the training program to freeze. People on the street stop mid-stride. Birds halt on the wing, frozen in mid-air. We see a world in which all change has ceased. We saw a very similar scene in *X2*, the second X-Men movie. This is also the premise of the 2002 movie *Clockstoppers*. Abuse of an ability to halt time (to undress women) is the theme of Nicholson Baker's comic novel *The Fermata*.

Unable to stop time in the way these science fiction fantasies suggest, we appear to have no choice but to reconcile ourselves to a world of constant change. This was very much the view of the ancient Greek philosopher Heraclitus. Born around 535 BC in Ephesus, Heraclitus established a world-view that in one sense remains with us today. Some have argued that every development in science, economics or political science is to some extent indebted to Heraclitus' philosophy.

However, his writing is famously obscure (and available to us only in fragments, in the form of more than one hundred independent sentences), so much so that he was nicknamed the 'Riddler' by his contemporaries and successors. As judged by his writings, he also comes across as arrogant and surly, and largely contemptuous of his fellow intellectuals.

Heraclitus pronounced that there is an account of reality – called the *Logos* – which describes the rhythm of nature and explains how all the objects, substances and processes in the world are bound together in a single structure. He compels us to listen to this account, but then rather unhelpfully admits that human beings are not usually able to comprehend it:

Of the Logos which is as I describe it men always prove to be uncomprehending, both before they have heard it and when once they have heard it. For although all things happen according to this Logos men are like people of no experience, even when they experience such words and deeds as I explain, when I distinguish each thing according to its constitution and declare how it is; but the rest of the men fail to notice what they do after they wake up just as they forget what they do when asleep.

His was a philosophy of opposites and of eternal change. The fact that we usually interpret the clash of opposites as the unleashing of destructive forces should not blind us to the fact that it is the tension between opposites that actually holds it all together. The world is a unity of opposites (think of night and day, war and peace, positive and negative, good and evil, Neo and Agent Smith). As a result, perhaps, of this tension between opposites, everything in the world is undergoing constant change: 'All things are in flux.' Famously, Heraclitus is supposed to have remarked: 'It is not possible to step into the same river twice', meaning that by the time we come to step in a second time, not only has the water flowed on and been replaced, but we ourselves have also changed.

If we set aside the flowery language, there is much we can interpret (or re-interpret) in Heraclitus' philosophy that appears consistent with what we know today. We only have to use the evidence of our perceptions to see that the world around us is in a state of constant change. Nobody's getting any younger. Things are not what they once were.

And it is here we come to one of philosophy's oldest challenges. To what extent can we trust our senses to deliver a reliable image of the world around us? Heraclitus was pretty clear: we can trust our senses and our senses tell us that everything is in flux. But not everyone thought the same way.

*

Parmenides was born into a wealthy and illustrious family around 510 BC, in Elea in southern Italy. Between them, Heraclitus and Parmenides admirably constitute the Heraclitean concept of a world unity forged by tension from polar opposites, because Parmenides insisted that Heraclitus had it quite wrong. We do not live in a world of constant change. In fact, nothing changes at all. Our impression of change in the world around us is an illusion delivered to our minds by our perceptions. Where does this notion come from? It comes from *reason*.[2] And so was joined an intellectual battle between reason and experience that would last to the present day, and will last well into the future.

According to Parmenides, everything is eternal and unchanging. Everything has always existed and will always continue to exist. We perceive a changing world because our senses deceive us.

These arguments are perhaps best illustrated by a couple of paradoxes devised by the philosopher Zeno, a disciple of Parmenides.[3] The most famous of these concerns the race between the Greek hero Achilles and a tortoise. Now, it is clear that Achilles had a strong sense of honour and fair play, because he agreed to give the tortoise a head start, no doubt confident of ultimate victory.[4] So, Achilles waits until the tortoise has reached a certain position – let's assume the half-way point – before setting off. By the time Achilles has reached the half-way point, the tortoise will have moved on a certain additional distance. By the time Achilles has reached that additional distance, the tortoise will have moved on further. By the time he has reached that further point, the tortoise will have moved further still. We can go on like this for ever, it seems. Each time Achilles reaches the point where the tortoise was, the tortoise has moved a little further ahead. It seems that Achilles will never catch up.

Here's another one. You shoot an arrow at a distant target. The

2. The belief that reason is the only sure way to knowledge is also sometimes called *rationalism*.

3. None of Zeno's original writings have survived and what today we refer to as Zeno's paradoxes come to us from the writings of others, notably Plato and Aristotle. It is not entirely clear that Zeno intended these paradoxes to be taken seriously.

4. If it helps, think Brad Pitt in the 2004 movie *Troy*.

arrow appears to fly through the air, describes a shallow arc, and strikes the bull's-eye.[5] How should we now think about the motion of the arrow whilst it is in flight? Suppose I take a photograph of the arrow with suitably high-speed film, one that can capture a moment without the object blurring. What would the photograph show? It would show the arrow in mid-flight, frozen in an instant of time much like the scenes in *The Matrix*, *X2* and *Clockstoppers*.

On looking at this photograph, we would be forced to accept that the arrow occupies a space equal to its own shape and size and that at this instant it does not seem to be moving. Are we being deceived? No, we're not. Our common sense should tell us that if we could stop time at any point in the arrow's trajectory, then we should see the arrow frozen in mid-flight. Within any particular instant of time, the arrow is not moving. If, as seems eminently sensible, we assume that the instant caught on film is representative of all such instants in time whilst the arrow is in flight, then we appear to be obliged to conclude that the arrow never moves.

Zeno's paradoxes are meant to challenge our preconceptions and prejudices about the everyday reality that we perceive. It is rather obvious to us that Achilles will overtake the tortoise, and the arrow will reach its target. But the mere fact that we hesitate – even for a moment – to answer questions about how such motion (and hence change) is achieved suggests that we should take Parmenides' challenge seriously.

I guess we should not leave these paradoxes without discussing attempts to resolve them. Interestingly, the commonly accepted resolutions require mathematical principles unavailable for more than at least fifteen hundred years, which must make Zeno's among the oldest and most sustained conundrums in human history.

For the sake of simplicity, let's assume that by the time Achilles starts the race, the tortoise has reached the half-way mark (it doesn't matter what units of distance we choose). By the time Achilles has reached the half-way mark, the tortoise has gone a further one-quarter of the distance, making a total of three-quarters. By the time

5. Well done.

Achilles has reached three-quarters, the tortoise has gone a further one-eighth of the distance, making a total of seven-eighths.

What we are describing here is a mathematical series with an infinite number of steps, or terms, starting with one-half, plus one-quarter, plus one-eighth and so on until we reach terms that are infinitesimally small. It is a property of such series that they are not 'open', they sum or converge to a single number, in this case the number one. It is not immediately obvious that a series with an infinite number of terms should sum to a finite number, but it does. With Achilles converging on the same point at a faster rate than the tortoise, we conclude that Achilles will overtake the tortoise and win the race.

Likewise, the photograph of the arrow doesn't tell us everything about what's happening to the arrow at that moment. The photograph doesn't tell us where the arrow was an instant before or where it will be in the next instant – it doesn't give us any information about the arrow's speed through the air. If we were to assume that the arrow travelled at one constant speed throughout, then the speed at any one instant is just this constant speed. If we wish to be more precise and determine what the actual speed of the arrow is at any given instant in its actual trajectory, then we would need to reach for the bag of mathematical tools known as calculus, which are in turn based on the convergence properties of infinite series involving infinitesimal divisions of space or time. At any instant in time, the arrow is stationary. But this does not mean that it isn't moving within a succession of such instants. In any instant in time, there is a difference between an object at rest and an object in motion.

Don't let the above resolutions fool you into thinking there's nothing more to be learned from Parmenides' challenge and Zeno's paradoxes, especially when it comes to our understanding of space and time. These resolutions are based on the assumption that space and time form a continuous, infinitely divisible backdrop against which we judge objects to be in motion. If you are inclined to think that this application of the mathematics of infinity and of infinitesimals to the real world is free from contradictions, try this task.

Set down a small reading lamp next to a clock. At some arbitrary time zero, turn the lamp on. After one minute, turn it off again. After a further thirty seconds, turn it back on. After a further fifteen seconds, turn it off again. Repeat this process, each time reducing by half the interval between switching the lamp on or off, just as Achilles reduces by half the distance he runs in pursuit of the tortoise. In the case of Achilles, we were quite happy to accept that by running the sequence one-half, plus one-quarter, plus one-eighth, he covered an infinite series of distance intervals that converged on the finish line. So we should here be content that after two minutes you have switched the lamp on and off an infinite number of times.

Now that you have completed the task, is the lamp on or off? On the one hand, it can't be on because each time you turned it on you then subsequently turned it off. On the other hand, it can't be off because each time you turned it off you subsequently turned it on again.[6]

You might reject this apparent paradox because you insist that you can't physically turn the lamp on and off an infinite number of times within two minutes. And yet a moment ago you were prepared to accept that Achilles can run an infinite series of distance intervals within a finite time.

This task teaches us that we should not take the proposed resolutions of Zeno's paradoxes as the last words on this subject. To paraphrase a famous Austrian, we'll be back.

We now turn to the ancient Greek philosopher Plato, an aristocratic Athenian born in about 427 BC, well connected with royalty and, as we would judge from our perspective today, with some rather anti-democratic political opinions. It would seem that he became friends with his great mentor Socrates when he was young, and left Athens in disgust when Socrates was executed in 399 BC, for corrupting the minds of the young (which meant encouraging them to think for themselves). Plato returned about twelve years later and founded the Academy, a school which survived for no less than nine hundred years.

Plato was no ivory-tower academic. He fought in the Peloponnesian war between Athens and Sparta and may have been decorated

6. This is one of a number of so-called infinite *super-tasks*. This lamp super-task was devised by James Thompson in 1954.

for bravery in a subsequent conflict. He travelled widely and had close connections with many political leaders both in Athens and elsewhere. His disappointment at the standards of behaviour of those in public office had discouraged him from pursuing a political career, and he founded the Academy with the purpose of developing the statesmen of the future, imbued with the values that Plato himself cherished. It is said that nobody ever saw him laugh.

Like all good philosophers, Plato drew on the work of his prede-cessors, notably both Heraclitus and Parmenides. He reconciled their opposing philosophies by acknowledging that, in a sense, both were right.[7] He developed a distinctive theory of knowledge based on the notion of things existing in the world as eternal and immutable *forms*. What we take to be the physical world around us is merely a world of appearances, or of experience, and the appearances of things only approximate the true nature of their forms. The forms are abstract-ions.[8] They are ideals related, possibly in a very obscure way, to the things as they appear to us.

In an attempt to explain what he meant, Plato developed a famous allegory which he included in *The Republic*. This is primarily a work not about experience, perception and reality, but about morality and politics. It attempts to answer the question of why we should try to be good, when bad people seem to have a much better time.

Imagine you are a prisoner in a dark cave. You have been a prisoner all your life, your legs shackled to the floor and your neck shackled to the wall so that you cannot move far and cannot look in any direction except forwards. You have never experienced the world outside the cave. You have never seen sunlight. In fact, you have no knowledge of a world outside your immediate environment and are not even aware that you are a prisoner, or that you are being held in a cave. It is dark in the cave, but you are not alone. You can't see your fellow prisoners but you have learned how to communicate with them. Their experi-ences are as limited as yours, but your world is not one of total dark-ness. You see men and women passing along the wall in front of you,

7. Philosophers have a habit of doing this. It is a cunning trick.
8. Under the influence of Pythagoras, it seems that Plato closely identified his forms with mathematical concepts such as numbers.

'carrying all sorts of vessels, and statues and figures of animals made of wood and stone and various materials'. Some are talking. As far as you and your fellow prisoners are concerned, the cave and the men and women you can see against the far wall constitute your reality. This is all you have ever known. But you are deceived.

Unknown to you and your fellow prisoners, there is a fire constantly burning at the back of the cave, filling it with a dim, sepulchral light. The men and women you can see against the far wall are in fact shadows cast by you and your fellow prisoners. When you hear them speaking, it is in fact you or another prisoner speaking, but the cave has an echo which makes it impossible for you to appreciate that the sounds are coming from you, not the shadows. Your world is a world of crude appearances of objects which you have mistaken for the objects themselves, 'literally nothing but the shadows of the images'.

One day, one of your fellow prisoners breaks free from his shackles and, succumbing to curiosity, walks out of the cave into the daylight. On the way he passes the fire. Outside he is temporarily blinded by the sunlight, and for some time prefers to skulk in the shadows that constitute the reality he understands and where he feels he belongs.[9]

Eventually his eyes recover, and he is astonished at the marvellous spectacle of three-dimensional shapes of objects and their vivid colours – Plato's world of forms, of a reality constituted by eternal and immutable objects-in-themselves. This is all so much more vivid than the reality he has known, of the shadows, of the objects-as-they-appear.

He scrambles back down into the cave to tell you what he has seen. But his descriptions are inadequate. How can he describe objects of three dimensions to people who have never experienced them? How can he explain what it felt like to see colours – intense greens and blues – to people who have never seen anything other than vague, dark grey shadows moving along the wall? It is clear to you that his 'escape' from the cave has driven him insane. You quickly grow tired of his

9. After recovering on board the *Nebuchadnezzar*, Neo asks: 'Why do my eyes hurt?' Morpheus answers: 'Because you've never used them.'

pleading, and kill him. You remain secure in the knowledge that reality is what you perceive it to be and there is nothing outside or beneath this. Plato wrote:

. . . the prison-house is the world of sight, the light of the fire is the sun, and you will not misapprehend me if you interpret the journey upwards to be the ascent of the soul into the intellectual world . . .

Plato's allegory was intended to convey the message that the reality that we perceive is based on the reality of the absolute, eternal, immutable, perfect forms of things-in-themselves. These forms exist in what has since been referred to as Plato's *world of ideas*. They lie outside the scope of our ability to perceive them. This should not be misinterpreted to mean that Plato's forms are just ideas, existing only in our minds. He took these forms to be quite real. In fact, the world of forms *is* reality. It's just that we can never perceive this reality for what it is; we can only ever perceive the shadows.

It is fair to say that Plato was never very precise about how his forms should be interpreted. On the one hand, we could conclude that these forms are properties that we ascribe to certain objects, as in 'this mountain is beautiful', or 'this is a damn fine cup of coffee',[10] in which case the forms are 'beauty' and 'goodness'. But then he goes on in *The Republic* to talk about the ideas or forms of a bed and a table, suggesting that when we perceive these everyday objects we see only vague shadows of the true forms of a bed and a table. I prefer this latter interpretation.

This would mean that, according to Plato, our perception of an everyday object such as a lemon is but a mere shadow of the true form of a lemon. If we take a second lemon from the refrigerator and study it hard we would conclude that it is slightly different in shape and size from the first. These differences represent imperfections. In fact, both are merely shadows of the one true form of a lemon, or the idea of a lemon. An alien visitor able to perceive such a true form, like the prisoner who escaped from the cave, could not even begin to describe it to us.

10. With acknowledgements to FBI Agent Dale Cooper in David Lynch's *Twin Peaks*.

There is an analogy here with the mice in Douglas Adams' *The Hitch Hiker's Guide to the Galaxy*. In this story we discover that the earth is, in fact, an organic computer built to work out the precise form of the question of 'life, the universe, and everything', for which the answer, already known from a previous computation, is forty-two. The beings who commissioned and paid for the earth are mice. But mice aren't quite how they appear: 'They are merely the protrusion into our dimension of vast hyperintelligent pan-dimensional beings. The whole business with the cheese and the squeaking is just a front.'

Using Plato's theory of forms, we might say that the mice of Adams' fiction are the shadows of the true form of mice. Just as we cannot perceive the true nature of mice because we cannot perceive more than three spatial dimensions and one time dimension, so we cannot perceive the world of forms. What Plato is really saying is that we can never hope to understand the true nature of reality because we are locked in the prison of our mortal senses. We are prisoners in the cave.

As I mentioned, *The Republic* is a work about morality, ethics and the political organization of society. It is in his world of forms that Plato finds the ultimate idea of goodness:

But, whether true or false, my opinion is that in the world of knowledge the idea of good appears last of all, and is seen only with an effort; and, when seen, is also inferred to be the universal author of all things beautiful and right, parent of light and of the lord of light in this visible world, and the immediate source of reason and truth in the intellectual; and that this is the power upon which he who would act rationally, either in public or private life must have his eye fixed.

One of Plato's more brilliant students was Aristotle, who had first trained in medicine before joining the Academy in 367 BC. Aristotle studied at the Academy for the remaining twenty years of Plato's life.

In that time he came to believe that Plato had got somewhat bogged down with his theory of forms, and came up with a very different description, which he set out in one of his own works called *The Metaphysics*. Specifically, Aristotle could not see how Plato's forms could help us to understand the dynamical nature of the world around us. We so obviously live in a world of change and if all the objects that we see are merely shadowy projections of true forms and these forms are eternal and immutable, then it is perhaps difficult to understand how any change can happen at all or, in particular, how new objects with new forms could ever arise.

So reality, Aristotle argued, must consist instead of both matter and form. Objects are made of physical stuff – matter – and this matter has potential for the reality of form (or structure, shape, and qualities such as colour, taste, and so on). A block of marble is a block of marble stuff with the potential for the form of a statue of Plato. Where does the statue come from? Was it always in the marble? Or was it waiting for a sculptor, carrying the *idea* of a statue of Plato in his mind? A seed is a small bit of living matter with the potential for the form of a flowering plant. Where did the plant come from? We might say today that the idea or form of the plant is coded in the genetic material contained in the seed.

Matter and form are logical components, but not real, separable components, of an object. If I smash the statue of Plato, I still have the matter but I no longer have the form except as an idea or an image in my mind. In essence, Aristotle put objects back into the world of experience. Plato had dismissed all the experiences delivered to us through our senses and urged us to use our powers of reason to penetrate to the true forms of things existing in the world of abstractions, of ideas. Plato argued that forms are primary, and our perceptions of their appearances (their shadows) follow. If the form of an object does not first exist in the world of ideas, then we can have no sensation of its shadow in the world that we perceive.

Aristotle was convinced that Plato had this back to front. He argued that we first perceive objects in the natural world, and then form abstractions and ideas about them in our conscious minds. In Aristotle's philosophy, the form of a thing is just a summary of its specific characteristics. In Plato's theory of forms, a lemon is yellow because it shares the form of yellow with other yellow forms. The form of yellowness is logically prior to the appearance of a yellow lemon. According to Aristotle, yellow lemons are logically prior to our idea of yellowness. We think of the abstract form of a lemon in terms of a certain shape, size, colour and taste (close your eyes and conjure it now in your imagination). We are able to do this because we have experienced the effects of many lemons using our senses. We have no innate idea of a lemon until we have experienced one.

Plato was seeking to escape from the cave, from the often brutal world of direct experience, to the infinitely purer world of the intellect, of ideas and forms. Plato's reality was one of thought and reason, one which projects into our world of perception much like Douglas Adams' mice. Aristotle brought all this back down to earth. His reality was one of perception and experience. Our thoughts about the forms of the things that we perceive are then shaped by our ability to classify and catalogue our experiences. With Aristotle, experience gained the upper hand in its battle against reason.

And there matters stood for about two thousand years. There were philosophers who came after Aristotle, but their preoccupations were different and in any case the Western world was overtaken by some major, tumultuous events a few hundred years after Aristotle's death. Much of the learning gathered during the flowering of Greek and Roman civilizations was lost as Europe stumbled into the Middle Ages. It is thought that Aristotle wrote some 170 works, but fewer than fifty, constituting about a fifth of everything he wrote, were preserved. Thomas Aquinas did much to help restore Aristotle's philosophy and science in the thirteenth century. But Aquinas was a scholar of the Roman Catholic Church.

The Church elevated Aristotelianism to the status of religious dogma. Aristotle was an inveterate collector and a classifier, and arguably the master scientist of his time (his influence on biology and zoology is felt even today). When the Church authorities embraced Aristotelianism, they pronounced on all matters not only of religious faith, but also of science. To contradict these views was to court disaster.

Substantial challenges to this orthodoxy were made in the sixteenth century by, among others, Nicolaus Copernicus. But the real break-throughs came largely in the seventeenth century, when the process of disentangling philosophy from theology was begun and formal scientific principles and methodologies were established. There was still much nervousness and trepidation, but it became possible once more to ask questions about the nature of our reality for which divine answers were not automatically supposed.

The battle between reason and experience was rejoined. And it quickly became clear that our concept of a reality independent of the human mind was going to struggle to survive.

5

Descartes' Demon

He felt that his whole life was some kind of dream and he sometimes wondered whose it was and whether they were enjoying it.
   Douglas Adams, *The Hitch Hiker's Guide to the Galaxy*

If, like me, you accept the Western notion of 'progress', then you will appreciate that much of this progress has been derived through systematically improving our understanding of the physical world. This improvement has, in turn, come through the application of rigorous scientific disciplines. We will devote a bit more time to these disciplines later but, for now, it is enough for us to acknowledge that one of the most important features of science as a way of developing an understanding of the world is that this is inevitably an understanding *from which we are removed*.

I don't mean physically removed, of course. I mean that scientific thinking is thinking from which our own personal, subjective perspective has been eliminated. The further we can get from our distinctively human, personal point of view, the greater the objective character of our resulting understanding.

Human beings might have started out believing they walked on a world which sat at the centre of the universe, supported or tormented by gods presiding over various aspects of nature. Nowadays we have largely given up this anthropocentric view – the view that we are at the centre of a universe organized just for our benefit and that higher beings have nothing better to do than muck about in our affairs. We have replaced this with a more objective view that puts us on a rather insignificant planet (a 'pale blue dot') circling a rather insignificant star in an otherwise undistinguished galaxy in a universe vast beyond human reckoning.

Some might complain that this progress has come with a fairly significant emotional or spiritual trade-off, but by getting our prejudices out of the way, by freeing ourselves from feelings about the way things *ought* to be and by being generally sceptical about what others have said about these things in the past, we have been able to understand the physical world much better (you might say that we have been able to understand the world as it really is). As a consequence, we have been able to manipulate and control our world in ways that have generally been beneficial to us – though not necessarily always beneficial to other species with which we share the world.

Like science, there are philosophical disciplines that are all about applying logical, rigorous thinking to distinguish clearly between our private, inner world of personal perspectives, experiences and internal mental processes and the outer world of physical things, and exploring questions about how these join up and how we can have knowledge of the external world. There are some who argue that science and philosophy in its broadest sense are distinct disciplines that try to pose and solve very different problems. I'll happily admit that an exploration of human morality and ethics is not something that can be conducted within the boundaries of traditional physical science. But I believe that problems concerning the nature of reality and our acquisition of knowledge of this reality are legitimate subjects for both science and philosophy.

From our current vantage point in the early years of our Western consumer-driven, technology-dominated twenty-first century, it is perhaps hard for us to understand and come to terms with a human culture founded on anything other than rational, scientific principles. But securing these foundations, shifting our perspective from one tormented by gods and devils to one dominated by evidence and reason, took many hundreds of years and demanded much personal sacrifice.

By the seventeenth century it had become possible to contradict the views of the Church authorities, provided this was done very, very carefully. In seeking to establish legitimacy for philosophy as a discipline distinct from theology, the French philosopher René Descartes still had to make sure he never arrived at conclusions that contradicted the Church. His aim was rather to use the power of reason and methods of logical analysis to get at already established 'truths'.

Descartes is rightly referred to today as the father of modern philosophy. Born in 1596 and educated by Jesuits, he had no reason to doubt the pronouncements of the religious authorities of his time. But he set about placing these views against the background of a much more rigorous and reasoned approach, intending to demonstrate their certainty in ways that did not rely simply on blind faith. Although many of his conclusions have long since been dismissed by the philosophers who followed, his approach represented a marked break with the past.

In his *Discourse on Method*, first published in 1637, he set out to build a whole new philosophical tradition in which there could be no doubt about the absolute truth of its conclusions. From absolute truth, he argued, we obtain certain knowledge. However, to get at absolute truth, Descartes felt he had no choice but to reject as being absolutely false everything in which he could have the slightest reason for doubt. This meant rejecting all the information about the world that he received through his senses.

Descartes supplied three reasons why he felt he could not trust his sensory perceptions and the experiences that resulted from them. First, he could not completely rule out the possibility that his senses would deceive him from time to time. Just as an optical illusion creates the impression that one of two measurably identical figures is larger than the other, so all his senses might play him false. Second, he could not be certain that his perceptions and experiences were not part of some elaborate dream.[1] Finally, he could not be certain that he was not the victim of a wicked demon or evil genius with the ability to manipulate his sensory inputs to create an entirely false impression of the world around him.

1. In *The Matrix*, shortly after Neo has taken the red pill, Morpheus asks him: 'What if you were unable to wake from that dream, Neo? How would you know the difference between the dream world and the real world?'

Descartes felt that there was at least one thing of which he could be certain. He could be certain that he was a being with a mind that has thoughts. He argued that it would seem contradictory to hold the view that, as a thinking being, he does not exist. Therefore his existence was also something about which he could be certain. *Cogito ergo sum*, he concluded. I think therefore I am.

It would still seem a big step from existence as a thinking being to conclusions about the existence or otherwise of physical objects in a material world. Remember that Descartes' philosophy was a product of its time and place. Having proved his own existence, Descartes went on to present a number of proofs for the existence of God, an all-perfect being which he established by logical reasoning must be a force for good and the foundation of our reality.

Descartes himself, he reasoned, had been created by God and has ideas of objects existing in the world which could come from himself, God, Descartes' demon or actual physical objects existing in an external reality. If his ideas are deceptions from any of the first three possible causes then this would mean that God was deceiving him or allowing him to be deceived, which contradicts the idea of God as an all-perfect being (deception taken here to be a source of imperfection in a good God). Descartes concluded that his ideas of physical objects are therefore the direct result of the existence of these objects in reality, thereby agreeing with Aristotle.

We are actually less concerned here with Descartes' ultimate conclusions about reality; it is the starting point for his philosophy that is of greater interest. He began by rejecting the idea that he could have certain knowledge of reality by relying on information received through his senses. Is this at all reasonable?

We can follow the logic of his argument by doing a simple experiment. You can either read what follows and use your imagination – in other words, treat what follows as a thought experiment – or, if you think it would help, you can actually carry out this experiment for yourself. The equipment you will need is readily available and costs little.

First of all, you should find some time in which you are free of the stress of modern living, time you can devote to some philosophical reflection, alone and without interruption. With some hours that you can devote to contemplation stretching before you, take two lemons from the refrigerator and cut one in half. Cut a thin slice from one of the halves. Place the whole lemon on a table in front of you. Light a lemon-scented candle. Dig out your copy of U2's rather overlooked album *Zooropa* from your CD collection and play track number four (called 'Lemon'). Turn up the volume as loud as you can without annoying your neighbours. With Bono's oddly high-pitched vocals echoing around the room, sit down at the table. Kick off your shoes and make yourself as comfortable as possible.

Hold one half lemon in your left hand and with your other hand pop the thin slice into your mouth. Try not to feel too self-conscious (after all, you are alone). Focus your eyes on the lemon on the table and fill your mind with its yellowness. Move your tongue over the slice in your mouth and taste the lemon's tart acidity, its sour sharpness. Rub your thumb and fingertips over the lemon half in your left hand and feel its soft, smooth yet bumpy texture. Draw a deep breath and inhale the lemon-scented air. Listen as Bono sings:

> She wore lemon
> To colour the cold grey night
> She had heaven
> And she held on so tight

With all five senses engaged in this way, experience the very essence of *lemon-ness*.

Is this real? Is what you are experiencing the combined result of the lemon, the candle and the recorded music, all of which really exist in the form you are perceiving them? If you were to put down the half lemon, remove the slice from your mouth and leave the room (so that you can no longer smell the candle or hear the music), what happens? Does the lemon cease to be yellow? Has it lost its sharp taste? Its soft, smooth bumpiness? Is the candle now odourless? Is the room silent?

Your first reaction might be to dismiss these questions as faintly ridiculous. Of course, the lemon is still yellow, sharp-tasting, soft, smooth and bumpy, the air thick with scent and the room filled with sounds. These are all physical properties of the lemon, the candle and the combination of CD, stereo system and the air that carries the sound waves, and all these things obviously continue to exist though there may be nobody in the room to perceive them. If you wait a little while and return to the room you know that the lemon will still be yellow, sharp-tasting and soft, smooth and bumpy. The candle will be burned down a little and the CD playing on the stereo may well have moved on to the next track.

Return to the room and find a comfortable seat. We need to force ourselves to go over this experiment once more and try, as far as possible, to remove our personal, subjective perspective from our analysis of it. We will discover that all these experiences, the perception of colour, taste, smell, the feel of an object and the hearing of sounds all derive from what philosophers call *secondary qualities*. As such, it can be argued, none of them are real.

Let's start with colour. The lemon's yellowness seems so obvious, so vital, so real, that it's hard to imagine circumstances under which we might begin to doubt its reality. But if we stick rigidly to the definition of reality that seemed so reasonable at the beginning – that reality is defined as independent of us, our ability to conceive it and form theories about it – then we will quickly come to the conclusion that there can be no such thing as colour at all, 'in reality'. We come to this conclusion because we have to acknowledge that the conception and experience of colour *exists only in our minds*. There is nothing about the properties of the surface of the lemon that can be connected with our conception and experience of the colour yellow.

Recall that we concluded from our discussion of social reality that elements of this reality, such as money, cease to exist on un-earth, our version of planet earth from which all minds (human and animal) have been removed. Sure, we said, there remain pieces of interestingly decorated paper or rectangular bits of plastic with a magnetic strip, but with no minds to interpret the information contained on or within these physical objects, with no minds to assign them a social function,

there can be no concept of money, and hence no concept of any underlying value that money represents.

This didn't cause us too much discomfort because, although money
is such an important part of our lived reality, we can accept that this
is an entirely collective, man-made concept, developed over many
thousands of years to ease certain aspects of social interaction. But
now we seem to be putting colour and other sensory perceptions in the
same category. How can this be? Surely, colour is not an invented concept; it is not a creation of human minds.

Is it?

The lemon, you might argue, has certain chemical and physical
properties that cause yellow light to be reflected from its surface. You
perceive yellow because it is coloured yellow and yellowness is an
innate property of all lemons (well, ripe lemons). Okay, let's follow
this line of argument and see where it takes us.

Lemon peel has a natural pigmentation which reflects certain parts
of the spectrum of visible light. This property can be reproduced in
artificial pigments, the first of which became commercially available in
the 1830s. Modern lemon pigment is made by forming solids consisting of tiny, lozenge-shaped particles from solutions of the chemical
barium chloride. Clearly, there is something innate in the chemical and
physical properties of natural lemon pigment or lozenge-shaped barium chloride particles that gives these things the property of reflecting
light the way they do. Whatever they are and by whatever physical
mechanism they operate, surely these properties exist independently of
our ability to perceive them?

We can admit that, from a scientific perspective, surfaces coated
with such pigments reflect photons of light – tiny particles of light
energy – with wavelengths in a certain region of the visible spectrum.
You might immediately want to identify this region of the spectrum
with the colour yellow, being that part which falls between orange and
green in the rainbow spectrum of colours, but be patient. Let's just
stick to the scientific facts that photons of light with a certain energy
and wavelength are reflected. These photons pass into your eyes and
are focused onto your retinas, forming an image of the lemon that is
reversed both left–right and top–bottom. To simplify the language a

little, I'm going to follow what happens next by reference to a single eye and a single retina.

The retina consists of collections of two different types of light-sensitive cells, called rods and cones. The rods are extremely sensitive but respond only to the relative intensity or brightness of the light – black-and-white and shades of grey in between. The less sensitive cones respond to light of different wavelengths (don't say colours – at least not yet). There are three different types of cones sensitive to different wavelengths of light such that, when triggered together, they can collectively respond to the entire visible spectrum. The photons interact with receptors in the rods and cones. These receptors respond to the number of photons (the intensity of the light) and their different wavelengths, stimulating chemical changes that eventually lead to the generation of electrical signals that pass down the optic nerve to the brain.

Science has a good explanation for each step in this causal chain of physical events, from reflection of photons of certain wavelengths from the surface of the lemon, through absorption of these photons by receptors in the retina and the specific details of the chemical changes that this triggers, to the generation of signals that pass to the primary visual cortex in the brain.

The brain is wired rather oddly. Signals from the left-hand sides of the retinas of both your left and right eyes (in other words, information gathered from your right visual field) pass to the visual cortex sitting at the back of the left side of your brain. Signals from the right-hand sides of your retinas (information from your left visual field) pass to the visual cortex at the back of the right side of your brain. The architecture and functions of the visual cortex are complex but we now have a fairly detailed understanding of how it works. There are groups of neurons that appear to respond to stimulation resulting only from the different wavelengths of light that have been absorbed by the retina. In a sense, the light from the lemon stimulates, or 'lights up', part of your visual cortex in a unique way.

So, what then? We are able to trace a series of physical and chemical events that start with the reflection of photons with a certain range of wavelengths from the lemon all the way to stimulation of certain parts of your visual cortex. But now we're stuck. No matter how hard we try, we will not find the experience of the colour yellow in any of this. Yellow is not a physical characteristic of the photons themselves. The photons are quite 'colourless' in this regard, being tiny particles of energy with wavelengths directly related to the amount of energy they contain. The cones in your retina are sensitive to different parts of the visible spectrum, but all you have here is a selectivity for photons of different wavelengths (and hence energies). The photons from the lemon will trigger the cones in a certain combination but this is all still physics and chemistry.

We can separate the chemical receptors and their associated proteins responsible for vision and dissolve them in a solution of nutrients in a glass beaker. If I now shine light on this beaker with wavelengths similar to those reflected from the lemon I can replicate the exact same physical and chemical processes that occur in the first stages of human vision. But we won't find yellow in any of this.

Clearly, electrical signals passing down bundles of nerve fibres are just that. The firing of neurons in your visual cortex is also a physical response to physical stimuli. The fact that your visual cortex 'lights up' in a certain way in response to the light from the lemon is key to your perception of the lemon, but it still does not give us yellow.

Think back to the character played by Arnold Schwarzenegger in any of the three *Terminator* movies. The Terminator is an artificially intelligent cyborg from the future.[2] He has mechanical eyes modelled on their human counterparts, which send images to some kind of 'heads-up' display and which (quite helpfully for this argument) appear to us the cinema audience as varying shades of red.[3] When the Terminator 'sees' a lemon in its visual field, the mechanical eyes send signals to the small but immensely powerful computer which is presumably (but doesn't have to be) located in its head. The computer stores a pattern in its memory corresponding to the size and shape of the lemon, and also records what wavelengths of light are reflected from it. It compares this record with others stored in its object database, runs its pattern recognition software, engages its artificial

2. Cyberdyne systems model T-101: living tissue over metal endoskeleton.
3. The 'heads-up' display is, of course, entirely for the audience's benefit, as there is nobody and nothing to look at such a display inside the Terminator's CPU.

speech module and says (in that unique way it has with words), 'Lemon. Yellow.'

Clearly, the Terminator has been engineered so that, given certain inputs, we get back certain outputs. But this engineering appears to be based on human experiences and knowledge of the secondary properties of lemons. In processing the inputs and delivering the outputs according to its programming, has the Terminator really *experienced* the colour yellow in the way we experience it?

It should by now be clear that it is only when you synthesize the information being processed by your visual cortex in your *conscious mind* that you experience the sensation of a yellow lemon.[4]

I think you know what's coming next. There is nothing in the chemical composition of the flesh of a lemon that we can point to and say this is its unique *taste*. For sure, there are natural acids in the lemon which possess certain groups of atoms which interact in predictable ways with chemicals in your taste buds which result in the transmission of electrical signals to your brain. But only when you interpret this information in your conscious mind are you aware of the lemon's sharp taste. The same argument can be applied to the scent of the lemon candle (chemicals interacting with your olfactory nerve resulting in signals passed to your brain), the touch of the lemon surface (signals from touch receptors in your fingertips passed up your spinal cord to the somatic sensory cortex in your brain) and even the sound of U2's 'Lemon' (compressions and rarefactions in the air interacting with your tympanic membrane, or eardrum, working through a complex mechanism ultimately producing signals relayed to your auditory cortex).

Without your mind, what do you have? Photons of different energies and wavelengths, chemicals containing distinctive groups of atoms, physical objects with certain surface properties, and compressions and rarefactions in the air. All producing different patterns of

---

4. Some philosophers use the term *qualia* in connection with mental states created by external phenomena but which are accessible only internally. Qualia stand at the crossroads of the mind–body problem and, as such, are the subject of considerable debate among contemporary philosophers and cognitive scientists.

electrical stimulation in your brain. In none of this physics and chemistry can we find colour, taste, scent, softness or melody. All are secondary qualities produced in your mind.

And remember, our starting point is that reality should be defined to be independent of us, our ability to conceive it and form theories about it. This is necessarily a reality that does not depend on the human mind for its existence. Without our minds, these secondary qualities cannot be real. The vast beauty of un-earth – the colour of its sky, the scent of a rose, the taste of a clear mountain spring, the sounds of trees sighing in the breeze, the texture of tree bark – has simply ceased to exist. It is now simply a world filled with physical objects possessing physical and chemical properties.

The discussion so far may appear rather mechanical or materialistic. It suggests, perhaps, that the unreality of secondary qualities really just depends on how we attempt to understand the relationship between body and mind. But I would argue that the conclusion does not depend on whether we take a materialist or dualist approach to the mind–body problem.

Recall that the materialists hold the view that mental states are the direct result of physical events unfolding in the brain and the development of specific brain states (such as those in which a certain part of your visual cortex 'lights up'). The mental states are either the result of some emergent properties of highly complex activity in the brain or they don't actually exist and there are only brain states.

Alternatively, the dualists hold the view that mental states are the result of some kind of mysterious ethereal 'mind substance' that exists separately from the physical brain but is somehow intrinsically connected to it. I don't believe it matters how mental states are produced, if indeed they are produced at all. The fact is that the activity generated in the physical brain somehow gives rise to experiences of the secondary qualities. These experiences are intensely personal and private. The simple fact is that we can't find the experience of yellow anywhere else but inside our minds, however our minds are meant to work.

Descartes was the most important dualist in the history of philosophical thought (his approach is often referred to as *Cartesian dualism*). He readily accepted the notion that the secondary qualities of objects do not exist except in our minds. He argued that when we perceive changes in these secondary qualities, they must be related in some way to corresponding variations in the objects themselves, although it may never be possible to discover the precise nature of this relation.

Despite how reasonable and sensible Aristotle might have seemed, we now find ourselves once again imprisoned in Plato's cave.

The pragmatist in you might still not be satisfied. The human mind, you say, is the result of evolution by natural selection operating through millions of years, leading to us, *Homo sapiens*. Does it make any sense to suggest that the human mind has evolved based on a brain with a sensory apparatus – sight, taste, smell, touch and hearing – that is not completely attuned to the physical reality around it? Put another way, would an organism that perceived the world around it very differently from the world as it really is be fit to survive?

You might accept that the concept of yellow exists only in your mind but you could argue that this experience is a direct result of the properties of physical objects in the real world with real *primary qualities* such as size, shape, density, motion and number. A lemon has real physical extension in three-dimensional space. Hold it to the light and light is reflected from its surface. The cones in your retina – we can now reveal – are sensitive to wavelengths of light that we associate with the primary colours red, green and blue. In the visual cortex are groups of neurons that respond to opposing colour messages. One group responds to red but is inhibited by green. Another responds to green but is inhibited by red. Another responds to yellow but is inhibited by blue. A fourth group responds to blue but is inhibited by yellow.

We have good evidence that our ability to recognize and remember the primary colours is not learned. It is not a matter of naming and language. Small children can recognize them long before they can name them. Anthropologists can tell you about native tribes that recognize all three though their language has words for only two. We recognize the primary colours because the human eye has evolved with three different types of cones, and this ability is a direct result of our genetic inheritance, in turn the result of evolutionary pressures. Why would this ability be selected if there is no evolutionary advantage? Why perceive colour if colour is not part of an external reality in which we must survive?

The same goes for the other elements of human perception. Colour brings our world alive and allows us to see.[5] Taste helps to tell us what is and what is not edible or poisonous. Touch, smell and hearing allow us to move around in the physical world and interact with it, detect prey or predator, sense comfort or danger. Surely our very survival must depend on our sensory apparatus delivering messages to our minds about reality as it really is?

This is a persuasive argument, but one that is ultimately insupportable. To see why, it is useful to consider what it is like to be a bat.

In our earlier discussion of social reality, we recognized that much of our day-to-day social interaction with other people leads us into a constant theorizing about what is going on in their minds and interpreting the way they perceive the world and form theories of their own. When I perceive the colour yellow, feel the surface of the lemon, taste it, smell the lemon-scented air and hear U2's music playing on my stereo, it seems very reasonable to suppose that, if I assume you are in possession of all the human faculties, you would have similar, if not virtually identical, experiences in my place. Your reactions may be different: maybe you don't like the taste of lemon, find the scent too overpowering or prefer Led Zeppelin to U2,[6] but although I can obviously never experience what you are experiencing, it seems a safe assumption that your experiences are similar to mine. Experiences are personal and subjective, but they can be shared, at least in this sense.

For now, let's accept the idea that there are indeed minds other than our own and that these minds have similar experiences when exposed

5. This is not a matter of being able to perceive the full richness of the visible spectrum. People who are colour-blind still perceive objects in shades of grey or shades of other colours. These are still colours. A world completely without colour of any kind would be invisible to us. Without colour of any description we would be blind.
6. Track 3 of *Led Zeppelin II* is called 'The Lemon Song'.

to certain external physical stimuli. You might argue that accepting this surely proves that these minds must be focused on the real properties of a real external world. The fact that we can all recognize the colour yellow must surely mean that yellow exists as a real property of a lemon.

I could counter this by forcing you to accept that your conception of the colour yellow could very well be different from mine (my yellow might be your green, for example), but I've never really liked this argument. Instead, I'd like to turn your attention back to an earlier stage, in which we said that we thought it would be unlikely that evolution would produce a dominant species that perceived the world around it to be very different from the way the world really is.

In 1974 the philosopher Thomas Nagel published a thought-provoking article in the journal *The Philosophical Review*, entitled 'What is it like to be a bat?'[7] Bats, as you probably know, collectively form some 950 different species, the largest with a rather terrifying six-foot wing span, and are the only flying mammals. They eat insects, fish, frogs, fruit and nectar and some (the vampires) drink the blood of other mammals. The smaller *microchiroptera* hunt for insects at night. Their relatively poor night vision gives way to sophisticated sonar, or echolocation. They emit high-frequency sounds, most of them way above the threshold of human perception. These sound waves bounce off objects around them, forming echoes which they then detect. This is not a quiet activity. If bat echolocation were all to take place in the range of human hearing, we would hear them screaming into the night air with the loudness of a household smoke alarm.

The bat uses the echoes to provide information about the objects around it and their sizes, shapes, directions, distances and movement. It is a finely tuned sensory apparatus. Bats have no difficulty finding and homing in on insects as small as gnats and can identify objects with the width of a human hair. They are odd little creatures, or as Nagel put it: 'Even without the benefit of philosophical reflection, anyone who has spent some time in an enclosed space with an

7. In David Lodge's recent campus novel *Thinks . . .*, this question is answered by students writing essays in the styles of Martin Amis, Irvine Welsh, Salman Rushdie and Samuel Beckett.

excited bat knows what it is to encounter a fundamentally *alien* form of life.'

When he asked what it is like to be a bat, Nagel did not mean that we should ponder what it might be like to have bat-like experiences, flying around in the dark catching insects. He challenged us to imagine what it is like for a *bat* to be a bat. What does the world look like, what passes for reality, from the bat's point of view? The bat is a highly evolved mammal, successful in its own ecological niche. If, like Doctor Dolittle, we could talk to one and ask it to describe its external reality, what would it say?

Humans do not emit high-frequency sounds from their mouths and use the echoes to gather information about the world around them. We cannot possibly imagine what it is like for a bat to be a bat because we lack the bat's sensory apparatus, in much the same way that we cannot begin to describe colours to someone who has been blind from birth. I obviously cannot know what a talking bat would tell me, but I would speculate that I would struggle to comprehend its description of reality.

Yet the bat and I (and you) supposedly occupy this same reality which, remember, exists independently of my (or the bat's) ability to conceive it. Just because I cannot understand what reality might be like for a bat does not mean that the bat's perceptions and experiences of that reality are any less legitimate than mine. What this implies is that evolutionary pressures lead to the selection of sensory apparatus that delivers a finely tuned *representation* of reality. What kind of representation depends on what kind of ecological niche a living creature is competing in. All that matters is that this is a representation that creates survival advantages. There is no evolutionary pressure to select a mind to represent reality as it really is.

We are locked in Plato's world of appearances.

There is no escaping the fact that reality as perceived and experienced by humans is the result of gathering, synthesizing and interpreting a myriad of physical and chemical events unfolding within it. The generation of secondary qualities such as colour, taste, scent, softness and melody is the result of this interpretation in our minds. This interpretation creates a representation of reality that is informed by the secondary qualities. These might be qualities that we can agree on and therefore share, one human being to another, but because there are other ways in which reality can be perceived and experienced of which we can never have knowledge we have to accept that we have no evidence to support an argument that our representation of reality – our reality of appearance – is identical to reality-in-itself.

You may now be feeling distinctly uncomfortable. It is, perhaps, relatively easy to appreciate the difference between primary and secondary qualities. When you look at a lemon you are seeing something – whatever it might be – giving rise to the sensation of a yellow lemon. You can sort of understand how its shape could be an intrinsic feature, a primary quality, of the real lemon that lies beneath the way it appears to you. Sort of. You can also understand that any attempt to interact with it, to look at it, taste it or touch it, would give you impressions that were not necessarily reflecting the true nature of the lemon. But now maybe there is something nagging at the back of your mind. Perhaps you are even a little afraid of it.

If logic demands that you reject the reality of the secondary qualities of physical objects, then surely you have to question the reality of their primary qualities, too. After all, if you are going to reject all the information about the physical world delivered to your mind by your senses, and using your senses is the only way you can gain information about the physical world, then surely this means rejecting everything.

Now you might really feel like Lewis Carroll's Alice, tumbling down the rabbit hole, grasping desperately for purchase on its smooth sides.

It is starting to grow very dark . . .

6

Brains in a Vat

What is real? How do you define real? If you're talking about what you can feel, what you can smell, what you can taste and see, then real is simply electrical signals interpreted by your brain.　　　Morpheus, *The Matrix*

The first philosopher to question seriously the distinction between primary and secondary qualities was George Berkeley.

Berkeley was born at Dysert Castle, near Thomastown in Ireland, on 12 March 1685, thirty-five years after Descartes had died from the rigours of a Swedish winter. He graduated from Trinity College, Dublin and in 1710, at the age of only twenty-five, published the work for which he is most remembered.[1] This was *A Treatise Concerning the Principles of Human Knowledge*.

According to Descartes and others who followed in his footsteps (most notably the British philosopher John Locke) physical objects possess primary qualities such as extension in space, shape, motion, density, number, and so on, all underpinned by the concept of material substance. These things are made of stuff, and this stuff exists independently of us. Secondary qualities such as colour exist only in our minds and therefore cannot be said to be independently existing real qualities of physical objects. This is a philosophical position generally known as *rationalism*.

Try as he might, Berkeley just couldn't see the difference:

1. The Berkeley district of San Francisco is named for George Berkeley, although Americans have adopted their own pronunciation. You say tomato, I say tomato . . .

But I desire any one to reflect and try whether he can, by any abstraction of thought, conceive the extension and motion of a body without all other sensible qualities. For my own part, I see evidently that it is not in my power to frame an idea of a body extended and moving, but I must withal give it some colour or other sensible quality which is acknowledged to exist only in the mind. In short, extension, figure, and motion, abstracted from all other qualities, are inconceivable.

Berkeley contended that it is impossible to separate primary and secondary qualities. We cannot conceive of objects possessing one and not the other, having shape but not colour, for example. Our thoughts and ideas about the primary qualities of objects are just that – thoughts and ideas – and are therefore no different in principle from thoughts and ideas we have of secondary qualities. If these secondary qualities exist only in our minds then so does everything. There is therefore no reason to hold on to the notion that we can have knowledge of anything at all beyond that which we perceive.

Berkeley's logic is merciless but compelling. We can hold on to the idea of an independently existing material substance, but at the cost of having to accept that we can ascribe no independently real properties to it, and can never hope to explain how this substance might give rise to the perceptions we have of it. In scientific reasoning, such an empty theoretical notion is often quickly eliminated as a useless appendage, by applying Occam's razor.[2]

On the surface, this poses an unavoidable conundrum. What causes me to have the perceptions that I have? Am I left to conclude that the only thing that exists is my mind?

This is not what Berkeley intended. What he was really stating was the rather obvious conclusion that our entire world is built out of perception and so our perceptions are the only things of which we can ever have knowledge. He argued that it is our perceptions that are the reality. It is impossible for us to ever have knowledge of a reality that we can't perceive, and so it is therefore meaningless to speculate about

2. Named for the fourteenth-century Franciscan friar William of Ockham. He is often credited with the statement: *entia non sunt multiplicanda praeter necessitatem*, or entities should not be multiplied beyond necessity. Although there is no evidence in his writings for a statement of precisely this form, it does appropriately reflect his logic.

the existence of such an independent reality: *esse est percipi*, essence is perception or 'to be is to be perceived', he concluded. Berkeley was the first philosopher to argue that empirical knowledge, which means knowledge acquired only through experience (and not abstract reasoning or theorizing) is the only valid form of knowledge.

Now, hang on a minute. Does this mean that when you leave the room – the one with the lemon, the scented candle and U2 playing on the stereo – everything in the room ceases to exist because you're no longer experiencing it? Is this like that old limerick about the tree in the quad?[3] Does this mean that the words you're reading right now on this page cease to exist when you close your eyes?

No, it does not.

Berkeley first establishes the simple truth that you can only ever know what you perceive. But he does not then go on to insist that, because of this, your entire world is necessarily an illusion or an hallucination. Quite the contrary. He accepts that there is something external to your mind (indeed, all our minds) that causes us to have the perceptions that we have. He is just not convinced that this cause is the material substance that we take to be the basis of an object's primary qualities.

Berkeley took holy orders and studied for a doctorate in divinity in 1721. He became the Bishop of Cloyne in Ireland in 1734. The cause of all our perceptions was, for him, fairly obvious. It is God.

His logic runs something like this. We have thoughts and ideas about objects in the physical world, but we have no evidence for the existence of these things beyond the evidence of our senses. Perception is reality and these things exist in the form that we perceive them only in thoughts and ideas in our minds. Our minds are therefore necessary to sustain this reality. But this reality is not continually flickering in and out of existence at the whim of our limited attention span. Reality is sustained by virtue of the fact that it is continually alive in the mind of an omnipresent God. The mountains, streams and trees of un-earth continue to exist even when there are no minds of mortal beings

3. There once was a man who said, 'God/Must think it exceedingly odd/If He finds that this tree/Continues to be/When there's no one about in the quad.' (Monsignor Ronald Knox.)

around because these objects are thoughts and ideas in the mind of God. This, in fact, is the conclusion of the anonymous reply to the famous limerick.[4]

We tend to be a little less satisfied with this answer today. But Berkeley's logic is pretty impeccable. Our knowledge of reality is derived exclusively from perceptions that give rise to thoughts and ideas in our minds. In itself this is not particularly mysterious. Thoughts and ideas come from us; they come from the 'inside out'. These can be thoughts and ideas about 'real' things but they can also be thoughts and ideas about imaginary things, such as unicorns, zombies or Gandalf. These imaginary things can come from nowhere else but our minds.[5] Put differently, our minds are the only places where such things can exist. Our perceptions come from the 'outside in'. What causes us to have these perceptions? From where else would they come but from another mind much like our own, but one that contains the entire world in thought?

Berkeley's argument is frustratingly difficult to refute. One notable attempt was made by Samuel Johnson, compiler in the eighteenth century of the first dictionary of the English language.[6] Johnson's biographer, James Boswell, tells the story:

After we came out of the church, we stood talking for some time together of Bishop Berkeley's ingenious sophistry to prove the nonexistence of matter, and that every thing in the universe is merely ideal. I observed, that though we are satisfied his doctrine is not true, it is impossible to refute it. I never shall forget the alacrity with which Johnson answered, striking his foot with mighty force against a large stone, till he rebounded from it – 'I refute it *thus*.'

4. Dear Sir, Your astonishment's odd:/I am always about in the quad./And that's why the tree/Will continue to be,/Since observed by Yours faithfully, God.

5. Okay, I appreciate that my thoughts about literary creations such as unicorns, zombies and Gandalf have been derived from my perceptions of them in books and films. But I can still create imaginary things in my mind for which I have never had perceptions. See, I've just thought of something that I don't have a name for. I have no idea what it is, but it has three heads and a body that resembles a rather large blancmange.

6. Fans of the British television comedy series *Blackadder* will, I fear, always think of Johnson as he was so memorably portrayed by the actor and comedian Robbie Coltrane.

But this doesn't work. Johnson may have confused visual perception with general perception, thinking that Berkeley's conclusion *esse est percipi* was to be interpreted as to be is to be *seen*. Had this really been Berkeley's conclusion, this would indeed have been easily refuted by the creation of any other kind of sensory perception, such as kicking a stone and so perceiving or experiencing it through the pain of a stubbed toe. But Berkeley's conclusion refers to *all* kinds of sensory perception.

All we can ever know is derived from our perceptions. We have by definition no access to any evidence of an independent physical reality causing us to have these perceptions, and if we reject the suggestion that these are thoughts in the mind of God, where does that leave us?

Suppose there exists an evil scientist who is able to remove your brain from your skull and keep it alive in a vat of nutrients (I'm afraid he disposes of your body). He is also able to preserve intact your optic nerve, your olfactory nerve, your gustatory nerves and the nerves leading to your somatic sensory and auditory cortices.[7] All these nerve endings would ordinarily be connected to the sensory organs in your body, but our evil scientist connects them instead to the output terminals of a vast computer. The nerve endings from your motor cortices are likewise connected to the computer's input terminals. All the neuronal pathways in your brain are preserved, all your short- and long-term memories are retained, together with your sense of identity and self.

So, make no mistake, the brain in the vat is you.

The computer is programmed to run a virtual reality simulation of the world that you know. The simulation produces output signals corresponding to the nerve stimulations required to reproduce this world in your brain, and thence in your mind. These electrical signals are fed into your brain, which is actually now sitting quite comfortably in a

---

7. Taste and smell are intimately linked. Our everyday sense of taste is actually three parts smell. Our taste buds can distinguish only four different types of taste – sweet, sour, salty and bitter (scientists are currently debating a possible fifth type). In addition we also rely on something called common chemical sense, involving thousands of nerve endings on the surfaces of our eyes, nose, mouth and throat.

vat. However, you interpret these signals in your mind as the world around you.

The computer simulation is fully interactive; when you think about raising your hand, signals from your motor cortex are interpreted by the computer, translated into the required simulations and then fed back to your brain. Your mind perceives that you have raised your hand. Although you have no hand, no face and no eyes, you receive signals that you interpret as your hand in front of your face. If you kick a large stone, the computer translates the signals from your motor cortex and feeds back the requisite signals to your visual and somatic sensory cortices and your pain centres. You see your foot lash out, and feel the pain.

The evil scientist has erased from your mind all memory of the operation he has performed. As far as you are concerned, nothing untoward has happened to you. Your life goes on as it did before.

This devilish brain-in-a-vat scenario is a philosophical concoction, and has become most closely associated with the contemporary philosopher Hilary Putnam. He wrote:

It can also seem to the victim that he is sitting and reading these very words about the amusing but quite absurd supposition that there is an evil scientist who removes people's brains from their bodies and places them in a vat of nutrients which keep the brains alive.

Although it might sound far-fetched, there is less fiction in this scenario than you might suppose. In the 1950s the Canadian neurosurgeon Wilder Penfield carried out operations on over one thousand patients suffering some form of brain damage.[8] In seeking out the damaged area, Penfield and his associates would expose the surface of the brain and stimulate it with electrodes. As there are no pain receptors in the brain (why would you need them there?) this whole procedure could be carried out under local anaesthetic. The patients could remain conscious and simply tell the surgeons what they felt.

Using this approach, Penfield was able to map out the surface of the somatic sensory and motor cortices, identifying which parts of the

8. Including his own sister.

brain are responsible for processing sensory inputs and which are responsible for motor responses. These maps can now be found in any textbook on neuroscience, and are often represented in terms of the projection of a homunculus ('little person') on the surface area of both halves of the cerebral cortex, suitably distorted in shape to reflect the strength of the sensation or response caused. Such diagrams show the relative importance in both sensation and movement of the hands (especially fingers and thumb), face (especially lips) and tongue.[9]

On stimulation of different areas, the patients would sometimes report sensations and would sometimes make involuntary movements. And when parts of their right and left temporal lobes were stimulated, some reported seeing and hearing things (sometimes separately, sometimes together). Some reported thoughts, recalled memories and experienced visual flashbacks. Some reported dream-like experiences.

So, could you be just a brain in a vat? If all your knowledge of the physical world around you is derived from your perceptions and your perceptions were being manipulated to give you the impression of reality, then how would you know otherwise?

If we extend this scenario (as Putnam does) to a situation in which all human beings are actually just brains in a vat, then we are firmly back in the territory of *The Matrix*. Instead of disembodied brains, the machine intelligence in the movie keeps whole human beings in separate vats of nutrients in the power plant, and feeds them a virtual reality simulation through cables connected to their brains. The simulation (the matrix) is so vivid that even when members of the human resistance enter the matrix, knowing that it is not real, their mental experiences can have physical consequences.

On failing to make the leap between two tall buildings in the 'jump program', a matrix-type simulation developed by the resistance for training purposes, Neo falls to the ground. Returning to the real world, he finds he is bleeding in his mouth as a result of the fall. 'I

9. The maps are almost mirror-images, but the division between sensing and motor response is not completely black-and-white. The motor cortex also receives some sensory input and stimulation of the somatic sensory cortex can sometimes produce movement.

thought it wasn't real,' he says. 'Your mind makes it real,' Morpheus replies. It becomes apparent that if they are killed in the matrix then they die in the real world: 'The body cannot live without the mind.'

We might debate the logical consistency or otherwise of the Wachowski brothers' film script,[10] but there's no denying the advances in virtual reality simulation that have taken place as computers have become ever more powerful, driven largely by the computer games industry (just compare the first ping-pong games from the 1970s with today's interactive, multiplayer, online games such as *Counterstrike* or *Medal of Honour*). Is it really so hard to imagine a virtual reality simulation so perfect as to be effectively indistinguishable from the 'real' world? If your imagination stretches this far, how can you then know that you're not already living in this virtual reality?

There are endless variations on this theme. In his exploration of the rights of individuals in society called *Anarchy, State and Utopia*, the contemporary American philosopher Robert Nozick describes a device he calls the experience machine. Fans of Steven Spielberg's film *Minority Report* will recognize this invention. Illicit trading of experiences recorded directly from people's cerebral cortex forms the basis of the 1999 movie *Strange Days*, starring Ralph Fiennes.

Plugging into Nozick's experience machine allows us to have any pleasurable experience we like, so vividly created in our minds that we take it to be reality. As Nozick suggests, we could experience writing a great novel, making a friend, or reading an interesting book.[11] Or we could choose from a library of other people's experiences. We could experience what it's like to be a member of the opposite sex having sex. We could experience what it's like to be Britney Spears or Madonna kissing at an awards ceremony. We could experience what it's like to be President George W. Bush, or Bill Gates, or Arnold Schwarzenegger.

Aside from the fact that the experience machine doesn't involve

10. In the quotation from the script used at the beginning of this chapter the Wachowski brothers forgot to mention hearing and, unless they were intending to advocate eliminative materialism, I might have said 'mind' instead of 'brain'.
11. But then, you already are.

the disembodiment of our brains, the most significant difference between this scenario and the brain in a vat is that plugging into the experience machine is entirely voluntary, at least as Nozick envisages it. It therefore brings with it all the issues about morality and free will, the difference between active doing and passive experiencing, already mentioned in relation to Cypher's betrayal in *The Matrix*. Nozick argues that plugging in is like committing suicide. We become no more than blobs of human flesh, blood and bone, a blank canvas on which an artificial reality is painted. Nozick feels that we wouldn't want to plug in, preferring to be ourselves and to do things for ourselves.

I'm not so sure. If it could be clearly and unambiguously demonstrated that an experience machine was entirely safe and without unpleasant side-effects, then I suspect it would actually be very popular.

To a certain extent, psychochemical drugs that can induce hallucinations or waking dreams can be thought of as local experience machines. Stanislaw Lem's book *The Futurological Congress* is a rather darker take on the brain-in-a-vat theme. When the hero, Ijon Tichy, awakes from suspended animation, he finds a utopian society of the future. In truth, this utopian society is created in the minds of its citizens through the use of drugs to change the nature of their perceptions. It is a 'pharmacocracy'. 'We owe our liberation to chemistry,' Tichy's colleague Symington tells him. 'For all perception is but a change in the concentration of hydrogen ions on the surface of the brain cells.'

With no moral constraints, many live out evil fantasies involving torture, rape and murder. Good or evil, it is all a false reality. Drugs pumped into the air (called 'mascons') are used to keep society passive and blind to the fact that a degraded world of 95 billion people is about to be destroyed.

A different but no less intriguing variation features in Peter Weir's movie *The Truman Show*. Truman Burbank (played by Jim Carrey) is living out his life in Seahaven, a re-creation of small-town America. No computers are involved, yet this is a simulation all the same. All his perceptions tell him that he is just an ordinary guy living an ordinary life. In fact, he has lived all his life inside a giant enclosed television studio that creates artificial night, day and weather systems, surrounded by five thousand hidden cameras and by actors under the direction of Christof. However, try as they might, the television crew can't always prevent the real world from intruding, and Truman becomes deeply suspicious when a series of improbable accidents prevents him from taking his dream trip to Fiji.

The acknowledged master teller of stories concerned with our sense of identity, perception and reality is the science fiction author Philip K. Dick. Though his work was largely the preserve of science fiction aficionados during his lifetime (he died in 1982, aged fifty-three), Dick's short stories and novels have been mined extensively by contemporary mainstream filmmakers. His stories lie beneath many popular English-language films, including *Blade Runner* (based on his novel *Do Androids Dream of Electric Sheep?*, published in 1968), *Total Recall* (based on the 1966 short story 'We Can Remember It For You Wholesale'), *Minority Report* (based on the 1956 short story 'The Minority Report'), *Screamers* (based on the 1953 short story 'Second Variety'), *Impostor* (based on the short story 'Impostor', also published in 1953) and, most recently, *Paycheck* (based on the 1953 short story 'Paycheck'). Dick wrote more than 120 short stories and forty-four novels, so there are surely more films yet to be made.[12]

One of the most extraordinary variations on the brain-in-a-vat theme comes from the Oxford philosopher Nick Bostrom. In an article published in 2003 in the journal *Philosophical Quarterly*, he explored the probability that at least one of the following three propositions is true: (i) we humans will become extinct before we can develop to a 'posthuman' stage of civilization;[13] (ii) any such posthuman civilization will have access to computer power so vast that time travel will be routine using computer-generated simulations of the past (so-called *ancestor simulations*); and (iii) we are almost certainly living in an ancestor simulation.

12. Let's hope they are better than *Paycheck*.
13. This is not wonderfully well defined but basically means a stage in our development in which we have such control over our genetic make-up, physiology, neurophysiology and neurochemistry that it no longer makes sense to classify ourselves as *Homo sapiens*, from both a physical and an emotional perspective.

Bostrom's argument is based on the observation of exponential growth in computer power in the last decades of the twentieth century. Some futurologists have projected this growth into the future. For example, the inventor Ray Kurzweil describes the computing power available in a current $1,000 personal computer as somewhere between that of an insect and a mouse. He estimates that a $1,000 personal computer will have the computing power of a human brain by 2020, and one billion human brains by 2050. Anticipated technological barriers (largely derived from the limitations of the physics of semiconductor devices) are, he argues, irrelevant. The barriers will be overcome by the invention of completely new technologies.

Actually, the required technology may already be known. Although this is an area of research in its infancy, computers able to operate at the quantum level might offer the potential for vast increases in computer power. There seems little ground for challenging the assertion that in the hundreds of thousands or millions of years it might take to reach a posthuman stage of development, computer power vast beyond current reckoning is likely to be available.

The last step is to assume that one consequence of such finely detailed simulations would be that the human beings so simulated (me, and you) would actually be conscious.[14] This is an important step in Bostrom's argument, and is based on the assumption that consciousness is substrate-independent. This means that any suitably complex computational structures and processes designed to mimic brain activity at the level of individual neurons can be regarded as conscious even though these structures and processes might be built of crystalline silicon rather than organic, carbon-based living matter.

Broadly speaking, Bostrom's argument is predated by the 1999 film *The Thirteenth Floor*, based on the book *Simulacron 3*, by Daniel Galouye. Present-day (or near-future) computer scientists have developed a computer system, situated on the thirteenth floor of a downtown Los Angeles corporate tower-block, able to run a detailed simulation of the Los Angeles of 1937. The simulation is

14. If you have ever played a computer game called *The Sims*, this might give you a moment's pause for thought.

populated by computer-generated people, some of whom are modelled on the scientists themselves, at least in physical appearance. As the simulation runs, the computer-generated people within it live out their lives as fully conscious beings. The purpose of the simulation is to allow people from the present to enter the simulated world by transferring or 'downloading' their consciousness to an appropriate target. The targets themselves suffer some discomfort as a result of having their consciousness displaced in this way, often waking in unusual places with no memory of how they got there or what has happened to them.

Once inside the simulation, the scientists can experience the reality of 1937 Los Angeles. Difficulties are created when the principal scientist, played by Armin Mueller-Stahl, makes a startling discovery. He has been using the simulation to indulge a passion for showgirls. He leaves a message within the simulation for his colleague, Douglas Hall, played by Craig Bierko, and returns to the present, where he is brutally murdered. Hall is clearly implicated in the murder, but suffers occasional blackouts and memory loss, often waking in unusual places with no recollection of how he got there or what has happened to him.

The denouement is clearly signposted: the present day is, in fact, an ancestor simulation run for the benefit of people from the year 2024. They are troubled by the fact that computer-generated people within a simulation have developed a capability to run simulations of their own, and have clumsily attempted to stop it.

If you could today gain access to a machine that could transport you back into the past so that you could observe moments from history, would you use it? Perhaps you would want to listen to Plato speak at his Academy? Watch the Bolshevik revolution unfold in Tsarist Russia? Watch England win the FIFA World Cup live at Wembley Stadium? Observe your mother and father falling in love? Find out who really killed JFK? There is no good reason to suppose that posthuman citizens will be less fascinated by their past. With access to vast computer power there is also no good reason to suppose that they would not be able to simulate history so exactly that it would appear to be real.

Bostrom concludes by arguing that unless we are now living in a simulation, our posthuman descendants will almost certainly never run ancestor-simulations. This is readily inverted. If the human race survives all potential doomsday scenarios and our posthuman descendants run ancestor-simulations on their vast computers, then we are almost certainly living in one:

If we are living in a simulation, then the cosmos that we are observing is just a tiny piece of the totality of physical existence. The physics in the universe where the computer is situated that is running the simulation may or may not resemble the physics of the world that we observe. While the world we see is in some sense 'real', it is not located at the fundamental level of reality.

All these variations on the theme of the brain in a vat share a common element. Whether evil scientist, belligerent machine intelligence, operators of experience machines, Lem's 'pharmacological dictatorship', directors of elaborate reality television programmes or posthuman civilization, there is always somebody or something in the role of Berkeley's God. All scenarios demand a 'God's-eye view', a fundamental level of reality, as Bostrom puts it, from which the hapless victims can be observed, trapped in their mental prisons.

When explored through fiction, the problems raised by the brain-in-a-vat scenario are usually resolved by one or more humans breaking free of their illusory reality and finding the 'real' reality. But if we were all really just disembodied brains in a vat then no such escape would be possible. How then, could we ever hope to know our true circumstances?

Putnam used the brain-in-a-vat scenario in his book *Reason, Truth and History* to argue that the scenario is, in fact, impossible. His argument runs like this. If we are really brains in a vat, then all our mental content is derived from a hallucination created by a computer programmed by an evil scientist. When we perceive mountains, streams, houses, trees and earth, no matter how real they seem, we have formed these mental representations based on artificial experiences with no reference to 'real' mountains, streams, etc. In fact, everything we perceive and therefore everything we think about is not real, in the sense that we understand this to mean a reality external to our minds (or the reality that the evil scientist supposedly occupies).

At this stage Putnam draws to our attention the properties of a so-called self-refuting proposition. An example of such a proposition would be: 'All general statements are false.' We can quickly see that this is a general statement which, if true, is self-refuting, because the statement says that all such statements are false. So it must be false.

Now consider the statement: 'We are all brains in a vat.' This, Putnam contends, is a similarly self-refuting proposition. In ordinary life (as opposed to science fiction) when I think of a tree I form mental representations based on my experiences of trees in the real world. My representation of a tree is causally connected to the existence of real trees. If I am merely a brain in a vat, then my mental representation of a tree is no longer causally connected to the existence of a real tree, as the electrical signals used to create a visual sensation of a tree in my mind are no longer derived from the tree, but from a computer program. I might perceive a tree, raise my 'hand' and 'say', 'Look – a tree!' But my mental representation no longer refers to a real tree. In fact, none of my mental representations any longer refer to anything that could be considered to exist in the real world, including brains, vats, brains in a vat in general and my brain in a vat in particular.

Nothing that we experience or think about in the vat bears any relationship to anything that could legitimately considered to be real, even though it might look real to us. Therefore thinking that we are brains in a vat also bears no relationship to anything real. If we are really brains in a vat, then the proposition 'We are brains in a vat' is self-refuting. The proposition is false and we are therefore not brains in a vat.

If you live in a world based entirely on deception, and you are not aware of it, then there is no reference point from which you can perceive otherwise. To see that you are indeed a brain in a vat in any meaningful sense you would have to be able to perceive that you are a brain in a vat. Your senses would need to be causally connected with your real brain in a real vat, existing in the real world. If you could establish such a causal connection, then it obviously can't be you in the vat. If you are really a brain in a vat, you can't establish the causal connection.

The fictional variations on the brain-in-a-vat theme all provide a reference point, a 'God's-eye view', such as the 'real' reality in *The Matrix* or the world outside the giant television studio in *The Truman Show*. In the formal brain-in-a-vat scenario, no such reference point is possible.

If we update Berkeley's conclusion from the eighteenth century to the computer-literate early twenty-first century, then we could say that we are simulations in the mind of God. Applying Putnam's argument would lead us to conclude that this is a self-refuting statement, although it's not clear to me just how persuasive this would be to someone who fervently believes in God. I can't help thinking that if there is a God then He would want us to know about Him, by giving us the relevant thoughts. Alternatively, if the evil scientist were really, really evil, wouldn't he or she want to torment us by giving us the idea that we might be brains in a vat?

This problem of reference is openly acknowledged in *The Matrix*. Shortly after Neo's liberation from the power plant, there is a scene aboard the *Nebuchadnezzar* in which the crew sit around discussing the awful manufactured food they have to eat.[15] One of the crew insists that it tastes like Tastee Wheat, an instant breakfast cereal they have experienced whilst in the virtual reality of the matrix. A debate ensues concerning how the machine intelligence could know what Tastee Wheat, or indeed anything, tasted like:

Maybe they got it wrong, maybe what I think Tastee Wheat tasted like actually tasted like oatmeal, or tuna fish. It makes you wonder about a lot of things. Take chicken, for example. Maybe they couldn't figure out what to make chicken taste like which is why chicken tastes like everything.

In fact, I'm not so persuaded by Putnam's argument. To see why, let's take another short diversion into science fiction.

Suppose you agree to participate in an elaborate experiment. Maybe you're suffering from some terminal heart condition and in order to prolong your life you agree to be the guinea-pig in a breakthrough surgical procedure. An expert neurosurgeon is going to remove your brain and transplant it into the head of a suitable body-donor, one whose

15. Which is, incidentally, grown in a vat.

own brain has died but whose body is being kept alive for this purpose. The donor has been carefully selected to be of the same race, sex and broad physical appearance, so as to minimize the risk of 'psychological rejection'.

The surgery is completed successfully. You remain you, but you wake up in a different body. The sense organs of your new body all seem to be functioning perfectly (actually, better than in your old body). You recuperate from the operation by taking long walks in the hospital grounds, breathing the wonderfully clear air that you thought you would never breathe again. Your new eyes linger on an oak tree that you remember from before your operation, one that you thought you would never see again. You marvel anew at the wonderful complexity of nature, and drink deeply of the sensations of being alive in a world that is now more compellingly real to you than it ever was when you took for granted your own place within it.

As you gaze on the oak tree you are causally connected with a real tree in the real world. Now, the brain inside your new skull is just a brain in an elaborate 'vat', being fed electrical signals by your new sense organs that you are interpreting as perceptions of the world around you. But, unlike the brain-in-a-vat scenario, you have no reason to doubt that through your new sensory apparatus you are causally connected with real objects in the real world. Everything is as you remember it. You have no reason to think this is all an illusion. You would therefore conclude from this that the statement 'I am the brain in my head' is not self-refuting. Even though your head no longer happens to be the one you were born with.

So far, so good.

You become aware that there is a wing of the hospital that is being kept discreetly off-limits to you. Nobody has told you that you are forbidden to enter this part of the hospital but you are subtly prevented from doing so by the hospital staff. From the window of your private ward you catch occasional glimpses of people entering and leaving this wing. These people do not dress like hospital staff. Intrigued, and by now well enough to seek a little excitement, you steal across to the mysterious wing in the middle of the night, and enter it unobserved.

You discover that the entire wing is one huge laboratory. At the console of what appears to be a vast computer there sits a technician. He has his back to you, his feet on the desk. He is engrossed in a book. (It happens to be this book, but this is merely a coincidence.)

Suddenly, he glances up at a large flat-screen visual display on the console in front of him. He is shocked to see himself on the screen. He mutters an expletive and turns to face you, but he doesn't look at you. In fact, he doesn't seem to see you at all. Instead, he is looking over your shoulder.

What you have until now assumed to be your heart beats faster as you slowly turn. Just behind you in a corner of the laboratory there lies a large, thick-walled glass tank filled with pale liquid, the colour of thinned blood. Inside the tank you can just make out a brain, each point on its surface connected to an uncountable number of thin copper filaments that spread out in all directions before bundling together to form a single cable. Alongside the tank is a panel giving a dazzling light display; countless tiny light-emitting diodes of different colours winking on and off, in some random pattern of activity.

You realize that you are looking at your own thoughts. It is your brain in the tank. You have been the guinea-pig for a rather different kind of experiment . . .

The point of this science-fiction horror story is that the brain in your head is really just a brain in a vat. Putnam's argument is based on the assumption that the brain in your head is ordinarily in causal connection with real objects in the real world, a connection mediated by your sense organs. This causal connection prevents us from concluding that the statement 'I am the brain in my head' is self-refuting. This is, perhaps, a perfectly natural assumption. But it *is* an assumption.

What is it about having your brain transplanted into another head that might invalidate this assumption? If we presume that everybody's sense organs work in much the same way to deliver much the same sensory perceptions, then it is hard to see why the assumption would be invalidated. But, as the story makes clear, once you have undergone such an operation you can no longer rely on these perceptions to reflect your real state of affairs. This just leaves you posing the question as to whether or not you can rely on the perceptions you are having right now.

We can always be more creative and think of ways in which it would be possible for an evil scientist or machine intelligence to capture and record every possible experience that humans can have and translate these into electrical signals prior to placing humans (whole or as disembodied brains) in a vat. But this has long since ceased to be the point. We could consider all these scenarios to be logically or even scientifically possible, and we could even go so far as to place a high probability on their occurrence. But this does not mean that they are occurring or will occur, or that we are experiencing any of these scenarios right now.

The simple fact is that we just don't know what gives rise to these perceptions. You can assume that the brain in your head is in causal contact with real objects, but you can never be certain. If we take the view that the only things we can be certain of are our perceptions then, as Berkeley contended, perception *is* reality. Because perception and experience take place only in our minds, it would seem that we have no choice but to give up our first assumption regarding the nature of reality – that it exists independently of us, our ability to conceive it and form theories about it. All we can really be certain of is that we exist as thinking beings that have perceptions and experiences.

If we are now obliged to give up our first assumption, what of the rest? Can we at least draw some comfort from the fact that whatever it is 'out there' that gives rise to our perceptions and experiences, it is at least logically consistent and conforms to laws that we have been able to construct from our experiences?

No, not really.

7

Are You Experienced?

Experience is not what happens to a man; it is what a man does with what happens to him.

Aldous Huxley, *Texts and Pretexts*

Through Berkeley, experience once again gained the upper hand in its battle with reason. Berkeley argued that perception and experience are everything and there is nothing further to intuit about the nature of reality by applying our powers of reason. His arguments led him to a philosophical position generally known as *idealism*, in which every object that makes up our perceived reality is no more than an idea in the mind of God.

If this gives you the sense that our grip on reality is starting to slip away, then be ready. In the hands of the eighteenth-century Scottish philosopher David Hume things suddenly got much more complicated.

Hume was born in 1711 near Edinburgh. Brought up a strict Calvinist in a wealthy family, he began to question religious doctrine when, at the age of fifteen, he left the University of Edinburgh to pursue his education privately, both in Scotland and in France. After initially considering a career in law, he turned to philosophy and spent more than ten years seeking support for religious arguments concerning the existence of God. 'Doubts stole in,' he wrote, 'dissipated, return'd, were again dissipated, return'd again.'

The result of this endeavour was *A Treatise of Human Nature*, first published anonymously in two instalments in 1739–40. In Hume's own words the book 'fell dead-born from the press', the little interest that it did arouse being largely critical. It was only many years later, when Hume had established a reputation as a historian, that the *Treatise* was recognized as a fundamentally important contribution to modern philosophy.

In his masterly summary of the works of the classical modern philosophers from René Descartes to Immanuel Kant, Richard Schacht says that of all the philosophers of this period, Hume may have been the most enjoyable to know. Pretty much all of Hume's writings stirred religious controversy at the time of their publication. The frontispiece to the first edition of the *Treatise* contains a Latin quotation which translates as: 'Seldom are men blessed with times in which they may think what they like, and say what they think.' On the advice of friends who wished to reduce his exposure to public censure, Hume arranged for his critical analysis of religion and the nature of God, *Dialogues Concerning Natural Religion,* to be published after his death.

Hume was a straightforward, no-nonsense sceptic. He agreed with Berkeley that we can never perceive anything other than our own ideas and can therefore have no knowledge of a reality external to our minds. However, Hume did not agree that this must mean that nothing at all exists outside our minds (other than the experiences given to us by God, as Berkeley would have it). He concluded simply that we have no means of knowing what, if anything, exists outside of ourselves and so the question itself is, broadly speaking, a meaningless one.

There may well be a reality 'out there' which is the direct cause of all our experiences, of tall mountains, streams, houses and trees, and these things may well exist independently of our ability to perceive them and form ideas in our minds about them. But, for Hume, experience is everything and cannot be transcended. We can have knowledge of the things we experience but absolutely no knowledge of what causes these experiences (be they real objects in a real world, evil scientists, demons, television programme directors, people from a posthuman future or God). There may be an independent reality but we have no way of establishing that such an independent reality exists.

Best, then, to deal with what we can know and not dwell too much on the things we can't.[1]

Hume's strategy was to consign all speculation about the nature of reality to a branch of philosophy known as metaphysics (meaning, literally, 'beyond physics'), and to deny any claim to knowledge achieved through metaphysical reasoning and speculation. He thereby established a philosophical tradition known as *empiricism*, where the word empirical is interpreted to mean purely experiential. Knowledge of the world that is not gained through direct experience is rejected as speculative metaphysics. This does not necessarily mean that there is no such thing as reality, but it does mean that we might have to temper our expectations. At best, we gain knowledge of an *empirical reality* – the reality manifested as effects that we can directly perceive. Just don't expect to be able to go beyond this empirical level. To do so is to engage in meaningless speculation.

Time to take a short break.

If you have ever visited the city of Prague in the Czech Republic then you will almost certainly have spent time gazing at the Astronomical Clock, positioned on one side of the Old Town Hall. The clock was built in 1410 by Mikulas of Kadan with the help of the astronomer and mathematician Jan Sindel, and tells the exact position of the sun and stars relative to the position of the earth. It originally displayed only astronomical information, but was decorated with flamboyant sculptures in 1490 by the master clockmaker Hanus and acquired some entertaining mechanical figures in the seventeenth and nineteenth centuries.

Local folklore has it that after completion of his work on the clock, the town officials had Hanus blinded with a hot poker so that he could never duplicate his work for any other town. In an act of revenge, he climbed the tower and sabotaged the clock. It remained silent for more than fifty years. The legend became a metaphor for stifled creativity during the years of communist oppression in former Czechoslovakia.

1. This was to be echoed many years later by the Austrian philosopher Ludwig Wittgenstein, who concluded his *Tractatus Logico-Philosophicus* with the statement 'Whereof one cannot speak, thereof one must be silent.'

The clock is divided into three parts, the walk of the apostles at the top, the clock dial in the centre and the calendar at the bottom. On the hour Death, represented by a skeleton, pulls a bell cord. Small windows open to the left and right and the apostles march past. The windows close, a golden cockerel crows and the hour is chimed. All of this is accompanied by a Turk shaking his head, a Miser watching his bag of gold, and Vanity admiring himself in a mirror.

The clock has three pointers, one each for the sun, the moon and the zodiac. Its movements are derived from three large co-axial gear wheels driven by the same pinion. The first gear contains 365 teeth and rotates the zodiac once each sidereal day,[2] the second contains 366 teeth and rotates the sun once each mean solar day and the third contains 379 teeth and rotates the moon in relation to the mean apparent motion of the real moon. The clock dial in the middle shows astronomical phenomena such as sunrise and sunset and the movements of the sun, moon and stars. A ball, half silvered and half black, rotates every lunar month to show the phases of the moon.

Even if you've never seen the Astronomical Clock, you can conjure its mechanical function in your mind and imagine what it might be like. It stands as a monument to our conception of a 'clockwork' universe. Once it is set in motion, its movements are entirely predictable. As the hour approaches, the tourists who gather in the square below do so with the expectation that they are about to see and hear Death ring his bell and witness the walk of the apostles, the result of the inevitable mechanical force of turning gears. Stand now and watch with me as the seconds tick by: watch as cause leads inevitably to effect.

Not so, said David Hume.

According to Hume the only thing we can be certain of is our experience, and we must be generally sceptical of everything we think we can learn from things that we can't directly experience. It follows then that no matter how many times we watch the Astronomical Clock strike the hour, we cannot conclude from this that the act of striking

2. A sidereal day is the time taken for one complete 360 degree rotation of the earth measured in relation to the fixed stars. It is on average about four minutes shorter than the more familiar solar day.

is a necessary consequence of the turning of the wheels in the clock mechanism. In his book *An Inquiry Concerning Human Understanding*, published in 1748 and a more popular version of Book I of the *Treatise*, he wrote:

. . . we are never able, in a single instance, to discover any power or necessary connexion; any quality, which binds the effect to the cause, and renders the one an infallible consequence of the other. We only find, that the one does actually, in fact, follow the other.

The relationship between cause and effect is so ingrained in common comprehension and understanding of the world around us that Hume's attack on it hardly seems credible. But what Hume was challenging us to do is examine what it is that we actually perceive when we see something causing something else to happen. What we see is that when this happens, *then* that happens. There is obviously no mysterious substance that we can point to and say, look, this is the cause. When we talk of something causing something else then according to Hume we go beyond our perceptions and start to speculate about something that we can't directly experience. And this is something about which we can't have knowledge.

When we see something causing something else to happen, what we actually perceive according to Hume is nothing more than the 'constant conjunction' of events pertaining to particular objects of perception. Experience reveals only one event followed by another. The more we observe the constant conjunction of particular types of events, the more we become convinced that one is the cause of the other. Hume asks what goes on in the mind of a man who has observed repeated sequences of events, with one always following the other:

What alteration has happened to give rise to this new idea of *connexion*? Nothing but that he now *feels* these events to be *connected* in his imagination, and can readily foretell the existence of one from the appearance of the other. When we say, therefore, that one object is connected with another, we mean only that they have acquired a connexion in our thought, and give rise to this inference, by which they become proofs of each other's existence: A conclusion which is somewhat extraordinary, but which seems founded on sufficient evidence.

When we stand in the crowd of tourists waiting for the Astronomical Clock to amuse us once more, our expectations are founded on a belief that events such as the turning of the gear wheels in the clock mechanism will eventually cause Death to pull the bell cord. We also assume that the future will resemble the past. Hume demands that we recognize this as an assumption that cannot rationally be justified based on our experience. The English philosopher Bertrand Russell made this point quite forcefully many years later: 'The man who has fed the chicken every day throughout its life at last wrings its neck instead, showing that more refined views as to the uniformity of nature would have been useful to the chicken.'

Hume is pulling firmly on the rug beneath our feet. Whatever it is that gives rise to the perceptions and experiences we have of the world (if, indeed, it is anything at all), this is simply beyond reckoning. We can have no knowledge of what the objects of sensation are 'really like', neither can we have knowledge of the connections between them that form such an essential part of our comprehension of the physical world. Cause and effect exists only in our minds – in the background – placed there through custom and reinforced through habit, right from the very first time when, as small children, we started to experiment with the objects we perceived in the world around us.

Now we are really in trouble. Not only does it seem that we have to abandon our first assumption regarding the nature of reality but now our second assumption regarding the logical consistency of this reality is under grave threat. Is there then an alternative to Hume's scepticism?

The answer is yes, but I really don't think you're going to like where it leads us.

Under Hume's influence, eighteenth-century philosophy had become starkly polarized between rationalism and empiricism, between reason and experience. In essence, the rationalist view maintains the existence of a reality founded on material substance and primary qualities that, while it may not be the naive reality of common sense, is nonetheless independent of the human mind. With suitable qualifications, our knowledge of this reality is derived from the nature of the independently existing objects within it. The empiricist view, associated with Hume, maintains that we can have no knowledge of what really exists (or what doesn't exist), we can only ever have knowledge of our perceptions and experiences.

This polarization is arguably the direct result of a strongly internalist view of the mind. My mind is a product of, and therefore firmly anchored to, my brain and is intensely personal and private. There is, then, a clear boundary between my inner world of thoughts and ideas and an outer world that may (or may not) cause me to have the perceptions and experiences that I have. The existence of this boundary gives rise to what some philosophers call the *matching problem*: how does my ability to gain knowledge of the world match up to a world presumably capable of yielding knowledge? The rationalist insists that through reason we gain a qualified form of knowledge of things that exist independently of us. The empiricist insists that we can only ever have knowledge of our perceptions and experiences.

Resolving the matching problem was one of the main tasks of the German philosopher Immanuel Kant, regarded by many as the greatest philosopher of modern times. Kant was born in 1724 in Königsberg (in what was then Prussia but which is now Kaliningrad in Russia). His life and work stand in marked contrast to his contemporaries and predecessors. His family was not wealthy, but he was able to secure a good education at the University of Königsberg and later became a lecturer there. Unlike Berkeley and Hume, who made their most significant contributions to philosophy before they turned thirty, Kant's greatest works were written after his fiftieth birthday. Most notable among these is the *Critique of Pure Reason*, published in 1781, when he was fifty-six.

Kant was greatly influenced by Hume's work, but came to deny Hume's conclusion that it is impossible to acquire knowledge through anything other than experience. The distinction between perception and experience on the one hand and the ultimate causes of these on the other was clear and unarguable, however. Kant therefore differentiated between what he called *noumena*, the objects or things-in-themselves, and *phenomena*, the things-as-they-appear as perceived and experienced by us. Noumena can have an existence independently of our ability to perceive them or form ideas about them whereas phenomena clearly cannot.

We might be tempted to think that we are back on track towards re-establishing our first assumption, but Kant insisted on a fairly significant trade-off. We can never have knowledge of the noumena, the things-in-themselves, because these are simply beyond experience. Hume would have said that noumena are therefore metaphysical and meaningless, but Kant argued that, through phenomena, the noumena impress themselves upon our minds because our minds have what he called *sensible intuitions*. We develop mental faculties that allow us to make sense of the world and these faculties enable us to develop intuitive knowledge. Developing these faculties makes perception and experience possible in the first place or, in other words, these faculties determine the form of perception and experience that we can have.

The form of experience precedes the content of experience. We may then ask: if the content derives from phenomena, the result of sense impressions ultimately caused by noumena, from what is the form of experience derived? From *pure intuition*, Kant said. Within this pure intuition Kant included our conception of space and time. He wrote:

What, then, are space and time? Are they real existences? Are they only determinations or relations of things, yet such as would belong to things even if they were not intuited? Or are space and time such that they belong only to the form of intuition, and therefore to the subjective constitution of our mind, apart from which they could not be ascribed to anything whatsoever?

Our first assumption concerning the common-sense nature of reality would have space and time as real existences, a kind of independent 'container' that objects can exist in and events can happen in. Empty the container completely so that there are no objects and nothing happens and, we would likely conclude, space and time still continue to exist. Some philosophers argued that there can be no absolute space or absolute time. They claimed that our conception of space and time are the result of the ordering of objects in certain relations with each other and events involving these objects occurring in relation with each other. They argued that there is no container. Take the object away and there is no space, no time. But these philosophers also maintained that such relations are real relations of real objects. Kant denied both of these different approaches to understanding the nature of space and time. Space and time are intuitions of our minds in order that we may have experiences of the appearance of objects and events.

Let's take a step back. Take your eyes away from these words and look around you. What do you see? You will perceive objects in your immediate environment (perhaps chairs, tables, fellow rail passengers, or whatever). Some of these objects are nearer to you and appear larger, some are further away and appear smaller. Your brain organizes this information so that you do not judge these objects to be necessarily larger or smaller, instead you judge them to have certain spatial relations one with another. This object is close, this one is further away. You conclude that these are objects in space. If pushed, you could even estimate the distances between them and draw them out on a piece of paper illustrating their spatial relations to you.

But just exactly where is this space supposed to be? Can you see it? Can you touch it? You might think these questions are a bit absurd. But no matter how hard you search for it, you will not find space. Space is not something that we perceive. We perceive objects to have certain relations one with another but the relations themselves do not form part of the content of our direct experience. The relations are the result of a certain synthesis of sense impressions in our brains translated by our minds, with the end result that we perceive objects in a three-dimensional space.

There is no solace to be found in modern neuroscience and cognitive science. Put yourself back in front of the Astronomical Clock, in Prague's Old Town Square. Now walk around, first to the left, then to the right, keeping your eyes fixed on the clock dial. What's happening? The answer seems obvious. You are moving around in relation to the fixed position of the clock, changing your spatial relation to it: now nearer, now further away, at one angle and then another. The clock and the space around it represent for you a specific 'frame of reference' against which you judge the spatial relations of the clock, yourself and your fellow tourists.

Where does this frame of reference exist? The most obvious way to think about this is in relation to your eyes. Again, for simplicity, we'll focus our attention on a single eye. When you look at the clock dial, light reflected from its surface enters your eye and forms an image on your retina. There is good evidence from cognitive science that this sensory information is processed in the brain and synthesized in the mind to create an eye-centred map of space. Close your eyes. You can still judge the position of the clock dial in front of you. Keep your eyes closed as you now walk to your left or right, forward or back. Chances are, if you now point in the direction in which you think the clock dial lies and then open your eyes, you will find that your judgement is pretty accurate.

The eye-centred map is not located in your retina, but in those parts of your brain where visual information is processed and, of course, as short-term memory in your mind. It is also a dynamic map that is acutely aware of your own position within it. People who have suffered damage to their brain's parietal lobe may also suffer from *optic ataxia*. They are unable to form a proper frame of reference in their mind and so experience great difficulty locating objects in relation to their own body.

When we put both your eyes together and combine their eye-centred maps, then the result is a spherical map of space located between your eyes.

Your eyes are constantly moving about. As you read these words you perceive your eye movements to be smooth as you move from one word to the next, from one line down to another. However, your eye movements are, in fact, very jerky movements called *saccades*. Look for these by watching your eyes in a mirror, and you will not see them. Look for them in the eyes of another in a mirror and you will see them readily. Clearly, an eye-centred map of space that was constantly jumping around in relation to our jerky eye movements would be difficult to cope with. The brain compensates for this movement, creating the mental impression of a fixed frame of reference against which we can judge the spatial relations of the objects around us.

None of this seems particularly remarkable. The brain organizes our visual sense impressions in order to create a fixed frame of reference in our minds, reflecting the real space of the reality in which we are moving and in which we are perceiving objects.

Not so fast. This fixed frame of reference is very much an intuition, as Kant had argued. Although vision is the principal sense with which we locate ourselves in relation to objects around us, it is not the only sense we use. Your brain also uses information from the somatic sensory cortex, from touch. It uses information from the auditory cortex, from your left and right ears, to create auditory maps; it is constantly processing information from your own bodily movements. Recent evidence from cognitive science points to the existence of multiple frames of reference in the brain and therefore multiple 'spaces', each linked to a different action or region of space.

Clues as to the origin of these multiple frames of reference can be drawn from patients suffering damage to various parts of the brain's parietal lobe, and from direct experiments. Neurons in a part of the parietal lobe called the ventral intraparietal area respond strongly to visual sensations but also respond to touch. The visual sensations are both eye-centred and head-centred, and seem to be focused on objects heading in the direction of our mouths. Neurons in the medial intra-parietal area respond to objects within reaching distance. Neurons in the anterior intraparietal area respond to the shape of our hand as we reach out to grasp an object. Those in the lateral intraparietal area track stimuli resulting from our eye movements, and carry information concerning the distance and direction of stimulation reaching the retina. The brain automatically compensates our mental image of the world for often rapid changes in the position of our eyes. All this activity in the parietal lobe does not result in any actions we might take in terms of bodily movements, but it does contribute to forming our memory of space and bringing to our attention objects in it and events occurring in it.

We are left to conclude that there is no unique frame of reference created in the brain. Such a frame is the result of a synthesis in our minds creating the *impression* of uniqueness, leading to the intuition of space. Now, this impression might be the result of a real, unique three-dimensional space within which a world of mountains, streams, houses and trees really exists. To take such a view is to insist that our knowledge of objects and the space in which they exist must conform to the objects themselves and space itself. But this insistence falls prey to the claims of empiricists like Hume, who argue that knowledge beyond direct sensory experience is impossible. So Kant turned this argument on its head. He insisted instead that the objects of our experience conform to our knowledge of them, and the intuition of space is necessary for us to have any knowledge at all. Space, we might say, is the mind's way of preventing everything from being in the same place.

What of time? Look away from this book once more at the objects around you. Perhaps you can see a clock inexorably ticking your life away. Out of the window you might see cars go past, or factories, houses, trees or fields rushing by if you are on a train.[3] But, just as with space, you will not be able to reach out and touch time. Time is not a tangible object. Your sense of time would seem to be derived from a sense of objects changing their positions, or changing their nature, from one type of thing into another. But even this is a false impression, Kant insisted. Time is, like space, a pure intuition.

There are subtle differences between space and time in Kant's philosophy. Space, he argued, is a form of *outer sense*, meaning that it is a form of intuition that precedes experience of objects outside of ourselves. The intuition of space makes the experience of external objects possible. In contrast, time is a form of *inner sense*, meaning that it is a form of intuition that makes possible the ordering (and, indeed, the having) of mental states. If we did not have mental states in time, then we would not be able to experience external objects as being in time. This fixes time firmly in our mental world.

Let's return (for the last time, I promise) to the Astronomical Clock. We are gathered in the Old Town Square at ten minutes to one o'clock, awaiting the inexorable turn of gears to cause Death to pull the bell

3. Actually, if you are sitting on a train on your way into London then time may seem to have stopped altogether. Trust me; this is an illusion.

cord and commence the procession of the apostles. How should we attempt to understand what's happening? We tend to interpret the flow of time always in only one direction and such that certain events are either past, present or future. So, as we wait for Death to do his thing, we could say that the event in which Death pulls the bell cord lies in the future. At exactly one o'clock, Death pulls the bell cord. We say that the event in which Death pulls the bell cord is happening now, it is in the present.

We are all suitably impressed and entertained by the display that follows. Ten minutes later, the display has finished and the crowd of tourists gathered in front of the clock is starting to melt away. We say that the event in which Death pulled the bell cord lies in the past.

So far, so good.

We now turn to the work of the English philosopher John McTaggart Ellis McTaggart. He was born John McTaggart Ellis in London in 1866. His family took the surname McTaggart as a condition of an inheritance from Sir John McTaggart, a maternal grand uncle, and so he became John McTaggart Ellis McTaggart. He studied philosophy at Cambridge and became a friend of the novelist Thomas Hardy. In his principal philosophical work *The Nature of Existence*, which was published in two volumes in 1921 and 1927, McTaggart denied the reality of space, time and material objects and insisted that all substance is spiritual. Reality is not material, but spiritual, and only individual minds, related to each other by love, can be considered to be real.[4]

McTaggart named the time series referred to by the terms 'in the past', 'in the present', and 'in the future' as the *A* series. These terms are obviously mutually exclusive. An event that is in the past cannot be in the present or in the future, and so on for the other possible permutations. Obvious, perhaps, but also in one sense contradictory. Look back at our experience in front of the Astronomical Clock. In the description given above, the event of Death pulling the bell cord was in the future, it was in the present and it was in the past. In fact, every event satisfies all the terms in the *A* series, even though they are

4. Hmm . . .

obviously mutually exclusive. This is *McTaggart's paradox*.

'Ah,' I hear you say, 'that's nonsense.' Quite clearly, the event in which Death pulls the bell cord indeed satisfies all the different terms in the *A* series but it does so at *different times*, at ten minutes to one o'clock, one o'clock and ten minutes after one o'clock. Okay, so let's try this. At exactly one o'clock, we could say that the event in which Death pulls the bell cord is present *in the present*. This same event is also past *in the future* and it is future *in the past*. These statements are all compatible, so there's no paradox.

But wait. At ten minutes to one the event is future *in the present*, at one o'clock the same event is present *in the present* and at ten minutes past one the event is past *in the present*. These statements are clearly incompatible, so our attempt to resolve McTaggart's paradox by shifting to a second level of terms in the time series has not succeeded. It should by now have become obvious that going to a third level will also fail.

It seems we have no alternative but to revert to what McTaggart called the *B* series. In this series events occur earlier than, are simultaneous with, or are later than one another. So, the event in which Death pulls the bell cord is earlier than another event in which you look at the clock at ten minutes past, it is simultaneous with you looking at the clock at one o'clock and it is later than the event in which you look at the clock at ten minutes to one.

McTaggart argued on this basis that the *A* series, our sense of past, present and future, *is not real*. We can only resolve the paradox by switching to a new set of terms that, unlike the *A* series, are individually true at any moment in time. For example, the statement that Death pulled the bell cord in the past is clearly not true for any time prior to or during the actual event of Death pulling it, whereas the statement that Death pulled it at a time later than ten to one is true at any time. By switching to the *B* series, we have given up our concept of *tense* which, McTaggart argued, is fundamental to our conception of time itself. He wrote:

The reality of *A* series, then, leads to a contradiction, and must be rejected. And, since we have seen that change and time require the *A* series, the reality of time and change must be rejected. And so must the reality of *B* series, since that requires time. Nothing is really present, past, or future. Nothing is really earlier or later than anything else or temporally simultaneous with it. Nothing really changes. And nothing is really in time. Whenever we perceive anything in time – which is the only way in which, in our present experience, we do perceive things – we are perceiving it more or less as it really is not.

Whether we accept McTaggart's arguments or not, this kind of thing only points up the great difficulty associated with grasping the nature of time from our perceptions and experience of the external world around us. Kant would not have been surprised by this difficulty. For him, time is a form of intuition, an inner sense originating in our minds that enables us to experience events involving objects as being in time.

Time, we might say, is the mind's way of preventing everything from happening at once.

In 1543, Nicolaus Copernicus had shocked the world by insisting the previous conception of a universe with the earth at its centre was wrong. Astronomical data could be interpreted and understood much more simply and easily, and predictions of astronomical events could be made so much more reliably, if it was assumed that the sun was at the centre of the universe and that the earth orbited the sun, once a year. Placing space and time in the context of pure intuitions, creating the very possibility of perceiving phenomena related to the objects of sensory experience was, Kant argued, no less a revolution in philosophical thought than was Copernicus' heliocentric universe a revolution in cosmology.

I have here treated Kant's main philosophical arguments in terms of an *imposition* on to objects in the noumenal world of the intuitions of space and time (and hence of cause and effect) and of the perception and experience of phenomena by our minds. Kant's writings are notoriously hard to follow and difficult to interpret, but this is a common interpretation and it is impossible to understand several of his proofs without it.

So, where does this leave us? On the one hand Kant seems to be agreeing with Hume that we can never have knowledge of the noumenal world, the world of things-in-themselves, as noumena lie beyond the possibility of experience. The reality that Kant is prepared to subscribe to is the purely empirical reality of direct experience, of phenomena, made possible through our mental intuitions of space and time.

On the other hand Kant's reasons for this conclusion are very different from Hume's. Hume argued that reality is empirical because we can never be certain of the existence of a world independently of our ability to perceive and experience it. Questions concerning the possibility of an independent reality are therefore meaningless meta-physical questions. For Kant, this is not a question of uncertainty concerning what we can ever know about things we can't directly experience. Kant is certain that we can *never* know anything about the noumenal world.

Whichever way we look at it, our common-sense assumptions concerning the nature of reality have been completely shredded. Space and time, cause and effect, the appearance of objects in the world around us, are all products of our minds. If we try to think about what it might now be like on a Kantian un-earth, where there are no minds to have perceptions, experiences and ideas, we find we cannot. We can't possibly imagine a world without space, without time. This shouldn't be surprising: our imagination must still conform to our intuitions, and our intuitions give us space and time as a framework in which to order our thoughts and mental images.

We seem to be stuck in a real bind. All our attempts to make sense of an external reality, from the level of social reality to the physical reality that underpins it, have broken on the rocks of the internal world of the mind. We are trapped. Locked in a mental prison from which there appears to be no escape. Only now, perhaps, do we comprehend the real power of Plato's allegory, especially if we extend it to include Kant's intuitions of space and time.

Is there a way out?

8

Doppelgänger

> I have to believe in a world outside my own mind. I have to
> believe that my actions still have meaning, even if I can't
> remember them. I have to believe that when my eyes are
> closed, the world's still there. Do I believe the world's still
> there? Is it still out there? . . . Yeah. We all need mirrors to
> remind ourselves who we are. I'm no different.
>
> Leonard Shelby, *Memento*

Our last hope lies in the recognition that virtually everything we have
so far considered about the relationship between the mind and the
world has been based on an implicit assumption. This is an assumption of the worst, most insidious kind. Worst, because it is not obvious that it is an assumption at all.

Everything we have considered so far has been founded on the
assumption of a clearly drawn boundary between the internal world
of the mind and an external world of some description, whether this
be an independent reality (noumenal or otherwise) or the result of the
machinations of a higher power, or a demon, or an evil scientist, or
posthuman beings from the future.

Descartes tends to be blamed for this assumption, somewhat
unjustly in my view. His dualist ideas about a mysterious mind substance have by now been largely laid to rest, but implicit in his philosophy was a clear distinction between mind on the one hand and the
physical world on the other. I would argue that this assumption is perfectly natural and derived from familiar sense experience. Our minds

are things we seem to carry around with us in our heads. The physical world is something we reach for outside of ourselves to see, hear, touch, taste or smell. What could be more natural?

If the first step towards understanding whether or not this is an assumption that can be justified is to recognize that it *is* an assumption, then the second step is to explore its content and its implications. To simplify this task a little, I'm going to restrict myself to a model that is in keeping with my own materialist predilections. From the perspective of materialism, mental activity is a higher-order emergent property of electrical activity occurring in the brain. I would be the first to admit that, whilst this might read quite reasonably on paper, it is of course no explanation at all.

I'm reminded of a cartoon used by the philosopher Daniel Dennett in his book *Consciousness Explained*.[1] The cartoon shows two scientists talking about a mathematical derivation chalked up on a blackboard. The second step of the derivation reads: 'Then a miracle occurs.' One scientist is saying to the other: 'I think you should be more explicit here in step two.' To say that mind is a higher-order emergent property of the brain is simply to say 'Then a miracle occurs', but using a set of words that implies something less than the miraculous. But still, this is about the best we can do within the limitations of our current scientific understanding of consciousness and the mind.

The materialist perspective has two consequences. The first is that my mental activity – thoughts, beliefs, desires, memories, and so on – is spatially located within my head. Nothing particularly earth-shattering about this, you might think. If we are prepared to set aside all the folklore and pseudo-science concerning the mind's ability to exert direct influence over objects in the physical world (also known as 'mind over matter') then we might come to accept that my thoughts are permanently confined inside my head with no capacity to go wandering off on their own outside.

The second consequence is that my mental content, the things that constitute my thoughts, beliefs, desires, memories, and so on, is

1. The cartoon in question comes from the magazine *American Scientist*, and appears on page 38 of the Penguin edition of *Consciousness Explained* published in 1993.

possessed by me and by me alone and does not depend on any feature of the external world. This is consistent with my assumption, repeated already many times, about the mind being an intensely personal, private place. We need to be careful to distinguish between how we acquire the mental content that we have and the nature of the content itself. Here we are focusing on the latter. No matter how I come to have the thoughts I have, the thoughts are mine and do not depend on features of the outside world.

These two consequences are quite distinct. I can claim to possess all my mental content quite independently of where this content might be located. It is a general observation of males that they sometimes think with a part of their anatomy that is not located in their heads, and this may sometimes lead to their undoing. *Possession does not imply location.* Likewise, this content might be located inside my head but – in a way that I will try to make clear below – it may not be wholly independent of the external physical world. *Location does not necessarily imply possession.*

Now that we understand the consequences of the assumption of a clear boundary between mind and world we can test it to see if it is really justified. Let's forget for a moment precisely what we have learned from previous chapters about what we can and cannot take for granted from information delivered to our minds by our senses. We are caught in a bind because we appear to be unable to gain knowledge of any kind of independent reality that may or may not exist outside of our mental world. The existence of the boundary between our minds and the external physical world means that we simply can't take for granted what (if anything) passes through this boundary. We can't be certain that our thoughts are not detached in some significant way from the precise nature of the external world, to the extent that even space and time become creations of our minds.

The assumption of a boundary means that we have divorced our minds from the world outside. So, here's the question. What if we take a leaf out of Kant's book and turn this argument on its head? What if we ask ourselves this: *Is thought of any kind actually possible without the outside world?* Can we convince ourselves of the existence of reality by the very fact that we can have thoughts at all? Descartes rather spectacularly put the mind centre-stage, since it was the only thing he felt he could be absolutely certain about. Kant's 'Copernican revolution' sucked the very nature of space and time inside the boundary, thereby also taking them centre-stage, inside the mind. In both cases the world that we perceive or the phenomenal world as-it-appears is a *product* of our mental capacities and intuitions. What we are proposing here is a Copernican revolution of a subtly different kind. We are seeking to put the physical world centre-stage, making mind a product of the world itself.

Remember that un-earth is a world without minds. We struggled even to begin to comprehend what this place might be like in a Kantian vision without space, and without time. With mind centre-stage, un-earth becomes incomprehensible.

What, then, might it be like to be a mind without a world to experience? *Anti-earth* is a place that I will not attempt to describe. Where un-earth has at least the appearance of a physical basis in mountains, streams, houses, trees and soft, brown earth, anti-earth has no physical basis whatsoever. It has no appearance. There are no objects on anti-earth – noumenal or otherwise – of which to have experiences. There are no experiences. There are no perceptions, no sensations.

To a certain extent, we do know something of what happens to a mind deprived of all sensory input. Even my local gym provides sensory deprivation facilities in the form of salt-water flotation tanks. Some people will pay good money for the opportunity to relax and unwind inside one. But such sessions are necessarily short. Extended periods of sensory deprivation can result in serious mental disturbance; victims report anxiety, depression, hallucinations and anti-social behaviour.

There was significant interest in the consequences of extended periods of sensory deprivation during two decades spanning the 1950s to the 1970s, most notably from the military forces of both Western democracies and Eastern communist regimes.[2] The West's interest was

2. Mild forms of sensory deprivation continue to be used for interrogation purposes, as illustrated by the notorious photographs of prisoners at Abu Ghraib prison, west of Baghdad in Iraq.

primarily defensive, derived from the concern that totalitarian regimes were using sensory deprivation and other techniques to brainwash their captives. This fear was portrayed to dramatic effect in John Frankenheimer's 1962 movie *The Manchurian Candidate* (though the brainwashing techniques used by the Koreans in the film were based on drug-induced hypnosis rather than sensory deprivation).[3]

But the Western military were not averse to experimentation with more offensive (and illegal) use of these techniques. In his book *The Guineapigs*, John McGuffin writes about the experiences of fourteen Irish political prisoners subjected to sensory deprivation experiments by the British Army in 1971, experiments that led to Britain's conviction at the International Court of Human Rights in Strasbourg. In an early chapter that traces the history of such experiments, McGuffin describes the 1958 work of the psychologist Donald Hebb, involving experiments on student volunteers:

To start with, the volunteers tended to sleep, but soon they found that it was becoming increasingly difficult to concentrate and they developed an acute desire for any kind of stimulation to break the monotony. Many then began to experience startling visual and auditory hallucinations and after a while were unable to distinguish waking from sleeping. Despite the high pay for just lying on their backs, few could last more than two days and the most anyone lasted was five days. Upon release they were given simple psychological tests which showed that their perceptions had become very disorientated – objects became blurred and fuzzy. More important from the investigators' point of view, while under the [sensory deprivation], they were found to be much more susceptible to *any* type of propaganda . . .

It seems that Hebb's experiments at McGill University in Montreal were sponsored by the Canadian Defense Research Board in order to understand the potential for the brainwashing techniques that American prisoners of war had been exposed to in Korea.

The result of extended sensory deprivation is mental disturbance verging on madness. Our minds simply cannot function properly unless they are in constant sensory contact with their physical

3. A remake directed by Jonathan Demme was released in 2004. The action has been updated from the Korean to the Gulf War.

environment. Some years after their experiences, several of those subjected to sensory deprivation experiments by British forces still suffered mental illness to varying degrees, from nightmares and headaches to depression and loss of concentration. One of the victims had to return frequently to a psychiatric hospital for treatment.

What, then, might we expect if we deprive of sensory input a young brain and a mind that has yet to be fully formed? We can already guess the answer. In 1959, neuroscientists David Hubel and Torsten Wiesel found that if they covered one eye of a young kitten for an extended period, then its visual cortex failed to develop properly and the kitten became blind in that eye. Although Hubel and Wiesel were awarded a Nobel prize for their work in 1981, the mechanism responsible for this failure of the visual cortex to develop properly was unknown until relatively recently.

In 2003, neuroscientists at the Massachusetts Institute of Technology discovered that this is not simply due to a lack of visual stimulation of the retina. The mechanism is actually chemical. Sensory deprivation results in the literal unravelling of the connections between neurons necessary for the transmission and processing of signals that ultimately lead to perception by the mind. The brain simply 'disconnects' the eye from which no useful information is being gained. This is why it is so essential to correct visual problems in young children. If deficiencies are not corrected, their young brains may become wired incorrectly, preventing the problem from ever being fixed.

Experiments in sensory deprivation should make it quite clear that the brain, and hence the mind, is very much a product of our experiences of the world around us. I have always quite liked the analogy between the brain and a particular type of information or software that is hard-coded in computer memory. Computer programs can be written that are then placed into so-called read-only memory (ROM) in a process called *burning*. We use this same language when we talk of burning a series of music tracks or a movie onto a compact disc or DVD. The information contained in the music tracks or movie is encoded and permanently stored in the medium. The brain appears to work in a broadly analogous fashion, except that the information it stores needs to be constantly refreshed or, at least, the pathways that are 'burned' into the brain need to be constantly exercised in order to keep them functioning properly.

But does this necessarily mean that, once my neural pathways have been formed, my thoughts are anything other than entirely my own, independent of the features of the world around me? To accept otherwise is to argue that my mental content is not just internal, it is not just inside my head. To accept this is to accept that, in a very significant sense, mental content is also *external* – it is also outside my head. How can this be?

Let's start by looking back at the nature of intentionality. Remember that intentionality is simply the property of our thoughts always being about things. We could assume that it is the objects that our thoughts are about that determine the content of our thoughts from the 'outside in', with the direction world-to-mind. In other words, the objects are 'out there', wherever 'there' is meant to be, and these objects cause us to have the thoughts we have. In this case, when I have a thought about water, for example, my thought refers to an external physical body of water, in a river, or a lake, or a glass. When I think about water, I mean the external physical stuff that we happen to call water. This doesn't mean that my thought must be based on words or names; I might simply mean an entirely sensory image, a series of visual, somatic sensory, auditory and taste signals that I translate in my mind as an image of wet, splashy stuff, good for drinking, goes hard when it gets cold.

This is different from the situation in which the content of my thought is derived internally, or from the 'inside out', in the direction mind-to-world. In this case, when I have a thought about water, the content of this thought is directed outwards and all the reference and meaning is just in my head.

Suppose that on the other side of the sun, occupying the exact same orbit as the earth but diametrically opposed to it, there exists an exact duplicate of earth which we can call *twin earth*. This planet shares earth's orbit around the sun and spins on its axis in the same way that the earth does, so that its days, seasons and years are the same as we experience them on earth. It also has its own moon, a carbon copy of our moon.

We can never see twin earth using an earth-based observatory, because wherever earth is in its orbit around the sun, twin earth is always on the other side. Further suppose that twin earth is populated by exact duplicates of all of us: me, you, President George W. Bush, all living duplicate existences. Right now, on twin earth, your doppelgänger is sitting in an exact duplicate of your present location, reading these exact same words.

Now, if all your thoughts about objects here on earth are internally derived, then in some way they are all dependent on you, your brain and your mind. We would expect your doppelgänger on twin earth, who remember is your exact twin, to have exactly the same mental content, because this is determined from the 'inside out'. He or she would be thinking the exact same thoughts.

If, instead, the content of your thoughts is derived from the 'outside in', from the existence of external physical objects such as mountains, streams, houses and trees in your immediate environment and with which you have established a causal connection, then your doppelgänger on twin earth, exposed to exactly the same mountains, streams, houses and trees, might be expected also to have exactly the same thoughts. With twin earth so defined, there is no way we can differentiate between the different origins of the content of these thoughts.

At least, this was the case until the early years of the nineteenth century, when chemists such as Louis Gay-Lussac in France and John Dalton in England argued over the interpretation of Gay-Lussac's law of combining volumes. The end result was an understanding that a molecule of water consists of one atom of oxygen and two atoms of hydrogen, in the combination we now write as H_2O. In itself this is not so remarkable. What is remarkable is that on twin earth the end result was an understanding that a molecule of water actually has a very different composition, which we write in terms of the formula XYZ.

To all intents and purposes, twin water is identical to water. It has the same physical properties (wet stuff, good for drinking, freezes at zero Celsius, boils at 100 Celsius) and the same appearance – it looks the same, sounds the same and tastes the same. On twin earth it is even called 'water'. But it is not the same. It is XYZ.

So, twin earth is not an exact duplicate of earth, after all. On twin earth the seas, lakes, rivers and streams (and clouds, reservoirs and hence human bodies) are actually filled with twin water, not water, though all the people on twin earth still call it 'water'. When you think of water here on earth, you have intentional states derived from the concept of water and its extension, H_2O.[4] When your doppelgänger on twin earth thinks of water, he or she actually has intentional states about the concept of twin water and its extension XYZ. When you think about water, whether you are familiar with its chemical composition or not, you *mean* H_2O. When your doppelgänger thinks about water, whether he or she is familiar with its chemical composition or not, he or she *means* XYZ.

Although you are identical in every way to your doppelgänger (except for the fact that your body is full of water, not twin water), it would seem that your thoughts are not, after all, identical. You might not be able to tell them apart, but the thoughts that you and your doppelgänger are having refer to different things. Does this mean, then, that all the reference and meaning contained in your thoughts about physical objects are determined by the very existence of these objects external to your mind? Does this mean that you can no longer be certain which thoughts you are thinking?

The contemporary philosopher Hilary Putnam (of brain-in-a-vat fame) thought so, and it is he who should be credited with the above twin earth thought experiment. Putnam used this thought experiment to argue that 'meanings just ain't in the head'. The meaning contained in our thoughts depends on the things with which we interact, or with which we form causal connections. You have thoughts about water because this is what you interact with. Your doppelgänger has thoughts about twin water because this is what he or she interacts with. Intentionality depends on context, on the establishment of

4. The word extension as used here simply means that the word water implies a whole bunch of other things, or extensions: wet stuff, good for drinking, freezes at zero Celsius, boils at 100 Celsius, consists of molecules of H_2O.

relationships between the content of your thoughts and the things that cause them.

Putnam's arguments have caused considerable debate in philosophy journals and books and, as far as I can tell, have been very successful in putting the case that the content of my mind is not just in my head. He argues that my mental content is not possessed uniquely by my mind and my mind alone but depends for its very existence on the placing of my mind within an external world.

But what about the location of this content? Does accepting Putnam's argument mean that in some obscure way my thoughts are happening in the world around me, that external objects are somehow doing some of my thinking for me?

No, it does not. It would be going much too far to suggest that inanimate objects in the world around you are capable of having your thoughts. What it does mean is that the *content* of these thoughts comes as much from the external world as from your internal mental world. If I take the external world away by depriving you of all sensory input for an extended period, then your mind can no longer function properly – you lose contact with a world that is responsible, at least in part, for the content of your thoughts.

The twin earth thought experiment has nothing to say about where your mental content might be located, but there have been many arguments put forward since Putnam's to the effect that your mental content is also, at least in part, located in the outside world. One of the most persuasive of these comes from the philosophers Andy Clark and David Chalmers and goes by the name of the *parity principle*. Their argument boils down to this. Much of our mental content is derived from the manipulation of objects that provide us with information. We tend to focus on the manipulation of these objects and the processing of the information as it occurs in our minds. Alice arranges to meet Bob on the street in front of the office on Wednesday at one o'clock in the afternoon. Alice therefore has this arrangement as a content of her memory. But, in truth, Wednesday is still nearly a week away and she's not good at remembering these things, so she puts the appointment into her Microsoft Outlook calendar on her laptop. Where is her mental content located now?

Fans of the 2000 movie *Memento* will recognize this problem. An insurance investigator named Leonard Shelby (played by Guy Pearce[5]) has suffered a head injury and can no longer make memories. To remember anything at all he has to leave Post-it notes for himself, and take Polaroid photographs. But this isn't enough. Notes and photographs can be easily lost. In one note he writes:

It's hard. I know it's hard. But you're a smart guy Leonard. You've got to figure out ways to keep yourself on the right track. The little notes aren't working out. Not for the more important stuff. You've got to find a more permanent way of writing things down.

He elects to tattoo some of the more important facts he has uncovered about his life and his circumstances on his own body. The movie unfolds backwards in time as Shelby tries to unravel the mystery surrounding the murder of his wife (and also his own injury, sustained during the murder).

Shelby manipulates the information that is made available to him by manipulating objects in the external world as a substitute for his own mental incapacity. Alice uses her calendar for entirely equivalent, though much less extreme, reasons. In Shelby's case, we can literally see what passes for the content of his memory in the form of his innumerable tattoos.

It is certainly a mistake to think that we carry about with us in our heads a perfectly recorded, highly detailed image of the world around us. Quite the contrary. We have learned instead to rely on the external world as a storehouse for much of what passes for our mental content. Just imagine for a moment that you are stopped in the street by a stranger who asks you for directions. Moments after giving directions, what do you remember? Can you describe the stranger in detail? In a series of experiments conducted on university students, they were stopped on campus by a stranger asking for directions. As they gave them, two men would pass between them carrying a door, hiding the substitution of one stranger for another. In many cases, the students

5. The film also stars Carrie-Anne Moss and Joe Pantoliano, and will therefore be well known to diehard fans of *The Matrix*.

would continue to give directions, oblivious to the fact that they were now addressing a completely different person.

The arguments put forward by Clark and Chalmers cover all aspects of how we gain mental content, including perception, reasoning and memory. Consciously or unconsciously, we interact with our environment, manipulate it and make use of it to represent things to us in ways that spare us the effort of having to force them directly into our minds. The end result is that our mental content is not just located in our heads.

It is at this stage that the materialist in me starts to get a little twitchy. To see why, let's extend Putnam's science fiction a little further. Remember, twin earth is always hidden from earth and there is no way we can know of its existence. Now suppose that some kind of superior alien intelligence has built a teleportation device and wants to try it out by playing some cruel tricks on earthlings and twin-earthlings. The aliens choose you. They beam you instantaneously to twin earth from your present location, sitting on the train reading this book, and simultaneously beam your doppelgänger to earth. You are transported to twin earth within the blink of an eye. As far as you can tell, nothing has changed. You are still sitting on the exact same train reading the exact same book. After a short time and for reasons best known to yourself, you get off the train, jump into a lake, thrash around and announce: 'This is water.' Though you get some very funny looks, nobody disagrees.

Let's take this step by step. The twin water in the lake has caused you to have certain visual, tactile and auditory experiences. You see twin water, it feels wet and it makes splashing sounds. But you have drawn on all your previous experiences of water on earth which, as John Searle would have it, form part of your mental background, to conclude that this is water, whereas it is really twin water. *You nevertheless think this is water*. Why would you think anything different? You certainly can't tell the difference. Putnam would say that your thoughts are now about twin water, and would conclude that this demonstrates that we can't be certain of our own thoughts. But there is at this stage no uncertainty in your mind.

As far as you are concerned, you have thoughts about water (and its extension H_2O). These thoughts have certain 'conditions of satisfaction', according to Searle. Whereas your perceptions are caused by objects in the physical world, with a direction that is incoming, or world-to-mind, your thoughts are outgoing, or mind-to-world. You may be fooled into thinking that all the conditions of satisfaction of your thoughts about water are met, but they're not. Despite appearances, this stuff is not water.

Contrary to Putnam, Searle argues in his book *Intentionality* that meanings are in the head and only in the head. These meanings are derived from our experiences of the physical world around us, in turn derived from sensory inputs – seeing, touching, tasting, smelling and hearing. These experiences also include everything we have ever been told and everything we have ever read, impressed on our brains through the formation of certain neural pathways and absorbed into our mental background.

Suppose that you work in a laboratory and can operate an instrument called a mass spectrometer (indulge me). This instrument can be used to identify the chemical components of substances such as water. After the incident in the lake, you take a sample of the water and analyse it with your mass spectrometer. You find that this is not water, it is XYZ. The conditions of satisfaction of your thoughts about water have not been met.

After a double-take, you check to make sure that the instrument is working properly. You run tests with samples of oxygen and hydrogen gas, which confirm that the instrument is working according to your expectations. You then analyse water samples from wherever you can find them. You are staggered by the results. Everything you have ever understood about the nature of water, right from your very first science class, is now being contradicted. You try more samples and use different instruments. You quickly become paranoid. All the water in the world has suddenly changed to XYZ. You ask your colleagues what has happened, and they look at you as though you have gone stark raving mad. How could you think that water is H_2O? They tell you that you seem to have been under a lot of pressure lately, and should maybe take a vacation. You eventually conclude that you have either gone mad or you are the victim of some incredible conspiracy . . .

Searle argues that meanings exist only in the mind because this is the only place they can exist. Nothing means anything on un-earth, where there are no minds. These meanings are projected 'inside out', mind-to-world. Our thoughts are internally derived from our mental background and pushed out into the world with varying conditions of satisfaction.

Taking such a position does not deny that the mind will struggle to function in the absence of sensory input. The sensory deprivation experiments would seem to suggest that the background is not something that develops in childhood and at some stage in life can be considered to be fully formed or complete. The background is not 'burned' into the brain once, like writing music tracks onto a compact disc. We continue to learn new things – forge new neural pathways – all our lives. That this might become more difficult with advancing years doesn't mean that it doesn't happen. With enough effort, old dogs can indeed learn new tricks. It shouldn't be surprising that the neural pathways become impaired, even 'overgrown', when they are not used because they are deprived of stimulation.

Mental content is precisely this: mental. It may well be that Leonard Shelby uses his tattoos as a reminder of important facts, but the first thing he has to do on waking is get them into his head by reading them. Alice will miss her appointment with Bob if she does not consult her calendar before Wednesday. No matter that the calendar represents for her a memory of the appointment created in the external world. If she does not get it back into her head then it represents no memory at all.

The fact that we do not carry a fully detailed representation of the world around with us in our heads is a simple reflection of the fact that we don't need to. We are efficient in our use of our mental capabilities (or, if you prefer, lazy). Students do not notice that the stranger they're giving directions to has been substituted because they're not paying attention. There's an awful lot that goes on in the world around us that we are not aware of and cannot later remember because we don't pay it any attention. Sometimes we'll drive a car to our destination and arrive without having any recollection of the journey. Have we driven dangerously? No, chances are we've driven perfectly safely, but the attention we've been giving to the act of driving has not been the kind that leaves persistent traces in memory.

On this argument, we seem to be right back where we started, with the boundary between mind and world firmly intact. With the boundary intact, it is perhaps difficult to build a defence against Plato's cave, Descartes' demon, or Kant's intuitions.

Whether or not you believe that there is a significant boundary between mind and world, it seems quite clear that our mental backgrounds have been formed by virtue of all the experiences we have had, all the things we have seen, touched, tasted, smelled and heard. All the things we have been told or have read. The direction of our perceptual experience appears to be firmly 'outside in', or world-to-mind. The sensory deprivation experiments make it painfully obvious that the mind cannot function without the world; that it is a product of the world and not the world that is a product of the mind.

You might by now have come to believe that you have reached the bottom of the rabbit hole. All around you is complete darkness, and silence. And I suspect that you have also by now grown weary of philosophers.

Perhaps you can draw some comfort from the fact that you have discerned progress of a sort in the philosophy of the last two and a half thousand years. But despite this progress, perhaps you also feel that you are still left with more questions than answers, and it is answers you now need.

There is little to dispute in the arguments we have studied carefully and tried so hard to understand. Yes, of course it is true that we can have knowledge only of the things we experience or can intuit and yes it is true that we cannot separate our understanding of reality from the operation of our minds. And yet, when all is said and done, you have lived your life quite happily under the assumption that the world around you is quite real and quite independent of your ability to conceive it and form theories about it.

Look around you at the collection of consumer goods you have assembled – maybe you have a wide-screen television, DVD player, stereo, refrigerator, dishwasher, espresso machine, microwave oven, and so on. These are surely all products of a technology founded on scientific understanding, an understanding surely underpinned by the presumption of an independent reality that can be manipulated to suit human purposes? A reality founded on natural laws, of cause and effect, of progressive evolution towards some kind of truth about the world as it really is. A reality of unobservable things like electrons buzzing along the mains cable into your home or office computer and dancing through its collection of transistors, resistors, capacitors, microchips and a myriad other electrical components that make the computer work. How could this not be real?

Maybe you now feel in need of an antidote to all the philosophy, from Heraclitus' world of flux through Plato's prisoners to Kant's intuitions to Putnam's twin earth experiment. Time to seek solace in the certainties of science.

I'm not sure how best to break this to you. Despite what you might think, you're still a long way from the bottom. There is still quite a way to fall.

PART THREE

Physical Reality
or
Are Photons Real?

9

Terra Firma?

All my life, I worshipped her
Her golden voice, her beauty's beat
How she made us feel
How she made me real
And the ground beneath her feet.
U2, *All That You Can't Leave Behind*

Philosophers tend to fret about what we can and can't know. As we've seen, the battle between reason and experience was joined by Heraclitus and Parmenides about two and a half thousand years ago and has been fought by philosophers ever since. Whilst we now think we know an awful lot more about the nature of our world, it is perhaps hard to see who is winning this particular philosophical war.

Kant's insistence that our perception of space, time, cause and effect is as much a creation of our minds as it is the result of real features of the external world might have persuaded some, but scientists are generally more pragmatic souls. Scientists deal with the world as they find it, and most do not have much time for deliberating on complex philosophical problems that appear to have no solutions. Besides, anyone with any experience of a world of objects moving through space and time (which means all of us) would surely conclude that these are features of the world that are uniform and predictable, and exist independently of our minds.

Scientists deal with a world of experience, one that can be manipulated and exposed to intense scrutiny through questions asked of it by direct observation and experiment. Even theoretical physicists are brought back down to earth by the need to make their theories relate to observable or measurable properties. Scientists would claim that they are no less rigorous in their thinking than philosophers, but they are generally prepared to take certain things at face value. Scientific reasoning is more concerned with the logical viability and testability (and, though it's not always admitted, the beauty and simplicity) of theoretical constructions developed to describe and explain the world as it is perceived and experienced.

Most experimental scientists assume that what they deal with every day in their observatories or laboratories is not only real but is real quite independently of themselves. If you were to ask them if they thought the objects of their studies were real, I suspect you would get some very quizzical looks. After all, it would surely be hard for any-one to justify the estimated two and a half billion dollars being spent building the Large Hadron Collider at the European Centre for Particle Physics (CERN) in Geneva if they were not convinced of the reality of the particles that they plan to study with it.[1]

Welcome to terra firma.

Now, we're not going to demand too much. We're not going to expect that science provides us with the ultimate answer to 'life, the universe and everything'. All we will ask is that science furnish us with answers to four basic questions concerning the constitution of our physical reality. What is space? What is time? What is matter? What is light? It is hard to imagine that we could have achieved our present level of technological sophistication without answers to these simple questions.

We should set aside any residual concerns we might have about the relationship between our minds and the world around us and concen-

---

1. A colleague reports the experience of once being escorted along the tunnel of a par-ticle accelerator by a physicist during a routine visit. The physicist advised him that there was nothing very interesting to see for the next few kilometres. As they walked along in silence, my colleague asked the physicist whether it had ever struck him that this whole enterprise was slightly mad. The physicist reflected for a moment then said, 'No.'

trate on what science has to say. Here, at least, we might expect to find some answers, not just more philosophical conundrums.

Space and time are closely inter-connected. Our sense of time is strongly linked to our perception of the motions of the stars, sun, moon and planets through space. The earth turns on its axis and day becomes night. The phase of the moon changes and February becomes March. The earth trundles around its solar orbit and wobbles on its axis, and winter becomes spring. With each orbit a year passes, we are a year older, policemen look younger and popular music becomes harder to appreciate.

If we're looking for a universal clock then surely we need to look no further than the heavens. The very idea of the universe as clockwork is deeply reassuring. When faced with the dizzying unpredictability of our social lives, it is encouraging to think that the physical foundations on which our lives are built are solid, dependable and predictable.

There are some[2] who will argue that this kind of predictability leaves no room for free will, but let's not be distracted. I, for one, am immensely reassured when the sun rises on a new day. It is enormously helpful for me to be able to find things in the places where I left them. Without a high degree of certainty and predictability in the physical world around us, it is clear that we would not be able to live.

To be fair, basing our measure of time on our immediate neighbours in the universe leaves us with some choices, because our neighbours sit at different distances from earth. We have chosen to use the sun, not least because it's that big yellow thing in the sky which fills our world with light. A solar day is the time between successive appearances of the sun on the meridian, which we divide (for historical reasons) into twenty-four hours. This would be fine if it were not for the fact that the earth is not only turning on its own axis, it is also moving around the sun. This means that the earth has to turn a little more than 360 degrees each solar day. Because the fixed stars are so much further away from the earth, it would actually make more sense to base our measure of time on the earth's rotation in relation to the

2. Philosophers, again.

stars. As already mentioned in Chapter 7, a sidereal day is the time taken for one complete 360-degree rotation of the earth measured in relation to the stars, and is on average about four minutes shorter than a solar day. Does this matter? It does if you're trying to predict the exact time of the next solar eclipse.

Astronomers have always been able to increase their status in society and their sense of self-importance by being able to predict eclipses. Remember how the hero of Mark Twain's *A Connecticut Yankee in King Arthur's Court* rescues himself from burning at the stake by pretending to work a magic much more powerful than Merlin's? He uses his knowledge of an impending eclipse at three minutes past noon on 21 June AD 528 and pretends to command that the sun's light be magically obscured. The trick would not have worked nearly so well if he'd been even a few minutes out.

Driven by the need for better time-keeping, astronomers wrought our present-day understanding of the clockwork universe from ever more detailed observations of the motions of the stars through space. This is an exemplary lesson in the triumph of scientific reasoning and therefore well worth retelling, if only very briefly.

The philosophers of ancient Greece had developed a picture of the universe that placed the earth at its centre. An essential element in this picture was the Aristotelian ideal of the perfect circle, and the motions of the stars around the earth appear to all intents and purposes to conform to this ideal. If we watch them long enough and track their motions through the night sky, distant stars appear to move in circles around the earth. However, as seen from the earth, the motions of the planets (the 'wandering stars') are far from circular. In about AD 150, the Greek philosopher Claudius Ptolemy attempted to explain the motions of the planets around the earth by constructing an elaborate theory based on epicycles (and much more besides). The epicycles were combinations of circles which at least preserved the ideal of circular motion. To a certain extent he succeeded, but as astronomical observations became more accurate he found that he had to make his model more and more complicated.

When the king of Spain was shown Ptolemy's model some eleven hundred years later, he remarked that if God had consulted him before embarking upon the creation, he would have suggested something simpler.

Science had the simpler answer. In 1543 Nicolaus Copernicus placed the earth in an orbit around the sun and placed the sun at the centre of the universe, and immediately resolved most of the complexities and anomalies of Ptolemy's model. Although it was still very dangerous to contradict Aristotelian wisdom, which had by now become religious dogma, it was still possible to argue that the universe behaved 'as if' the sun were at the centre. It helped that Copernicus' orbits were still circular.

Whilst studying at the University of Copenhagen in 1560, the eccentric Dane Tycho Brahe witnessed a partial eclipse of the sun. He was so struck by the fact that this eclipse had been predicted by astronomy that he decided there and then to commit the rest of his life to the art of exact astronomical observation.[3] Brahe spent about forty years building a vast compendium of the most accurate observations ever made of the positions of the planets and the visible stars. On his death in 1601 these data were inherited by his successor Johannes Kepler, a young mathematician recruited by Brahe a year earlier to help make sense of his observations.

The data that Brahe had collected on the motion of the planet Mars around the sun suggested that it could be generalized as a circular orbit. A circular orbit did fit the data, to within an accuracy of about eight minutes of arc, and it is a credit to Kepler that he considered this was not good enough. Brahe's observations were more accurate than the predictions and so, Kepler reasoned, the motion couldn't be circular. The result of about twenty-five years of incredibly hard labour using Brahe's data was, as we now know, Kepler's three laws of planetary motion.

The planets move not in circular orbits around the sun, but in *elliptical* orbits with the sun at one focus. This means that any given planet

---

3. Brahe also fought a duel with another student (his third cousin, Manderup Parsberg) over which of them was the better mathematician. It's not clear who won, but Brahe had part of his nose sliced off. For the rest of his life he wore a false nose made of silver and gold.

is closer to the sun for some parts of its orbit and more distant for other parts. Kepler also noted a balance between the distance of the planet from the sun and the speed of its motion in the orbit. A planet moves faster around that part of its orbit that takes it closest to the sun, and more slowly in that part that is more distant, such that a line drawn from the sun to the planet sweeps out equal areas in equal times.

Finally, Kepler also discovered a relationship between the mean radius of a planet's orbit and the time taken for a planet to complete one trip around the sun (called the period of the orbit). He found that the ratio of the cube of the mean radius to the square of the period is approximately constant for all the planets in the solar system.[4]

There is nothing in Kepler's laws that suggest an explanation or a theory as to why the planets move around the sun in the way they do. The laws are simply generalizations of many thousands of astronomical observations. But Kepler's laws provided clues to an understanding of the basic physics of planetary motion which do explain why they move the way they do. The theory that underpins them and makes sense of them is Isaac Newton's theory of motion combined with Newton's theory of universal gravitation, which he first published in 1687.

Newton's second law of motion connects the acceleration of objects with their mass and the force applied to them. The harder I push an object the more it accelerates. Newton's law of gravitation connects the force acting between two objects with their masses and the inverse square of the distance between them. If we combine these laws,[5] then we immediately find a relationship between the cube of the mean radius of the orbit and the square of its period – Kepler's third law.

Here we see a natural progression from Ptolemy's epicycles, to

4. For example, the mean radius of earth's orbit is about 150 million kilometres and it obviously takes on average a little over 365 days to complete one round trip. For Mars, the equivalent figures are 229 million kilometres and 687 days. So, for earth the ratio of the cube of the mean radius to the square of the period is 25.3 billion billion cubic kilometres per square day, for Mars it is 25.4.
5. This is easy to do in the case of circular orbits, but a little more difficult for elliptical orbits.

Copernicus' heliocentric model, to Kepler's empirical laws to Newton's laws of motion and gravitation. We need not be detained by the fact that understanding did not tumble out quite as neatly as this short summary would suggest. Here, surely, we have science leading us relentlessly closer to the truth about reality as it really is; a mechanical clockwork constructed in a frame defined by an absolute time, and an absolute space, that had survived for all eternity.

Newton's physics was a physics of absolutes. He even had an answer for those with incessant philosophical questions as to just where this absolute space was supposed to be found.

Go out into the garden. Tie one end of a rope to the handle of a bucket and tie the other end around the horizontal branch of a tree, so that the bucket is suspended in mid-air. Fill the bucket three-quarters full with water. Now turn the bucket so that the rope becomes more and more twisted. When you feel you can't turn the bucket any more, let go and watch what happens. The bucket will spin around as the rope untwists itself. At first the water in the bucket remains still. Then, as the bucket picks up speed, the water itself starts to spin and its initially flat surface becomes concave – the water is pushed out towards the circumference and up the inside of the bucket by the force of the rotation. Eventually, the spinning water catches up with the spinning bucket, and both spin around at the same rate.

Over your shoulder, Newton smiles. 'Look,' he says, 'absolute space. Can you see it?'

Here's the logic of Newton's argument. The surface of the water becomes concave because the body of the water is moving. This motion is either absolute or relative. But the water remains concave as its rate of spin relative to the bucket changes, and it remains concave when the water and the bucket are spinning at the same rate. The concave surface cannot therefore be caused by motion of the water relative to the bucket. It must therefore be caused by the absolute motion of the water. Absolute motion must therefore exist. Absolute motion can only exist in absolute space. Absolute space exists. QED.

So much for space and time. What of matter and light?

For Newton matter was simply a question of weight and quantity of material substance, which became much more tangible with the refinement of the concept of mass. Newton freed material objects from the relativity of gravitational attraction, which determines what an object weighs, and established that objects have an intrinsic mass related to their inertia, a measure of their resistance to acceleration. If an astronaut enjoying the experience of 'bunny-hopping' on the moon suddenly attempts to change his direction of motion, he quickly discovers that although he weighs less on the moon, he nevertheless retains all his mass. The 1989 movie *For All Mankind*, an anthology of clips from moon landings spanning the four-year period 1968 to 1972, shows a number of astronauts coming to grief as they struggle with the significant difference between their weight and their mass, a difference so counter-intuitive from all their previous experience of earth-bound physics. The result is a startling visual tribute to Newtonian mechanics.

Weight is relative, mass is absolute, and the transition to absolutes made Newton's a truly universal physics.

Newton also extended the scope of his mechanics to explain the properties of light and concluded that light consists of tiny particles, or corpuscles, which should in principle be subject to the same laws of motion as ordinary physical objects. This was his conclusion despite the fact that several of his contemporaries had advanced compelling theories of light based on wave motion.

It is hard to conceive descriptions of light that could be more different. A visual metaphor for Newton's light corpuscles would be infinitesimally small balls of some rubber-like substance, silently streaming through space in straight lines and bouncing off objects in all directions, like tiny rubber bullets. Contrast this with waves rippling outwards on the surface of an otherwise still pond, marking where a stone has been thrown. The waves are disturbances in the water, and it is the disturbance that moves outwards, not the water. The ripples move outwards as a result of the gentle up-and-down movements of the water in a uniform sequence.

In the years following Newton's death in 1727, experimental evidence continued to accumulate for the wave theory of light. One experiment stood out as particularly compelling. Imagine an apparatus consisting of a thin blackened metal plate with two narrow parallel slits and a piece of photographic film, with the film placed behind the slits. We shine light with a narrow range of wavelengths (or colours) on the plate with the slits. The light passes through the slits and we record the result on the photographic film. We see a pattern formed on the film consisting of a series of alternating bright and dark bands, called *interference fringes*.

We can interpret this result by invoking the wave properties of light. The light, we say, consists of waves that are forced to squeeze through the narrow slits, spreading out beyond much like the ripples on the surface of the pond. The waves from the two slits overlap with each other and, where wave crest meets wave crest, the result is a larger crest. Where crest meets trough, they cancel each other out and the result is stillness. Such constructive and destructive interference of the waves produces the pattern of fringes. We can see similar interference effects in the splashes of colour reflected from a shallow pool of water whose surface is contaminated with oil, or from the surface of a soap bubble. These variations in colour are produced by the interference of light reflected from the upper and lower surfaces of the thin film of oil on water, or the inner and outer surfaces of the soap bubble.

The wave theory of light proved ultimately irresistible. With this modification, there were very few aspects of the world that Newton's grand physics of the cosmos could not explain in terms of the mechanical interplay of physical forces, material particles and wave disturbances, all acted out within the container whose walls were absolute space, governed by the universal clockwork of absolute time. Its laws represented deep, underlying physical principles that govern the behaviour of all objects, all mass, all motion, throughout the entire universe.

These laws were certain. There was no doubting them. Let the philosophers worry away at problems of their own making, but there was little room for any doubt about what Newton's physics was telling us about the real world.

Like Alexander, a physicist of the late nineteenth century might have wept, for it really did seem that there were no more worlds to conquer.

There were some cracks in the plasterwork of Newton's great edifice, however. His force of gravity was, in truth, a little mysterious. In all of his mechanics, force is a physical phenomenon exerted through contact between one object and another, just as one billiard ball causes another to move by colliding with it and so imparting energy to it. Gravity appeared to be an influence felt through mutual action-at-a-distance between objects, exerted instantaneously, with nothing but empty space in between.

Throw an apple (or, if you prefer, a lemon) high into the air. What causes it to fall back? Gravity, of course. But how? What is it that reaches up and pulls it back? Some physicists invented a hypothetical, all-pervading, tenuous form of matter called the *aether* that was meant to fill up the space between objects and carry the force of gravity from one to another.

A very different problem was awarded a similar solution. Just as the ripples on the surface of the pond are ripples *in* water, and sound waves are compressions and rarefactions *in* the air, so all wave motion requires a medium to support it. Waves must be waves in something. What, then, were light waves meant to be waves in? The answer was again the aether. Light waves were meant to be waves in a stationary aether which fills all of space.

But if space was meant to be filled with aether then it was reasonable to expect certain physical consequences. Earth's motion through a stationary aether was expected to give rise to a drag effect. This meant that there should be measurable differences in the speed of light depending on the direction it is travelling relative to the earth. In precise experiments conducted towards the end of the nineteenth century, no such effect could be found.

Then there was this little problem with the speed of light itself.

If you have ever passed through a busy airport, then you will almost certainly have travelled on a moving walkway. Now you can stand on this walkway and let it carry you along at a speed of, say, five kilometres per hour. Or you can carry on walking along the moving walkway, as most self-important businessmen tend to do, usually with a mobile phone clamped to their ear. If you walk at five kilometres per hour along a walkway that is moving at five kilometres per hour then you are obviously moving at a total of ten kilometres per hour.

Recall the plot of the 1990 movie *Die Hard II*, in which Bruce Willis reprised his role as the New York cop John McClane. Suppose McClane is entering the empty, half-finished airport building in search of a satellite communications terminal so that he can make an urgent call for help. It is dark, but he's carrying a flashlight. As he walks along, at five kilometres per hour, light from the flashlight streams ahead of him and reveals a bad guy, lying in wait. He fires his Colt M4 assault rifle, releasing a deadly bullet with a muzzle velocity of 3,259 kilometres per hour. He climbs onto a moving walkway, and carries on walking. He is now moving at ten kilometres per hour. He fires his rifle again. What is the speed of the bullet this time? And what is the speed of the light from his flashlight?

If you conclude that the bullet now leaves the rifle with a total velocity of 3,264 kilometres per hour measured relative to a stationary bad guy, then you'd be right. Emboldened, you might be tempted to say that the speed of the light must also be whatever it was when McClane was walking plus five kilometres per hour, the speed of the moving walkway. But now you would be wrong. The speed of the light never changes. It remains constant, irrespective of the speed of its source.

The speed of the light is so fast compared to the moving walkway that this fact might not trouble you. But if we were to imagine that the walkway could move much faster, say at about one billion kilometres per hour (about 90 per cent of the speed of light), then the fact remains that the speed of light is still unchanged. McClane travels along this walkway, never more than a few steps behind the front of the light beam. If he moved any faster he would start to catch up with it. If the bullet behaved the same way, then he would be able to see it hovering a short distance from the barrel of the gun.

*

And so we come at last to a young technical expert, third class, working at the Swiss patent office in Berne in 1905. Albert Einstein had struggled to find a way to reconcile the failed attempts to find evidence for the aether and an apparently universal speed of light, independent of the relative motion of the source, with any kind of Newtonian interpretation of space and time. Eventually, he gave up. Undaunted, he turned the problem on its head. He asked, instead, what kind of theory we get if we take these undeniable experimental facts at their face value. What happens if we assume that every observer in the universe, whether stationary or in constant motion within their own spatial frame of reference, always perceives the laws of physics to be the same? What happens if we assume that the speed of light is a universal constant?

The result was Einstein's *special theory of relativity*.

The consequences are bizarre. If the speed of light is to be constant, then this must be because the sources of light travelling at different speeds have different times. The seconds, minutes and hours for one source must be different from those of the other. This property is not restricted to sources of light. *Time slows down the faster any object is moving.* John McClane can never quite catch up with the front of the light beam, because time slows almost to a halt the closer he gets to it.[6]

Suppose Alice and Bob are twenty-fifth century twins. Alice climbs aboard a spaceship, accelerates out of earth orbit and undertakes a long journey to Proxima Centauri, a tiny red dwarf star that forms part of the triple Alpha Centauri system in the constellation Centaurus and which happens to be the nearest star to our own sun. She travels at a constant speed of 90 per cent of the speed of light. On reaching her destination, she slows down, turns around and accelerates back to the same constant speed, and so returns to earth.

Back on earth, Bob monitors her progress anxiously. As far as he is concerned, her total round trip takes a little under nine and a half years. However, as far as Alice is concerned, her trip has taken less

6. I say almost, because the simple fact is that he can never actually reach the speed of light. As he accelerates closer and closer to this limiting speed, his mass (or, if you prefer, his resistance to further acceleration) increases towards infinity.

than half this, a little over four years. Her twin brother is now older by more than five years.[7]

The weirdness doesn't stop here. Measurements of distance become a matter of relative speed as well. Alice's sleek spaceship contracts in length as it travels at 90 per cent of the speed of light to less than half its original (stationary) length. This is usually interpreted not as a physical contraction, in which the atoms that make up the spaceship and everything in it all bunch up closer together, but as a contraction in space itself. At speeds close to that of light, one metre is no longer a metre measured relative to a stationary observer carrying a metre rule.

We might be inclined to dismiss these wild claims if they hadn't all been fully confirmed by experiment.

The full import of Einstein's breakthrough was understood a few years after publication of his first paper on relativity in 1905. The mathematician Hermann Minkowski pointed out that space and time had lost their independent meaning. It was necessary to abandon the Newtonian concept of a three-dimensional container full of absolute space in which a universal clock kept absolute time. It was no longer possible to say than an event occurred at some point in space and at some point in time. It is, however, possible to use a particular recipe to combine space and time and say that an event occurs at a particular point in *spacetime*. With the advent of Einstein's relativity, the physical world became four-dimensional as space and time began to blur into each other.

With no absolute space or absolute time, change as something that happens within an objective time interval becomes an illusion, as Parmenides, Kant and McTaggart had all once argued. There is only my subjective 'now' against which I judge everything to be past, present or future.

*

7. This is the famous twin paradox, although it is not, in fact, a paradox. Some physicists disputed that there would be an age difference between Alice and Bob because, relatively speaking, Bob has had the same experiences of relative motion as Alice. However, Alice is the only one of the two to have experienced acceleration by travelling in the spaceship and this destroys the symmetry between their circumstances.

Einstein wasn't quite done yet. His theory of relativity was 'special' simply because it could deal only with frames of reference at rest or moving at constant speeds. This theory had eliminated absolute distances and absolute time intervals, but it left absolute acceleration intact. When it came, eleven years later, Einstein's general theory of relativity eliminated that too, and incidentally explained how gravity is meant to work.

We are by now familiar with the visual metaphor of spacetime as a stretched two-dimensional rubber sheet, which heavy masses such as stars and planets distort in a third dimension, each dragging the sheet down and making a deep well. Objects on the surface of the sheet that roll too closely to one of these wells will be pulled down into it or, put another way, objects that stray too close to a planet's gravitational field will be pulled towards the planet through gravitational attraction. In Einstein's general theory, the action-at-a-distance implied by Newton's gravity is replaced by a *curved spacetime*.

Space and time had now not only blurred, they gained a *geometry* that could be straight or curved, depending on the presence of matter.

The arguments that Newton had used in connection with his bucket had perhaps contained another of those insidious assumptions, the kind that don't make their presence immediately obvious. Newton had assumed that when speaking of relative motion it was necessary only to consider the motion of the water relative to the bucket. Why consider any other objects? How could the concave surface of the water be the result of the presence of the tree, or the ground, or your house, or you, or Proxima Centauri, forty thousand billion kilometres away?

Einstein argued that the spinning water accelerates not absolutely, but relative to all the matter in the universe around it. If the water were stationary and all the matter in the universe were spinning, the surface of the water would still become concave, owing to the distortion of spacetime around a spinning mass that has subsequently been called *frame dragging*.

We should be careful not to gloat over Newton's discomfort, however. If we were somehow able to remove all the objects in the universe, leaving only the spinning bucket, we have grounds to believe that the surface of the water would still be concave. Space and time may themselves not be individually absolute, but spacetime might be. On 20 April 2004, the US launched Gravity Probe B into earth orbit. The probe is an incredible feat of twenty-first century engineering. It's purpose is to search for evidence of frame dragging by the rotating earth. It has spent the last year in earth orbit accumulating the data needed to prove frame dragging one way or the other. Results were not yet available at the time this book went to press, but I would encourage interested readers to follow progress on the web.[8]

In any case, with the appearance of Einstein's relativity, Newton's absolute space and time were gone, perhaps forever. And more deeply disturbing revelations were yet to come.

The quantum revolution was begun one day in October 1900. The German physicist Max Planck lit a slow-burning fuse which exploded almost thirty years later into the most profound shock for our human comprehension of the nature of matter, light and physical reality.

In order to solve some minor problem in what was almost a backwater of physics, Planck found himself to his horror having to claim that light energy is not continuous, pouring from one material object to another in a continuous stream, as had always been assumed. He had to argue instead that light comes in discrete lumps, or *quanta*.

Planck wasn't quite sure what to make of this conclusion, but Einstein certainly was. In his magically productive year of 1905, Einstein not only accepted the idea of light quanta (which were called *photons* many years later), he went on to use the idea to explain other puzzling phenomena and made predictions that could be tested experimentally. His predictions were proven experimentally some ten years later.[9] The result was quantum theory.

What was going on? Could it be that after so many physicists had fought so hard to establish a wave theory of light it was now going to turn out that light was, after all, made up of 'particles' of energy?

The answer was yes. And no. There was no denying the wave properties of light. Interference, and its explanation in terms of wave

8. You can find the Gravity Probe B website at http://einstein.stanford.edu/.
9. It was this work – not relativity – that was to win Einstein his Nobel prize for physics in 1921.

phenomena, was here to stay. But there was no denying the particle-like properties of light, either. In some wholly obscure way, light was both wave and particle.

But if light waves could be light-particles, could other, larger particles also be waves? This was the question that the French physicist Prince Louis de Broglie[10] asked himself. In 1923 de Broglie combined his work on radio waves and his interest in chamber music with the model of the interior of an atom that had been developed by the New Zealander Ernest Rutherford and the Danish physicist Niels Bohr some ten years before. This is the familiar planetary model of the atom, which at the time represented our best attempt at understanding the fundamental constituents of all matter.

In this conception, we imagine a small positively charged nucleus made up of protons and neutrons and containing most of the atom's mass concentrated at the centre. This nucleus is surrounded by orbiting negatively charged electrons, much like planets orbit the sun. This is a compelling model perhaps, but one that contradicts virtually every known physical law for electrically charged particles.

De Broglie thought instead of an electron in an atomic orbit as a kind of musical instrument. Just as musical notes are produced by so-called *standing waves* in the strings or pipes of musical instruments, so de Broglie imagined the electron orbits to be much like standing electron waves. Not everyone agreed. Some called his idea *la Comédie Française*. But it was already too late.

De Broglie, and subsequently the Austrian physicist Erwin Schrödinger, turned the picture of a tiny self-contained negatively-charged particle orbiting the nucleus into a picture of a negatively-charged electron wave 'cloud' of varying amplitude surrounding the nucleus.[11] Where was the electron in this picture? It had lost its

10. Pronounced 'de Broy'.

11. If you're struggling a little with the idea of the amplitude of a cloud, it might help to think instead of the difference between light summer clouds (low amplitude) and heavy, dark, wintry clouds laden with rain to come (high amplitude). The idea of an amplitude is not directly interchangeable with the idea of the *density* of a cloud in this sense, but in quantum physics the two properties are intimately related. Moreover, if we think of the density of the cloud in terms of the *probability* that it will yield rain, then we do start to get a sense of the connection between amplitude and probability in quantum theory.

definition. It had become a phantom. Within the confines of its cloud it was at once everywhere and it was nowhere.

It was suggested that the amplitude of the cloud in a particular region of space tells of the *probability* of finding the electron in that place. In other words, the electron cloud represents our *knowledge* of the state of the electron in the atom. When we make a measurement, there is a certain probability that the electron will be found 'here', close to the nucleus, but there is also a finite probability of it being found 'over there', further away from the nucleus. In this interpretation there is absolutely no telling which answer you will get before you look to see where it is. This seemed to leave everything to chance.

Many physicists found this interpretation unpalatable. Despite having laid the foundations for the development of quantum theory, Einstein rejected this kind of probability interpretation, famously remarking that 'God does not play dice.'

It was at this point that Niels Bohr and the young German physicist Werner Heisenberg decided to go right back to the beginning. Within the electron cloud it seemed we had lost track of precisely where the electron had got to. We had lost track of its position, speed and direction as it moved around the nucleus. So, the physicists began with some fairly searching, fundamental questions, such as: What do we actually mean when we speak about the position of an electron in space?

Supposing you wanted to track the path of an electron, its position and speed as it travels through space (or spacetime). The most direct way of doing this would be to use a very powerful microscope. But, according to Heisenberg, we immediately run into a problem. Our instrument relies on photons that are as 'large' in energy terms as the object we are using them to study. Each time a photon bounces off an electron, the electron is given a severe jolt. This jolt means that the direction and the speed of the electron are changed in ways that are unpredictable. Although we might be able to obtain a fix on the electron's instantaneous position, the sizeable interaction of the electron with the device we are using to measure its position means that we can say nothing at all about the electron's speed or the direction in which it's going.

We could use much lower-energy photons in an attempt to avoid this problem and so measure the electron's speed and direction, but the microscope would then lose resolution and we must give up hope of determining the electron's position.

Heisenberg reasoned that the exact position of the electron on the one hand and it's speed and direction on the other cannot be measured simultaneously. To determine these quantities requires two quite different kinds of measurement and the measurement of one property with certainty excludes the simultaneous measurement of the other with certainty.

This is Heisenberg's famous uncertainty principle. It can be traced back to the wave-like and particle-like properties of fundamental constituents of matter such as electrons.

Initially, Heisenberg's own interpretation of his uncertainty principle ran as I have just described. He believed that his principle placed fundamental limits on what we can measure. The electron had become a phantom within a cloud of probability simply because it is physically impossible to track its progress through the space inside the atom any more precisely.

Bohr vehemently disagreed with Heisenberg and they argued bitterly. Bohr believed that quantum theory tells us not what we can measure, but what we can *know*. He believed that although wave behaviour and particle behaviour appear mutually exclusive, these are not in fact contradictory, they are complementary behaviours of the fundamental constituents of matter and light.

According to Bohr, we can never know the 'true' properties of photons or electrons. We can, however, bring out their complementary wave-like and particle-like behaviour by choosing what kind of experiment to perform. We can only acquire knowledge of the complementary behaviour, not the true behaviour, and so this represents a fundamental limit on what we can ever know about physical reality.

It is often assumed that Heisenberg's uncertainty principle means that we can never be certain about anything, or, at least, we can never be certain about the values of the physical quantities we measure. This is a misconception. There is no restriction placed on the certainty with which we can measure any physical quantity that features in the uncertainty principle.

However, the principle does say that there exist physical quantities that are connected (they are sometimes said to be *conjugate*), such that if we measure one quantity with absolute certainty, this means that there is an infinite uncertainty associated with the other. So, if we measure the position of an electron with absolute certainty (we might say that in doing this we have made the position a 'real' property of the electron), then there is an infinite uncertainty associated with its speed and direction (these properties are not 'real' in this sense).

After centuries of scientific investigation, in which successive layers of the structure of the material world had been peeled away, what did we find? We learned that the material world around us (including ourselves) is composed of atoms and of chemical compounds formed from different combinations of atoms. Digging more deeply, we discovered that atoms themselves are composed of smaller, more fundamental objects – protons, neutrons and electrons, and that light consists of bundles of energy called photons.

Each step took us further and further away from our world of direct experience. But we had the expectation that, with more refined and sophisticated instruments, we would continue to extend ways of gathering experience and would keep on uncovering ever smaller and ever more fundamental versions of the things we can perceive directly.

We might have anticipated that we could not go on doing this forever – we could not expect to go on uncovering ever smaller and ever more fundamental bits of matter *ad infinitum*. We might have expected that we would eventually run into a brick wall: we would hit something tiny, ultimate and indivisible, something final. But Bohr is telling us that we have instead run into a much more fundamental limit on our ability to know the 'true' nature of physical reality, one that has nothing to do with the limits of our inventiveness, and everything to do with the way that nature is wired at the quantum level.

At this level, waves and particles have become the shadows in Plato's cave, or Kant's phenomena. We can never escape from the cave into the world of light, or look upon the world of noumena. We can see the wave shadows and the particle shadows, but we can never see the things that cause them.

On the surface, this has nothing whatsoever to do with the existence or otherwise of a boundary between mind and world. There might be a sense in which the wave and particle shadows represent the limits of our mind's ability to perceive and comprehend nature, but Bohr intended his concept of wave–particle complementarity to be taken as a fundamental principle of the physical world, not of our mental world.

Space and time have once again become illusions. And here, right at the heart of the structure of physical matter and light, we find ourselves once again fretting about what we can and can't know of reality.

Were we being naive in supposing that science could give us the answers?

10

Rise of the Danish Priesthood

So we do it again, exactly the same except now without looking to see which way the bullets go; and the wave pattern comes back. So we try again while looking, and we get particle pattern. Every time we don't look we get wave pattern. Every time we look to see how we get wave pattern, we get particle pattern. The act of observing determines the reality.
Tom Stoppard, *Hapgood*

Perhaps we're getting too carried away. After all, the peculiar effects of Einstein's relativity only occur when objects travel at speeds close to that of light. This is hardly something to get nervous about at the kinds of mundane speeds with which we move about the surface of planet earth. Our problems with our understanding of the fundamental constituents of light and matter are a little more disconcerting, but surely there's still little doubting the reality of mountains, streams, trees, houses and soft brown earth. Mountains do not interfere. If I run through a forest of densely packed trees my physical being is not spread out like a light wave when I emerge from the other side. So, electrons and photons are both waves and particles. Is that something to get worried about?

Whether this matters or not really depends on your point of view. Bohr and Heisenberg believed that we can never have knowledge of the 'true' nature of reality and (much as Hume had done) they argued that to speculate about it is largely a waste of time. They insisted that what we have to deal with are the effects and sensations that can be created by manipulating physical objects using laboratory instruments and observed by us. In other words, if we do *this* to *that* object under *these* circumstances, then we can expect to get *this* result. And there's nothing more to it than that.

As they nagged away at the problem of interpretation at Bohr's institute in Copenhagen, Bohr, Heisenberg and the Austrian physicist Wolfgang Pauli argued at length, long into the night. Eventually, they reached a compromise. They developed an interpretation of the relationship between quantum theory and physical reality that became known as the *Copenhagen interpretation*. This interpretation categorically denies that there is anything to be gained from thinking that we can ever discover the true nature of physical objects 'as they really are'. It emphasizes instead the nature of the relationships between physical objects and the instruments we use to expose their properties and behaviour to observation. It is an interpretation that appears to take us right back to square one.

The Copenhagen interpretation insists that the properties of fundamental objects like photons or electrons do not exist unless they are exposed to something with which they can interact, such as a measuring device. In one sense, such objects do not have independently real properties at all; their properties become real only when they undergo the right kinds of interactions. Now this is not a matter of philosophical interpretation, or semantics. If we think of the photons or electrons actually possessing these properties independently of any interaction then at best we may be misled, at worst we will be quite wrong.

This point is best illustrated by reference to the two-slit experiment described in the last chapter. Recall that we interpret the interference fringes to be the result of the overlap of the waves spreading out beyond the slits. Constructive and destructive interference of the waves produces a pattern that takes the form of a series of light and dark bands that appear on the photographic film, once we have developed it.

But now we recall that, according to Planck and Einstein, light consists of self-contained bundles of energy called photons. And, according to de Broglie, light and matter exhibit a basic wave–particle duality. So, let's reduce the brightness of the light so that, on average, only one photon at a time passes through the apparatus. What happens now?

What we do see is that when one photon impinges on the film, it interacts with the chemicals in the photographic emulsion and triggers a series of chemical changes that serve to amplify the event. After developing the film,[1] the result is a tiny white dot that indicates 'a photon struck here'. This is entirely consistent with the idea that the photon is a self-contained particle, a quantum or 'atom' of light-energy. As successive photons pass one at a time through the slits, each is registered as a tiny dot on the film. If we wait long enough to ensure that we have recorded a large number of such events, one after the other, we discover that the dots are grouped into a series of bright and dark bands. We have recovered the interference pattern.

Although we can see the interference pattern only when we have recorded a large number of photons, one after the other, each event must be governed by wave interference. If it wasn't, then there would be no restriction on where each photon could impinge on the film and the end result would be a random scatter pattern of dots. The fact that we see dark fringes at all must mean that there are places on the film (and hence regions of space in front of the film) where the photons can never be found. These are equivalent to regions of space where we have destructive interference.

There is no alternative interpretation. If we understand the interference pattern to arise from the alignment of crests and troughs in a series of overlapping waves, then this is what must happen to each and every individual photon that passes through the slits.

We could try to understand what's happening by assuming that the

1. Explanation for would-be photography buffs: Photographic emulsion is made up of millions of tiny crystals of a silver salt (called silver halides). The photon interacts with a silver salt crystal, and the crystal (and some of its neighbours) break down to give a black silver deposit. We then use developing chemicals to break down more crystals and so amplify the initial deposit to create a visible image. We then treat the film with further chemicals to convert any remaining silver halides into colourless salts, so the film is no longer sensitive to light. This is the negative. We then pass light through the negative onto light-sensitive paper and so create the positive.

individual photons pass through only one slit or the other, before impinging on the film. However, it is fairly easy to show that if this were really the case, then the interference pattern would disappear. The photon cannot split into two, with one half passing through one slit and the other half passing through the other slit. Splitting it in two would in any case halve its energy and so double its wavelength (and hence change its colour), and we can easily confirm that the photons passing through the apparatus have the same colour they start out with.

We are left with no choice but to conclude that each individual photon has in some bizarre way passed through both slits simultaneously and interfered with itself, before interacting with the photographic emulsion. But how can this be? How can a fundamental, indivisible particle be in two different places (actually, many different places) at the same time?

By their very nature, waves are spread through space. They are *delocalized*. They are disturbances that pass through many points in space at any particular moment in time (think again of the ripples in the pond). Particles, on the other hand, are by definition *localized*. Particles are either 'here' or 'there'. Whether we imagine the particles to be tiny bundles of energy or bits of matter, or infinitesimally small rubber balls, the fact that they are particles makes them by definition localized in space. Our problem in trying to make sense of the results of the double-slit experiment with single photons is that we can't push localized, indivisible particles simultaneously through two slits that are separated in space.

We have no choice but to drop the idea that photons are localized bundles of energy, and think instead in terms of the photon's wave properties. We conclude that the photon wave corresponding to a single photon passes through both slits, spreads out beyond these slits and interferes. The photon wave that reaches the photographic film therefore has strong variations in its 'brightness' or amplitude (the height of the resulting wave). The amplitude has been strengthened in some regions of space through constructive interference and weakened in other regions through destructive interference.

The amplitude of the photon wave in a particular region of space is related to the probability of observing the photon in that place. The photon wave represents a 'cloud of probability' gently washing up against the film, just like the electron cloud mentioned in the last chapter represents the probability of finding the electron at different points in space. The photon is much more likely to be eventually observed as a particle in a region of space where the amplitude of its wave or cloud of probability is large. The photon wave therefore has a higher probability of interacting with the photographic emulsion in regions where it has high amplitude. After many photons have been recorded, the end result is a pattern of bright and dark fringes that mirror the amplitude pattern of the wave of a single photon.

This might seem quite reasonable as far as it goes, but we're not out of the woods yet. The amplitude of the photon wave that impinges on the photographic film tells us where the dot *might* be formed, it does not tell exactly where it *will* be formed.

In the early 1930s, the mathematician John von Neumann recognized that this kind of measurement involves two very different types of process. Up until the moment at which the photon interacts with the photographic film, we can describe what happens to the photon wave using the mathematical equations of quantum theory. The theory tells us that the wave evolves smoothly in space and time – much like the ripples on the pond – passing through the two slits, spreading out and interfering to produce the pattern of amplitudes that we will eventually recognize as interference fringes. But at the moment of interaction, the moment of measurement, something quite different happens.

The photon wave undergoes an instantaneous change from its delocalized state before measurement to its localized state after measurement. Before the change there is a probability of interaction at any one of a large number of points on the film, reflecting the delocalized nature of the photon wave. After the change these many possibilities have been reduced to only one actuality – the photon has been detected 'here', and nowhere else. This change is now commonly known as the *collapse of the wave function*. The cloud of probability somehow falls in on itself to produce certainty at one, and only one, location on the film. The photon is first localized and then absorbed by the photographic emulsion, triggering a series of chemical changes that eventually produces a tiny white dot.

We have arrived at a paradox. A quantum object such as a photon behaves as a wave or as a particle, depending on what kind of measurement we choose to make. If we look to see how we get the wave interference pattern by trying to follow the individual paths of the photons through the apparatus, then we just get a random particle pattern – a scatter pattern of dots. If we don't look to see how we get the wave pattern, then we get the wave pattern. We quickly discover that we can't do both simultaneously. We can get the wave pattern with single photons only if we don't look to see how we get it. We might think that this is because we lack the ingenuity to conceive of an instrument that could show both types of behaviour at the same time. But, according to the Copenhagen interpretation, this is something we can't do because such an instrument is simply inconceivable.

Under Bohr's forceful and dominant intellect, the Copenhagen interpretation was rapidly established as the only viable interpretation of the new quantum theory. It became dogma. The physicists of the 'Copenhagen school' became the new high priests of quantum theory, and hence high priests of physical reality itself.

There were some heretics, however. The most notable dissenters within the community of physicists at the forefront of the development of quantum theory were Einstein and Schrödinger. Both physicists had minds of their own and were not easily cowed. The intellectual confrontation between Einstein and Bohr, which took place at a number of international physics conferences held in the late 1920s and early 1930s, became one of the most famous debates in the entire history of science.

Einstein believed that the collapse of the wave function implies a peculiar, 'spooky' action-at-a-distance. Here's why. Before measurement a single photon in the two-slit experiment is delocalized – its cloud of probability is spread over an extended region of space. At the moment of measurement, the wave function collapses and the photon becomes localized instantaneously. It definitely appears 'here', and therefore definitely does not appear 'there'. If 'here' and 'there' are very far apart, the act of measurement would appear to change the physical state of the photon (from delocalized to localized) far from the point where the measurement is actually made. Einstein believed that this kind of action-at-a-distance violated one of the most important principles of his special theory of relativity, the principle that the speed of light represents an ultimate speed that cannot be exceeded.[2]

Perhaps this doesn't cause you too much discomfort. After all, you might say, photons are rather odd things. They are rather ephemeral. They are massless little bundles of pure energy, so maybe it is not so surprising that, like some will-o'-the-wisp, they can be both 'here' and 'there' before a measurement, then suddenly 'here' when a measurement is made. But remember that de Broglie insisted that wave–particle duality extends to all quantum objects, including bits of matter that have mass. Interference effects have been observed in the laboratory with electrons, neutrons and molecules containing as many as sixty atoms.

Now this, I would contend, is discomforting. Our instinct is to regard bits of matter with mass as particulate: they can only be in one place at a time. The observation of interference effects is evidence that fairly large bits of matter can also behave as delocalized waves. Where is the mass in such a wave? How does it get from everywhere it has a high probability of being found to precisely 'here', where it is actually found? Now this is surely spooky.

Some have found this argument quite puzzling, and it is worth a short diversion to understand why. Let's return to Alice the pioneering astronaut of the twenty-fifth century. She leads the first mission to Proxima Centauri, about forty thousand billion kilometres distant. On arrival, she is overtaken by tragedy. Her husband, Bob, who remained behind on earth, is killed in an accident.[3] Alice does not know this yet, as it will take a little over four years for a radio transmission communicating this information to reach her from earth. But,

2. Don't forget that Einstein's general theory of relativity is all about eliminating the action-at-a-distance implied by Newton's theory of gravity. So he was especially sensitive to yet another kind of action-at-a-distance implied by quantum theory.
3. Sorry to have wrong-footed you. Bob was the twin brother last time, but I need him to be the husband this time.

surely, this does not alter the fact that she became a widow instantaneously with her husband's death? Doesn't this immediate change in
Alice's status from wife to widow involve the same kind of principle
as a photon changing from a cloud of probability in which it can be
here or there to being an actual photon which is actually here? If this
is indeed the case, then this is hardly spooky.

But no, it is not the same. Those who have argued on this basis are
guilty of confusing an element of social reality with an element of
physical reality. As we saw in Part I, the institution of marriage and
the status in society of a woman whose husband dies is only real for
as long as there are minds to be aware of and to believe in the institution and collectively make it real. When Bob dies, no physical action
is exerted on Alice's mind. The social reality of Alice's widowhood is
manifested physically in the form of a death certificate or an
announcement, but only in places where the certificate or the
announcement can have an immediate physical influence on other
minds. Nothing happens to Alice at all until she hears of her husband's
death, four years on. Alice is a widow only in the minds of all those
people on earth who have learned of Bob's death. Alice does not
become a widow in her own mind until four years later. This is hardly
instantaneous and, of course, it is not in violation of the principles of
special relativity, as the news of Bob's death has to travel from earth
to Alice at speeds no faster than that of light.

Einstein believed that quantum theory is somehow incomplete. He
initially preferred to take the view that quantum objects like photons
and electrons are, in reality, localized particles that are somehow guided
along different paths that, statistically, result in the appearance of wave-
like behaviour. Quantum theory is incomplete, Einstein argued, because
the theory has nothing at all to say about the 'real' quantum objects,
how they might be guided and how their statistical properties might
arise. He chose to attack the Copenhagen interpretation by developing
a series of intellectual puzzles to prove that the theory is incomplete.

However, each time Einstein thought he had outwitted the
Copenhagen interpretation, Bohr came back with a clever solution.
On one occasion Bohr even used Einstein's own general theory of rel-
ativity against him. Einstein remained stubbornly unconvinced. He

conceded that Bohr's solutions to his puzzles appeared to be satisfactory, but in his view they still contained 'a certain unreasonableness'.

In fact, when forced to defend the Copenhagen interpretation against Einstein's challenges, Bohr had reverted to the argument that it is the inevitable and sizeable disturbance of the observed system that causes the problem.

For example, suppose we tried to demonstrate that a photon does indeed pass through only one of the slits at a time in a two-slit experiment, even in situations where we observe wave interference effects. We might develop an ingenious device that could 'see' the photon in the space just beyond either of the slits without in any way disturbing the photon's trajectory, without knocking it off course. But, Bohr argued, when we try to use even this device we discover that it still disturbs the wave properties of the photon – it spoils the alignment of crests and troughs – in a way that is guaranteed to destroy the interference pattern. Bohr found himself arguing that it is this disturbance that places a fundamental limit on our ability to acquire knowledge in a quantum world.

This, of course, was Heisenberg's original interpretation of his own uncertainty principle and was the focus of his big argument with Bohr. It is an interpretation that is still generally widespread today.[4] It says that what limits our ability to acquire knowledge at the quantum level is the sheer size of the interaction (in terms of energy) required to gain such knowledge in relation to the size of the object under study. We can't 'look' at quantum objects without changing them in a fundamental way because our instruments are just too 'clumsy'. It implies that the limit of what we can know about reality is imposed by a fundamental limit to our ingenuity to devise measuring instruments.

At first sight, there seems to be no getting around this. Yet this is exactly what Einstein needed to do. He needed to develop a thought experiment in which it is possible in principle to acquire certain knowledge of the state of a quantum object without disturbing it in any way, thereby demonstrating that quantum objects do indeed have

4. It is also wrong, as we will see.

measurable properties all along whilst at the same time denying Bohr an escape route through the 'clumsiness' defence.

At stake in this debate was nothing less than our comprehension of the very essence of physical reality.

Quantum objects possess many other kinds of properties in addition to exhibiting wave-like and particle-like behaviour. To avoid getting caught up in the intricacies of quantum physics, I'm going to reach for a visual metaphor to take us through the next bit. Like all metaphors, this one is imperfect in many ways and I will try to point out its imperfections as we go along. Anyone wishing to delve a little more deeply into the science is welcome to consult the books on quantum physics listed in the bibliography, including my own.

I have no idea what the cloud of probability corresponding to a photon wave looks like, but let's imagine that it looks like some kind of shimmering, ghostly vapour, like a cheap special effect from an episode of *Star Trek*.[5] We can't see inside the cloud and so tell what properties the photon has, until we make a measurement on it. But we can suppose that somewhere inside this cloud there exists the potential for a particular property of the photon. It doesn't matter precisely what this property is. It is sufficient for us to note that this is a property manifested in terms of a direction. The photon will be found to have either a vertical, v, or a horizontal, h, direction when measured against an arbitrary reference direction that we impose at the moment we make the measurement.

To keep things really simple, let's imagine that we make a measurement by simply asking the photon what direction it has relative to our reference direction.[6] This reference direction can be any direction we like. So, a photon comes along with its shimmering cloud of probability. 'What is your direction relative to due north?' we ask. At

5. I'm thinking of the 'beings of pure energy' that would appear from time to time when the production had run out of money to buy proper alien costumes.

6. If this is a bit too much for you to swallow, here's a very brief summary of what's really happening. The 'vertical' direction corresponds to the detection of a photon polarized in the vertical plane, measured relative to some arbitrary laboratory axis. A 'horizontal' photon corresponds to detection of a photon polarized in the horizontal plane. Asking the question is then synonymous with making a polarization measurement by passing the photon through a linear polarization analyser, and detecting it.

the precise moment we ask this question, at the moment we make a measurement, the cloud collapses instantaneously into one of only two possible answers. Either we get the answer v or we get the answer h.

The cloud has a 50 per cent probability of collapsing to give a v-answer, and a 50 per cent probability of collapsing to give an h-answer, just as tossing a coin will give the answer heads or tails. Before it collapses it can be thought of as being in some kind of obscure combination of the two – what physicists call a *superposition* – a mixture of vertical and horizontal states, with both answers equally probable.

Although we only ever get one answer or the other, the reference direction we use is, in fact, quite important. If I ask the photon what its direction is relative to due north, then for this particular photon I am precluded from making a measurement – asking the question – in any other direction (such as due east). I can ask only one question, specifying one direction, at a time. Now this may be because I lack the ingenuity to devise an instrument that would allow me to ask questions such as 'What is your direction relative simultaneously to both north and east directions?' Or it may be due to the fact that nature isn't wired this way, there is no sense in which the photon can have more than one direction simultaneously and the question is therefore meaningless.

The fact that I can't simultaneously make a measurement against more than one reference direction at a time is equivalent to saying that the properties vertical and horizontal relative to one direction (such as north), are complementary to the properties vertical and horizontal relative to another direction (east), just as wave-like and particle-like behaviour are complementary properties of all quantum objects.

This means that if I do make a measurement against one reference direction, and I get the answer v or h, then I conclude that I have absolute certainty about this answer (I could say that the property v or h is 'real' for this reference direction). I must also accept from Heisenberg's uncertainty principle that there is now an infinite uncertainty associated with the answers v or h measured against any other reference direction: these answers cannot be 'real'.

So, the real properties of the photon are at the mercy of my choice of reference direction.

We now perform measurements on a series of identical photons. Think of the photons streaming silently through space towards us, forming a beam. We randomly pull some of the photons out of the beam and ask them for their directions relative to a reference direction (let's stick with due north for the time being). After we have made many such measurements, we end up with equal numbers of v-answers and h-answers. We know we will get equal numbers of each answer, but we cannot tell which answer any individual photon will give until we ask it. The answers are not pre-determined.

Can this be right? After all, we only ever get v-answers or h-answers. Isn't it therefore appropriate to apply Occam's razor here and assume that each individual photon cloud contains a mechanism or a recipe that pre-determines either vertical or horizontal all along? Couldn't the cloud actually be a v-cloud or an h-cloud and making the measurement – asking the question – simply be our way of finding out which it is, much as we look at a coin to discover if we got heads or tails? Couldn't we just forget about this superposition nonsense? The beam of identical photons would then be made up of an equal mixture of photons with v-clouds and h-clouds. This is entirely consistent with the answers we obtain, and is a lot easier to understand.

According to the Copenhagen interpretation the answer to this question is a most emphatic no. The properties of quantum objects are not real *until they are measured*. There are no v-clouds or h-clouds, there are only clouds with probabilities for each possible result and the measurement collapses the cloud into one or the other. Complementary properties of photons such as vertical and horizontal measured against different reference directions cannot be simultaneously real. What I get depends on what reference direction I use, and I can only ever deal with the probabilities for particular answers, not certainties.[7]

*

7. If you're not yet convinced by this argument, I should point out that the properties vertical and horizontal are not the only properties a photon can have. Photons can also be measured to reveal clockwise and anti-clockwise properties. Both clockwise and anti-clockwise properties can be recovered by creating specific kinds of superposition of vertical and horizontal. What properties are we going to find? This depends on what measurement we make. And I can only ever furnish you with the probabilities of getting all the different possible results.

In 1935, working in collaboration with Boris Podolsky and Nathan Rosen, Einstein developed what was to become the single most important challenge to the Copenhagen interpretation, a challenge that was to shake the interpretation of quantum theory to its very core. The Einstein–Podolsky–Rosen thought experiment (which from now on I will abbreviate as the *EPR experiment*) involves measurements made on one of two quantum objects that have interacted and moved apart. We will jump straight to a version of the EPR experiment that allows us to make use of our metaphor.

We now have two photons and so need some way to distinguish them. We'll call them 'green' and 'blue'.[8] Because they have interacted, their joint properties are intimately linked by the physics of their interaction. Let's suppose that their properties are constrained by the physical laws governing their interaction to be such that, if the answer for the green photon is vertical relative to some reference direction, then the answer for the blue photon must also be vertical relative to the same direction. Similarly, if the answer for the green photon is horizontal, then the answer for the blue photon must also be horizontal. This restriction is demanded by the physics of the interaction (we could think of this as a 'law of aligned photons').[9] Again we have no way of knowing what the actual answer will be until we set a reference direction, ask the question and collapse the cloud.

Alice and Bob help to perform this experiment for you. You have set up a device in which the interaction can take place in a laboratory on a deep space station that lies equally distant from earth and Proxima Centauri. The space station therefore lies about twenty thousand billion kilometres from earth. The pairs of photons so created scatter off in all directions. After waiting a couple of years for the photons to make their journeys to Proxima Centauri and earth, Alice interrogates a single green photon on Proxima Centauri and Bob

8. This is not an arbitrary choice. Some of the most successful practical realizations of the EPR experiment have made use of photons with wavelengths corresponding to green and blue.
9. Again, for those of you who are interested, in two-photon experiments involving cascade emission from excited atoms the 'law of aligned photons' is actually the law of conservation of angular momentum.

interrogates its blue photon partner on earth. The photons are now separated by a distance of forty thousand billion kilometres.

Alice asks her green photon what direction it has relative to due north. Bob does the same for his blue photon. We expect the answers to be perfectly correlated. If Alice gets a v-answer (or an h-answer) then we expect that Bob will also get a v-answer (or an h-answer).

Now let's stop and think about this for a minute. Suppose Alice and Bob agreed that they would always use a reference direction of due north. Further suppose that Alice gets a v-answer. This must mean that Bob will also get a v-answer. There is no uncertainty associated with Bob's blue photon any longer. That the blue photon must give a v-answer is absolutely certain. For this specific reference direction, the vertical direction is now a 'real' property of the blue photon, even though Bob hasn't measured it yet. When applied to the blue photon, the Heisenberg uncertainty principle demands that there is now an infinite uncertainty associated with the answers v and h for any other reference direction.

You might now begin to sense the trap that Einstein, Podolsky and Rosen have so cunningly set. Suppose that Bob is devious. He might have agreed with Alice before they parted that he would always use a reference direction of due north, but what if he now chooses due east? The fact of the matter is that he is going to get an answer – v or h – no matter what reference direction he chooses. Suppose Bob now chooses due east and gets an h-answer. When he and Alice eventually get together again to compare notes they will conclude that for Bob's blue photon the properties v and h were 'real' – they were absolutely certain – for both north and east reference directions. Heisenberg's uncertainty principle and the Copenhagen interpretation categorically deny that this is possible.

We concluded earlier that the properties vertical and horizontal were complementary for different reference directions because we could ask a photon only one question, about one direction, at a time. The EPR experiment subtly undermines this position. Now Alice and Bob can ask a pair of correlated photons questions about two different directions at the same time. We seem to have arrived at a situation in which we can discover what the properties of the blue photon are through a measurement Alice chooses to make on another photon forty thousand billion kilometres away. There seems to be no way that the 'clumsiness' defence can be used here.

So there it is. All of these different properties of the blue photon must be real, hidden somehow inside the cloud of probability, and yet there is absolutely nothing in quantum theory to tell us what they are, or how they come about.

Einstein, Podolsky and Rosen concluded simply that quantum theory is incomplete. When they published their paper, it represented a bolt from the blue. It had all the pioneers of quantum theory in turmoil, with some claiming that they would have to start all over again because Einstein had shown that it didn't work.

Bohr's response, when it came a short time later, was essentially a restatement of his principle of complementarity. EPR had assumed that any measurement Alice chooses to make on the green photon *does* not in any way affect the possible answers from a subsequent measurement on the blue photon. Bohr argued the contrary. No matter how strange it seems, when Alice chooses to measure the properties of the green photon against a specific reference direction this *does* directly affect the properties that the blue photon can have, no matter how far away it is. The reality of the properties of the blue photon are, Bohr maintained, indeed determined by the measurements Alice chooses to make on the green photon, and EPR's assumption is not valid. This happens instantaneously, despite the fact that a conventional signal travelling at the speed of light would take a little over four years to get from Proxima Centauri to the earth.

Bohr insisted that it is the measuring device itself that defines the elements of reality that we can observe or, to keep faith with our metaphor, it is the nature of the questions we ask that defines the reality. Where Morpheus in *The Matrix* insisted that 'your mind makes it real', Bohr insisted that it is our measurements that make it real. Without measurement, there is nothing but clouds of probability.

However, Bohr's insistence on the correctness of the Copenhagen interpretation is bought at a high price. In their thought experiment, EPR had created a pair of quantum objects that have become 'entangled' in spacetime. This entanglement allows for correlations between the pair to be established over potentially vast distances. There is no getting around this. If Bohr is right, making a measurement on one of them collapses the wave function and this immediately connects one with the other, implying a spooky action-at-a-distance that appears to violate one of the basic principles of Einstein's special relativity.

Something, somewhere seems to have gone horribly wrong.

EPR's assumption that it should be possible to make measurements on the green photon without in any way disturbing the blue photon is often referred to as *Einstein separability* of the photons. The kind of reality implied by this separability is therefore sometimes called *local reality*, meaning that as the photons separate following their inter-action, they behave as distinct, self-contained objects with properties that are unique to one and independent of the other.[10]

In contrast, the Copenhagen interpretation says that the photons are not Einstein separable and they are therefore not locally real. As a result of the interaction, we have created a pair of photons that are now inex-orably entangled with one another. Up to this point we have thought of the photons as individual clouds of probability, each determining its own possible measurement outcomes, giving its own answers. This is where the metaphor breaks down. Once they are entangled, there can be no individual clouds of probability. There is only one cloud corre-sponding to the entangled pair. In some highly obscure way the cloud becomes stretched out over a distance of forty thousand billion kilo-metres. As soon as Alice performs a measurement on Proxima Centauri, the cloud collapses and she obtains a v-answer (or an h-answer). Instantaneously, Bob on earth obtains a v-answer (or an h-answer).

To paraphrase the *X-files*, before the measurement the properties of the photons are 'out there', somewhere, and we appear to be able to exercise remarkable powers over their reality by choosing just what kind of question we ask.

But at what point in the process of measurement is this collapse meant to occur? We might have naively assumed it to be the moment a quan-tum object interacts with a measuring device, but is this assumption

10. Local reality does not mean that the photons should be thought of as always local-ized in space.

justified? After all, a measuring device is itself composed of quantum objects – electrons, protons, neutrons, atoms and molecules. Why shouldn't we assume that the interaction takes place on a quantum level? The problem is that the collapse is itself not contained in any part of the mathematical structure of quantum theory. The theory itself gives us no clues whatsoever.

Later in 1935 Schrödinger drew on some extensive correspondence he had had with Einstein to show up the apparent absurdity of this situation. He shifted the focus of the discussion from the microscopic world of sub-atomic quantum objects to the large-scale world of everyday life. The result was to become known as the *paradox of Schrödinger's cat*.

Imagine a small steel chamber containing a device to measure the vertical and horizontal properties of a photon. As before, there are two possible answers. The photon is initially present in a cloud of probability that represents a superposition of these, such that it has a 50 per cent chance of giving a *v*-answer and a 50 per cent chance of giving an *h*-answer. The measuring device is connected to a phial containing deadly poison. If the device obtains a *v*-answer, the poison is released. If it obtains an *h*-answer, the poison remains safely contained in the phial. We place Schrödinger's pet cat inside and close the chamber.

Through a small window in the chamber we send in the photon in its superposition state. We close the window so that there can be no further interactions with the outside world. This also prevents us from peeking.

Remember that in quantum theory we can only know the probabilities of getting vertical or horizontal answers. We have no way of telling in advance which of these answers we will actually get.

So, what happens? Let's examine this thought experiment in stages. The photon enters the chamber. At this stage we would describe the cloud of probability as a superposition of vertical and horizontal answers. The photon interacts with the device. We might be tempted to say that the cloud of probability collapses at this stage to give either a vertical or a horizontal answer. If it collapses to give a *v*-answer, the cat is doomed. If it collapses to give an *h*-answer, the cat survives.

But, as Schrödinger pointed out, we have absolutely no evidence to indicate where exactly in the chain of events the collapse is supposed to occur. There is nothing to stop us assuming that, on interaction with the photon, the device itself enters a superposition state, an equal mixture of its response to the vertical and horizontal answers. This would mean that the phial of poison also enters a superposition, a mixture of the states corresponding to the situation in which the poison is released and the situation in which the poison is contained. Finally, the cat itself enters a superposition, an equal mixture of dead cat and live cat.

What happens now, when we lift the lid of the chamber? Does this act trigger the collapse of the wave function? Is our choice to lift the lid (or not) going to determine the fate of the cat?

Schrödinger did not intend for us to take this thought experiment too seriously. However, this paradox does pose some serious questions. The Copenhagen interpretation insists that we resist the temptation to ask what physical properties a quantum object (or a cat) actually has before we make a measurement on it, as such a question is quite meaningless. As far as the Copenhagen interpretation is concerned, Schrödinger's poor cat is indeed trapped in a blurred state, suspended between life and death, for it is simply meaningless to speculate otherwise until we lift the lid, and look.

Why worry? After all, this stuff about wave–particle duality, games with vertical and horizontal photons and diabolical animal experiments appears interesting but maybe, after all, this is ultimately a matter of semantics. Some of the most dazzling intellects of the twentieth century had amused themselves with a stimulating philosophical debate centred on thought experiments that nobody would ever actually carry out. So what?

We might be worried because quantum theory is the most successful theory of physics ever devised, and if we can't find reality here, at what seems to be the very bottom of the rabbit hole, then perhaps we're going to struggle to find it anywhere else.

Everything hinges on the completeness of the theory itself. If the theory is not complete, then there may be hope yet for reality. Einstein and Schrödinger had challenged the completeness of quantum theory and the intellectual integrity of the Copenhagen interpretation. Bohr had defended them. In the end, the views of the Copenhagen school prevailed, if only through the inertia of many at the time who dismissed the arguments as just so much philosophizing.

In the 1940s and 1950s, whether you believed in an independent reality or not appeared really rather secondary to the simple fact that quantum theory worked so wonderfully well. The Copenhagen interpretation became an entrenched view, a perspective so common that it was no longer even acknowledged to be a view for which there could be serious rivals. It became accepted wisdom, and as such not worthy of questioning. By the early 1960s, the grip of the Danish priesthood was strong.

Nobody dreamt that any of this would actually be tested in the laboratory.

I I

For Whom the Bell Tolls

It is a very important experiment, and perhaps it marks the point where one should stop and think for a time, but I certainly hope it is not the end. I think that the probing of what quantum mechanics means must continue, and in fact it will continue, whether we agree or not that it is worth while, because many people are sufficiently fascinated and perturbed by this that it will go on.

John Bell, *The Ghost in the Atom*

The Copenhagen interpretation insists that reality at the quantum level is fundamentally weird. Make no mistake, if this interpretation is the correct and only one then we can give up hope that we will ever understand the nature of the reality of matter and light at this basic, physical level; further, we will be forever trapped in Plato's cave, able to observe nothing more than the wave shadows and the particle shadows.

The challenge presented by the EPR experiment is therefore fundamental. If quantum theory is indeed incomplete then completing it might give us an opportunity to penetrate the shadows and look upon the real world perhaps at an even more basic level.

Hold onto your hope. We're not at the bottom of the rabbit hole yet.

If quantum theory is incomplete, what might a complete theory look like? Einstein had hinted at an alternative statistical interpretation, in which quantum probabilities and quantum uncertainty are replaced by statistical probabilities and the uncertainty of plain, old-fashioned, common-or-garden ignorance.

Suppose you toss a coin. What result are you going to get? Heads or tails? Well, of course, you don't know until it comes to rest on the ground. But you do know that there's a 50 per cent probability that you'll get the result heads and a 50 per cent probability that you'll get the result tails. You obviously can't know which until you look, but you don't regard this as particularly mysterious or spooky.

You settle for probabilities because you know that the actual result is determined by a large number of variables, such as the force with which you toss the coin into the air, the amount of spin you put on it, the force and direction with which it hits the ground, and so on. It is nevertheless apparent that the result you get is the direct consequence of the operation of all these different variables from the moment you launch the coin into the air until the moment it comes to rest on the ground. You resort to probabilities because you are ignorant of precisely how all these variables are going to affect the outcome.[1] You are ignorant of these many variables because you do not control them. But you would not doubt that the outcome of tossing the coin is pre-determined by them, whatever they are.[2]

If we were to assume that a photon in a superposition of vertical and horizontal states behaves just like a tossed coin, then we would be extending quantum theory in a very specific kind of way. We would be implicitly assuming that the quantum cloud of probability is no different from a statistical probability, which we use because we are ignorant of all the different variables that might pre-determine the answer. We can simplify this a bit by summarizing all these variables and

1. If you were somehow able to know how all these variables were going to affect the outcome then you could predict with certainty (100 per cent probability) whether you were going to get heads or tails. If you could extend this capability to include other games of chance then you could have some real fun in a casino . . .
2. In fact, in March 2004 there appeared news reports of a beautiful Hungarian blonde and a couple of Serbian gamblers accused of using high-tech laser gadgetry in London's Ritz casino to scan the speed of the ball moving on a roulette wheel and phone the results into a high-speed computer, which predicted where the ball would come to rest. They were just narrowing the range of unknown variables.

reducing them to one; a single variable that represents the physics of the interaction from the moment the photon is created to the moment it is measured, to the moment we ask the question. Just as we don't know all the variables that determine the outcome when we toss a coin, so we don't know the variable that determines whether we will get a v-answer or an h-answer on measuring the photon. In other words, the variable is 'hidden', but we could nevertheless consider it to be physically real.[3]

Let's go back and see what such a local hidden variable theory implies for the EPR experiment. To keep things simple, I will assume that the hidden variable is represented by a tiny pointer and dial that lies 'inside' the photon, hidden or veiled beneath its cloud of probability. This internal dial tells in which direction the photon state is actually pointing all along, and we can imagine that it is marked north, south, east and west.

Asking the question is now a bit like posting a letter. The pointer on the internal dial points in a specific direction set by the physics of the interaction that created the photon, but we don't know which direction it is. Unfortunately, we can't simply look at the dial and so discover this direction. Instead, we have to be more devious. We choose an external reference direction and compare this with the internal pointer direction. If by chance we happen to get the two directions lined up, much as we line up the edge of a letter so that it will fit through the slot in the postbox, then we are guaranteed to get a v-answer. If the directions do not line up (we hold the edge of the letter at the wrong angle so it won't fit through the slot) then we are guaranteed to get an h-answer.

We allow for a bit of latitude either way. If the internal pointer direction and the reference direction are within ±45 or ±135 degrees of each other, then we can expect that we will get a v-answer. This is

3. We need to be a little careful here. Einstein argued that quantum theory is incomplete and favoured an alternative statistical interpretation of quantum probability, but he was not an advocate of hidden variable theories. It seems he believed that all these problems would be resolved in an elusive grand unified theory, or 'theory of everything'. More on this in the next chapter.

like saying that the postbox has a wide slot so that a letter pushed at an oblique angle of up to 45 degrees off the long axis of the slot will still fit through and so get posted. Any angle outside these ranges will give an *h*-answer (the letter doesn't fit through and is not posted).

The best way of working out what will happen is to consider some specific examples. Suppose that the internal pointer is pointing due north. Obviously, if we set our reference direction to due north then the two directions are aligned and we will get a *v*-answer with certainty: the letter is posted. If, instead, we set the reference direction to north-east, then this is just within 45 degrees of the internal pointer, so we would expect to get another *v*-answer, also with certainty: the letter is still posted (just). Any reference direction between these two, such as north-north-east, will similarly give a *v*-answer. Using a reference direction outside the range (such as due east) will give an *h*-answer (the letter is not posted).

So far, so good. Nothing particularly mysterious about this. Now I want you to stick with me for this next bit, because the results are profoundly disturbing and so well worth a little effort.

We are now in a position to extend this logic to include all possible internal pointer directions. With the internal pointer pointing north, then all of the above reference directions, north, north-north-east and north-east, will give *v*-answers. We can abbreviate this series of answers as *v-v-v* for the three reference directions in the order I have written them. We can expect to get this same combination of answers for all internal pointer directions ranging from north to north-east. However, as the internal pointer moves clockwise beyond north-east, then it moves out of the range of, first, the north reference direction, then the north-north-east reference direction and finally the north-east reference direction. The pattern of possible answers changes from *v-v-v* to *h-v-v* to *h-h-v* and eventually to *h-h-h* as the internal pointer direction changes from north to south-east. At this point, it comes within ±135 degrees of the north reference direction and gets picked up again as a *v*-answer, just as the letter would still fit through the slot if you flipped it through 180 degrees. We pick up a *v*-answer first in the north direction, then the north-north-east direction and finally the north-east direction. The pattern changes from *h-h-h* to *v-h-h* to *v-v-h* and eventually back to *v-v-v*. For future reference, these results are summarized in the table below.

Range of Internal Pointer Directions	Reference Direction			Statistical Probability
	North	North-north-east	North-east	
	v	*v*	*v*	25%
	h	*v*	*v*	$12\frac{1}{2}\%$
	h	*h*	*v*	$12\frac{1}{2}\%$
	h	*h*	*h*	25%
	v	*h*	*h*	$12\frac{1}{2}\%$
	v	*v*	*h*	$12\frac{1}{2}\%$

A glance at this table quickly reveals that what we're really charting here is the overlap between the areas swept out by different ranges of internal pointer directions and the 'hourglass' shape imposed by our choice of reference direction. Where the areas overlap, we will get a *v*-answer. Where they don't overlap, we will get an *h*-answer.

This table also summarizes the statistical probabilities for the various answers. These are calculated simply from the number of times we would expect to obtain each combination of answers assuming that the internal pointer directions are uniformly (and statistically) distributed from north to south.[4] This is what Einstein meant when he talked of statistical probabilities. The pattern is repeated for internal pointer directions from south back to north so when we consider

4. The percentages are consequently just the proportions of the areas swept out by the different ranges of internal pointer directions to the area of the semi-circle stretching from north to south, as you can readily see from the table.

the full 360-degree range of possible internal pointer directions the percentage probabilities are the same.

For a reason that will hopefully become apparent below, I now want to take a look at some simple relationships between these sets of results. Suppose we carry out experiments on a sample of 1,000 photons, pulled at random from a beam. How many would we expect to give us a v-answer using a north reference direction and an h-answer using a north-north-east reference direction (let's abbreviate this as N-v/NNE-h)?

If we assume that the internal pointers of the photons in the sample are uniformly distributed over all directions on the internal dial, then we can get the answer directly from the table. There is only one entry with v in the north column and h in the north-north-east column, corresponding to internal pointer directions south-east to south-south-east, so the answer is $12\frac{1}{2}$ per cent. In a sample of 1,000 photons, this would give us 125. In other words, in a randomly-drawn sample of 1,000 photons with internal pointers distributed uniformly over all possible directions, then we would expect 125 to have pointer directions in the range south-east to south-south-east. These photons would be expected to give the measurement combination N-v/NNE-h, with certainty.

How many photons would be expected to give a v-answer using a north-north-east reference direction and an h-answer using a north-east reference direction (call this NNE-v/NE-h)? This combination is only possible with internal pointer directions south-south-east to south-east so the answer is again $12\frac{1}{2}$ per cent of 1,000, or 125. The sum of these two, N-v/NNE-h plus NNE-v/NE-h, is 25 per cent, or 250 photons. It is obviously no coincidence that this is equal to the total number of photons giving a v-answer using a north reference direction and an h-answer using a north-east reference direction, N-v/NE-h.

Stop and reflect on this observation for a moment. What we are really saying is that the number of photons with internal pointer directions in the range south-east to south-south-east, when added to the number of photons with internal pointer directions in the range south-south-east to south, is equal to the number of photons with internal pointer directions in the combined range south-east to south. If you think this is a statement of the blindingly obvious, be reassured. It is.

Now this is all very interesting, I'm sure you'll agree, but it is also not much use to us. Remember that we can only ever ask one question of each photon, specifying only one reference direction, at a time. It is quite simply impossible for us to show that a photon will, for example, give a *v*-answer in a north direction and an *h*-answer in a north-east direction at the same time.

This is where the EPR experiment now comes into its own. Let's return to Alice and Bob, on Proxima Centauri and earth respectively, making measurements on the green and blue photons. If Alice makes a measurement on a green photon using the north reference direction and gets a *v*-answer, Bob can make use of the law of aligned photons and infer that the blue photon would have given a *v*-answer *if* he had used this reference direction. Instead he uses the north-north-east direction and between them Alice and Bob count how many pairs of photons give the combined results N-*v*/NNE-*h*, where the first entry N-*v* now refers to the green photon and the second NNE-*h* entry refers to the blue photon. They are perfectly at liberty to do this provided they assume that when Alice makes a measurement on the green photon forty thousand billion kilometres away this can in no way affect the answer that Bob will get from the blue photon. They assume that the photons are Einstein separable, and locally real.

We can conclude from this that in a randomly selected sample of 1,000 pairs of correlated green and blue photons, the number of green photons giving a *v*-answer for the north direction and blue photons giving an *h*-answer in the north-north-east direction (N-*v*/NNE-*h*) is, as we concluded above, $12^{1}/_{2}$ per cent, or 125 photon pairs. Similarly, the number of pairs giving NNE-*v*/NE-*h* answers is also $12^{1}/_{2}$ per cent, or 125. The sum of these two is equal to the number giving N-*v*/NE-*h* answers, which is 25 per cent or 250.

We can now anticipate that nature may be a little more devious than this simple local hidden variable theory allows. It is clear from the table that we would never expect to get combinations such as *v*-*h*-*v* or *h*-*v*-*h* for the three reference directions we have chosen. However, it is not impossible to imagine a more elaborate local hidden variable theory that might allow such combinations. If these combinations were possible, they would increase the number of pairs of photons giving N-*v*/NNE-*h* answers and NNE-*v*/NE-*h* answers and their sum would then exceed 25 per cent. We would therefore have to qualify our conclusion, such that we would say that the sum of the numbers of photons giving N-*v*/NNE-*h* and NNE-*v*/NE-*h* is greater than or equal to the number giving N-*v*/NE-*h*. This conclusion, which applies to all possible local hidden variable theories, is known as *Bell's inequality*, first stated by the Irish physicist John Bell in a paper published in 1966.

We are about to get to the pay-off. All this stuff about internal pointers and reference directions and so on is fairly straightforward although it is a bit esoteric. It is very difficult to connect any of this with what might really be going on 'inside' a real photon. We have assumed that a photon is a bit like a letter, a measurement a bit like pushing the letter through the slot in a postbox. Unlike a conventional postbox, the slot can be turned through all possible directions and the letters are coming at us from all possible directions, too. We have nevertheless made some simple assumptions about how many letters will go into the postbox (*v*-answer) and how many won't (*h*-answer) for three different orientations of the slot. We extended this to the situation where we have two correlated letters and two slots, one on Proxima Centauri and one on earth. Allowing for some deviousness on the part of nature, we concluded that the number of letters giving one combination of results added to the number giving a second combination must be greater than or equal to the number giving a third combination. This conclusion applies to local hidden variable theories of all kinds.

So, what does quantum theory predict? Quantum theory predicts that the number of pairs of photons giving N-*v*/NNE-*h* answers added to the number giving NNE-*v*/NE-*h* answers is about 14.6 per cent. In a randomly selected sample of 1,000 pairs of photons, this implies a total of 146. The number of photons giving N-*v*/NE-*h* answers is 25 per cent, just as we obtained in our local hidden variable example, implying a total of 250 photons.

We conclude from this that 146 is greater than or equal to 250.

Stay calm. You should be worried, but it is important at this stage to be worrying about the right things.

The first thing to note is that you haven't made a mistake with any of the arithmetic. Quite clearly, 146 is not greater than or equal to 250, so you can be at least reassured about this. What this does mean is that quantum theory makes predictions which break the rule of Bell's inequality. The reason why is fairly plain from our earlier discussion. According to the Copenhagen interpretation of quantum theory, the photons in the EPR experiment are not Einstein separable. There are no internal pointers. At least, there are no internal pointers that exist for each photon independently of the other.

One way of thinking about the quantum theory prediction is that the two photons in the pair interfere with each other. Like destructive interference in the two-slit experiment, this interference between the two photons in each pair reduces the numbers of photons giving specific combinations of answers below that predicted if the photons are assumed to be independently real. The two photons interfere with each other even though they are separated by a distance of forty thousand billion kilometres, and when Alice makes a measurement on the green photon this *does* affect the answer that Bob will get from any subsequent measurement he makes on the blue photon. Quantum theory is unequivocal on this point.

The question is now this: is it right?

Yes, it is right. Experimentalists picked up on Bell's inequality not long after it was published and started to develop and refine the kinds of experimental techniques necessary to put the inequality to the test. Through the 1970s to the present day, experiments of ever greater sophistication have been carried out which demonstrate fairly unambiguously that photons in an EPR experiment do indeed break the rule of Bell's inequality.

The most widely known of these experiments were performed by the French physicist Alain Aspect and his colleagues in the mid-1980s. Further experiments performed since then have demonstrated entanglement between photons measured at observer stations in Bellevue and Bernex, two Swiss villages outside Geneva almost eleven kilometres apart. Not quite the forty thousand billion kilometres between Proxima Centauri and earth, but certainly enough to make the point.

Entanglement involving three and four photons has also been demonstrated in experiments that do not depend on Bell's inequality in order to prove the case against local hidden variables. The conclusions are by now pretty inescapable.[5] Quantum theory succeeds and all classes of local hidden variable theories that could possibly be conceived fail. In truth, there are some loopholes left. But experiments that close these loopholes individually have been performed and only a very grand conspiracy on the part of nature, involving exploitation of several loopholes simultaneously, can keep alive any vestiges of hope for local hidden variable theories. And, as Einstein once said, the Lord is subtle, but he is not malicious.

Whatever reality is, at the quantum level it is not local.

Time to take stock. Reality is not local and it is not at all clear what this means. Before we go on to consider what we might do next, we have to face up to the stark contradiction between two of the most successful theories of the twentieth century – quantum theory and special relativity. Quantum theory says, unequivocally, that reality is not local and that the fates of two quantum objects that have interacted at some time in their past history are still in some highly mysterious way bound to each other, no matter how far apart they get. On the surface, this mysterious connection appears to involve faster-than-light communication between two distant objects, the possibility of which special relativity categorically forbids. We appear to be caught between Scylla and Charybdis, between an unequivocal quantum theory and a forbidding special relativity. We have reached an impasse.

To understand how physicists are currently navigating their way around this impasse, it is helpful to take a look at a couple of examples of the 'practical' uses of entanglement from the frontiers of modern physics research.

5. I, for one, am convinced.

The fact that there can be serious consideration of practical applications of entanglement tells you everything you need to know about physicists' remarkable powers of resilience. We might puzzle over what entanglement and breaking the rule of Bell's inequality mean for our understanding of physical reality, but physicists (especially experimentalists) deal with the facts as they find them and are not given to worrying overmuch about what they might mean at a philosophical level. They tend to ask of themselves a rather different question: if entanglement is an experimental fact, what can we do with it?

There are two areas of current research relevant to our discussion here. The first concerns the use of entangled photons to provide a secure form of encryption for secret messages. Suppose Alice wishes to send a secret message to Bob. There are any number of methods available to her, including modern cryptography based on the mathematical properties of so-called modular functions, used for most commercial transactions carried out via the internet. All such codes are, however, potentially breakable. Before you start to panic about the last purchase you made on the web, you should be aware that breaking modern encrypted messages (such as those carrying your credit card details, for example) requires computer power so vast that this is not possible with present-day technology. These messages may one day be vulnerable with future technology, however.

Alice is not satisfied with any of the current cryptographic techniques, so she turns to quantum physics (this is a particularly sensitive and secret message). She sets up a central source of pairs of entangled photons, keeps the green ones for herself and sends the blue ones to Bob. They each measure the properties of their photons by asking the question of each photon in turn using randomly chosen reference directions. They each record the reference directions they used. Perhaps Alice selects the sequence north-east, south, east-north-east, north-west, north, west, south-west-south, . . . etc. Perhaps Bob uses the sequence south-west, south, west-south-west, south-east, north, north, south-west-south, . . . etc. They both also record whether they got a v-answer or an h-answer for each measurement. They encode a v-answer as the binary digit 1 and an h-answer as the binary digit 0. They then publicly exchange information about the sequence of reference directions they used, without saying what kinds of answer they got.

For those measurements in the sequence in which they have both successfully detected a photon and used the same reference direction, they both know that the answers will be correlated (because of the law of aligned photons). By comparing their lists of reference directions and disregarding measurements for which the directions were not the same, they will both arrive at an identical sequence of binary digits (such as . . . , 0, . . . , . . . , 1, 1, . . . , 0, . . . , 1, etc.) known only to Alice and Bob. The result is a sequence of binary digits (or bits) that is entirely random. But it is an entirely random sequence that is known to both Alice and Bob and only to Alice and Bob. They can now use this bit sequence as an encryption key,[6] allowing them to use conventional methods to send secret messages to each other, secure in the knowledge that only they know the key.

How can they be so certain the key is safe? Let's assume an eavesdropper (traditionally referred to in the scientific literature on this subject as Eve) is somehow able to intercept the entangled photons before they reach Alice or Bob and so learn the sequence and the encryption key. Eve would have had not only to intercept the photons and ask them their directions relative to her own reference directions, she would also have had to arrange for the photons (or duplicates) to be transmitted to either Alice or Bob to avoid arousing suspicion. But now Eve has a problem. Because she has had to make measurements on the photons in order to learn the sequence, the wave functions of the photon pairs have already been collapsed. Any photons subsequently sent on to Alice or Bob will no longer be correlated to the extent predicted by quantum theory.

Alice and Bob can check periodically for the presence of an eavesdropper simply by carrying out tests of Bell's inequality. If the photons

6. An encryption key is a recipe used to code the message. Here's a simple example. We could use a 0 in the bit sequence to code a letter in the message with the previous letter in the alphabet (for example, 'e' becomes 'd'), a 1 codes a letter in the message with the subsequent letter in the alphabet ('e' becomes 'f'). So, the bit sequence 01101 codes the message 'Alice' as 'Zmjbf'. We can decode the message by applying the encryption key in reverse.

no longer break the rule of Bell's inequality, they know immediately that their photons have been intercepted by an eavesdropper and can discard the encryption key as unsafe.

Now each element in the bit sequence that is used as an encryption key is learnt by both Alice and Bob instantaneously as the measurements are made. But, it can be argued, this is just a sequence of randomly generated bits, not a coded message carrying 'meaningful' information, or useful knowledge. Einstein's special theory of relativity is founded on the principle that there can be no transmission of meaningful information (such as this object is over here, travelling in this direction with this speed) faster than the speed of light. In order for Alice and Bob to communicate meaningful information or useful knowledge to each other (rather than a meaningless, random bit sequence), they must first publicly exchange information about the reference directions they have used. Such public exchange involves a conventional transmission of information, at speeds no faster than that of light.

This is the sleight-of-hand that physicists employ to argue that the apparent faster-than-light communication involving entangled quantum objects does not in fact conflict with special relativity. If we accept this argument, then we are left to ponder just what kind of information is transmitted when a measurement is made and the wave function collapses, if indeed any information is transmitted at all.

The second area of active research concerns teleportation. Suppose Alice, on Proxima Centauri, wishes to send a photon to Bob on earth. She could obviously just flash a light in the general direction of earth and wait a little over four years for it to get to Bob, but Alice is rather impatient. Instead, she develops an experimental arrangement which allows her to entangle one of her green photons with another blue photon, created on Proxima Centauri independently of the photon pairs that she and Bob have been experimenting with. She doesn't need to know anything about the state of this second photon other than it precisely matches the colour of Bob's photons.

Alice now performs measurements on both photons, which are destroyed in the process. The consequence of one particular kind of measurement is to cause the wave function governing Bob's blue photon on earth to collapse into whatever state the blue photon on Proxima Centauri had before Alice entangled her green photon with it. Now it is a simple fact of quantum theory that photons with identical characteristics (such as colour and properties such as v- or h-orientation) are actually indistinguishable. To all intents and purposes, Alice has sent the blue photon from Proxima Centauri to earth, instantaneously.

Okay, so this is hardly like beaming Captain James T. Kirk aboard the *Enterprise* from the surface of some hostile planet, but teleporting photons is science fact, not science fiction. Teleportation of this kind is not restricted to single photons. Reports have appeared of the teleportation of laser beams consisting of billions of photons across the laboratory. Most recently, physicists have successfully teleported charged atoms.

There is a catch, related once again to the physicists' sleight-of-hand. Not all the different kinds of measurements that Alice can make will necessarily convert Bob's photon into a teleported photon. So in order for Bob to recognize his photon as a teleported photon, Alice must first tell him what reference direction she used and, most importantly, what answers she got.[7] In fact, if she tells him the answers she got from all the measurements she made on a succession of photons, Bob can use this information to convert all his blue photons into teleported photons. Once again, the act of teleportation itself would seem to be instantaneous, but meaningful information carried by a teleported photon requires a conventional communication to recover it. And a conventional communication can travel no faster than the speed of light.

Some physicists may have reconciled themselves to the apparent contradiction between quantum theory and special relativity, but the problem still nags. It is fair to say that nature herself is indifferent to any concerns we might have with our own theories and quietly gets on with her inscrutable task. Nevertheless, the inherent contradictions in the theory, combined with a determined reluctance to accept that we

7. Fans of *Star Trek* will appreciate that it is necessary for Scotty to know just who is being beamed aboard and the coordinates of their location. This requires a conventional communication – a request to 'Beam me up, Scotty.'

will never escape from Plato's cave, have led some theorists to develop alternatives to the Copenhagen interpretation.

I should confess that I'm no big fan of the Copenhagen interpretation. I don't really like the idea that there should exist a fundamental limit to our ability to acquire knowledge of and comprehend the physical world. But be warned. Wandering the paths of alternative interpretations is not for the faint of heart. It is a measure of the scale and nature of the problems with our understanding of reality at the quantum level that most of the alternatives are more bizarre even than the orthodox interpretation.

The alternative interpretations come in all sorts of different flavours, but we can organize them into two basic types. There are interpretations which seek to make the collapse of the wave function a real physical phenomenon, and there are those which seek to eliminate it completely from the theory.

If you look around, I can pretty much guarantee that you will not see any object in a superposition state, an overlapping combination of opposing properties such as up–down, left–right, top–bottom, dead–alive, and so on. I can further guarantee that you have never seen an object in such a superposition and you never will. Why?

Superpositions of objects are fairly common at the quantum level, at the microscopic level of photons, electrons, atoms and small molecules. Why are they not common at the level of macroscopic objects, of cats, people, trees and houses? Perhaps the simple fact that we never see macroscopic objects in superposition states is itself a clue.

Although fairly common, superposition states (of which entangled states are a specific variety) are actually very delicate and they are destroyed very easily. By this I mean that the circumstances under which a superposition can be maintained must carefully set up and preserved in order to measure the properties of the superposition. Any experimental parameter that causes the crests and troughs of the quantum waves to become misaligned will destroy the superposition. This presents us with another potential clue.

In one alternative interpretation, quantum theory is extended through the introduction of a kind of frictional force, called *decoherence*, which rapidly results in the misalignment guaranteed to destroy a superposition. This force originates from the presence of many other quantum states of other objects with which the object in a super-position state can interact. So, if we create a superposition and place it in intergalactic space where it can't interact with anything else, then it may persist for a considerably long time. If, however, we place the object in a laboratory vacuum, for example, then interaction with even the few atoms or molecules that still persist in such a vacuum causes misalignment and effectively collapses the wave function within a hundredth of a millionth of a billionth of a second. That's not instantaneous, but it is very fast.

It goes without saying that interaction with anything of macro-scopic dimensions, such as a piece of photographic film or a cat, will collapse the wave function even faster than this. This is why we never see a superposition in our macroscopic world of direct experience.

This extension of quantum theory is intuitively appealing (though perhaps annoying to science fiction writers). To a certain extent, it has entered mainstream physics and appears to be broadly accepted by most physicists who worry about how to deal with the interface between the microscopic world of quantum objects and our macro-scopic world of cats and the humans who observe them.

But this interpretation does not quite provide the complete answer to all our problems. Decoherence can help explain why we never see a superposition, but it does not explain why we get one answer in preference to the other. We ask the question and we get a v-answer rather than an h-answer. Decoherence theory tells us why we see one or the other and not a blurry mixture of both, but it cannot tell us why v and not h for this particular measurement. And decoherence does not remove the need for some kind of spooky action-at-a-distance, if this is indeed what it is.

Although John von Neumann never himself appears to have used the term 'collapse of the wave function', the idea nevertheless originated in the mathematical treatment of quantum measurement contained in his book *The Mathematical Foundations of Quantum Mechanics*, which was first published in 1932. So what did von Neumann figure was going on?

He held the view that all of physics would one day be shown to be reducible to quantum physics and he saw no reason to believe that macroscopic objects could not exhibit quantum behaviour. As to the question why we never see superpositions of macroscopic objects, his answer was simple, if rather startling.

Imagine a photon in a superposition state, an equal mixture of v- and h-orientations. The photon interacts with some kind of macroscopic measuring device. We could suppose the device flashes a red light if a v-answer is recorded or a blue light if an h-answer is recorded. Von Neumann saw no reason to suppose that the device itself wouldn't enter a superposition state under these circumstances, with both red and blue lights 'half-flashing' at the same time. The mixture of red and blue light enters your eyes and impinges on your retinas, which also enter a superposition state. The signals are transmitted down your optic nerve to your brain, which also enters a superposition state. So what happens then?

You already know the answer. Von Neumann suggested that the wave function collapses when the superposition encounters a conscious mind. As we learned in Chapter 5, there is nothing in the physics involved in each step in the process from detection of light by your eyes to the transmission of electrical signals to your brain that is not entirely predictable and understood, using physical principles. If you are happy to accept the idea that the measuring device enters a superposition, then there is every reason to expect that your brain enters a superposition, too. But you are never conscious of macroscopic objects in superposition states, so between your brain entering a superposition and you registering the result in your mind, something changes. That change is the collapse of the wave function.[8]

We would have further to suppose that it only takes one conscious mind to collapse the wave function, or else it would be possible that some of your fellow human beings are wandering around like zombies, in states of suspended animation, waiting for their minds to be collapsed. Are cats conscious beings? If they are, then perhaps

8. Readers with an appetite for vicious circularity might at this point like to return to the beginning of Chapter 5, and keep reading until they disappear in their own cloud of probability.

Schrödinger's cat is at least spared the discomfort of being both alive and dead at the same time.

For a time, Einstein was quite taken with another possible alternative. What if Bohr got it completely wrong? What if physical reality consists not of waves *or* particles, as required by Bohr's principle of complementarity, but of waves *and* particles?

The idea is that quantum objects are real particles, with fully determined properties such as v- and h-orientation, set by some physical interaction and following pre-determined trajectories through space. The difference is that, unlike the straight-line trajectories we would expect such objects to follow in Newtonian physics, the quantum objects follow trajectories set by their *associated waves*.

These are 'pilot' waves. When a single photon passes through a two-slit apparatus, it is the pilot wave that passes through both slits, spreading out beyond and overlapping to give constructive and destructive interference just like a conventional wave. The photon itself then passes through only one of the slits (it is always localized) but follows a path beyond set by the pattern of amplitudes of the pilot wave. The photon is guided along a path of high amplitude from the slits to the photographic film, where it is detected. After many photons have passed through the two slits, one after the other, the result is an interference pattern that reflects the pattern of amplitudes of the photons' pilot waves.

Einstein's flirtation with this approach didn't last. He had encouraged de Broglie to pursue this line of reasoning, but his enthusiasm for it quickly drained away. When this interpretation was resurrected in the 1950s by the American physicist David Bohm, it became known as the de Broglie–Bohm theory. Einstein tended to think of it as 'too cheap'.

The pilot wave theory is an example of a non-local hidden variable theory. As such, it is not invalidated by the results of experiments designed to test Bell's inequality, as local hidden variable theories are. There is no collapse of the wave function as such in this theory, but by its very nature it is non-local, so all the spooky action-at-a-distance remains. Today, the theory has some ardent supporters, but these are few in number.

*

The last alternative we will consider is perhaps the most bizarre of all. We might ask what evidence we have that the collapse of the wave function does actually occur. We would have to admit that we have none. Physicists use the idea of the collapse in order to rationalize the relationship between a photon before measurement, which may give any one of a number of possible answers each with a certain probability, and the same photon after measurement, which has given one answer, and only one answer.

Ah, I hear you say. It gives only one answer in this universe, but what about all the others?

In the many-worlds interpretation of quantum theory, there is no collapse. We get all possible answers. It's just that we don't get them all in the same universe. This interpretation implies that there exists a breathtakingly large number of 'parallel' universes (referred to collectively as the *multiverse*), all running in different spacetimes. An interference pattern, then, is the manifestation of interference between parallel universes. A photon gives a v-answer, and you write this down in your laboratory notebook. At the same moment of measurement, the same photon also gives an h-answer, in a parallel universe. The parallel you writes this down in your parallel laboratory notebook. Little wonder that the many-worlds interpretation has been called *schizophrenia with a vengeance*.

It is quite hard to turn aspects of modern quantum physics into movie storylines, but the many-worlds interpretation, with its evocation of parallel universes, has inspired a few. In James Wong's *The One*, released in 2001, it is not only possible to travel between these parallel universes but by killing all the different versions of yourself in these universes the you that remains becomes stronger and more powerful. The film is largely a vehicle for the martial arts star Jet Li, with several concepts borrowed from *The Matrix*.

The 2002 movie *Cube 2: Hypercube*, draws on a little more quantum physics, with multiple dimensions and time shifts. However, it relies on that old favourite beloved of conspiracy theorists, the menacing and mighty military-industrial complex, and never rises above the level of hokum. It would seem that the definitive script, one that properly exposes and explores the consequences of modern theories of quantum physics, has yet to be written.

You might by now be running out of patience. This is all very interesting, you might exclaim, but what are photons, electrons and other quantum objects, really? The truth is, nobody knows.

The conventional, Copenhagen interpretation of quantum theory insists that we can never know. Under different kinds of circumstances and in different kinds of experiments we will get different kinds of behaviour. The behaviour – the phenomena – is all we can ever know. We have a highly elaborate theoretical structure that we can use to predict the probabilities for all the different possible answers, but don't expect this structure to give us certainties or tell us how or why.

If this makes you uncomfortable, pick an alternative interpretation. At this moment in the history of physics, you are perfectly at liberty to make a free choice.

We have failed to find reality at the lowest physical level, the level of contemporary quantum physics. It seems that we can never know what photons, or electrons, or protons, or neutrons really are. The objects that constitute everything we see and everything we are appear set to remain elusive and mysterious.

We are now very close to the bottom of the rabbit hole, but there is still a little way to fall. If we can't find reality at our present level of understanding of the physical world, is there any hope that we might be able to find it in theories yet to come? If we were able to look upon the ultimate, one true theory of everything, would we see an unambiguously independent reality smiling back at us?

12

Reality in Loops and Strings

> *Interestingly, according to modern astronomers, space is finite. This is a very comforting thought – particularly for people who can never remember where they have left things.*
> Woody Allen

> *Time is that quality of nature which keeps events from happening all at once. Lately it doesn't seem to be working.*
> Anonymous

In J. R. R. Tolkien's *The Return of the King*, Pippin and Gandalf wait anxiously for the impending battle with the forces of Mordor before the gates of Minas Tirith, a battle that will determine the fate of Middle Earth. Pippin is wondering what has become of Frodo, and asks if there is any hope. Gandalf replies: 'Just a fool's hope, as I have been told.'

And this is what we are left to grasp for. We have failed to find reality in the fundamental quantum constituents of matter and of light. But we're not yet at the end of physics. One of the last remaining hurdles to be cleared requires that quantum theory and general relativity be brought together in a single quantum theory of gravity or a 'theory of everything'.

This, however, is no trival task. Quantum theory and general relativity are like two sub-critical masses of plutonium. They are safe and work well enough if we keep them apart, but they have a tendency to explode when brought together. Now, a theory of everything may have something different again to say about space and time and – who knows? – about matter and light, too.

Just a fool's hope, as I have been told.

Left to its own devices, and coupled with advances in experimental particle physics derived from building a succession of ever more powerful particle accelerators (or 'atom smashers'), quantum theory has changed its shape several times in the last seventy years without changing fundamentally what it has to say about physical reality.

The English physicist Paul Dirac was the first successfully to bring together quantum theory and special relativity, discovering antimatter along the way.[1] It was recognized shortly afterwards that quantum theory had to be a theory not of particles,[2] but of the fields characteristic of the forces between particles, starting with a quantum version of the classical electromagnetic force field between two electrically charged particles, such as a positively charged proton and a negatively charged electron.[3]

A proper quantum field description yields further particles as the quanta of the fields, responsible for carrying or transmitting the electromagnetic force between the charged particles. These particles carry the 'action' of the force from one place to another, from one particle to another, thereby ensuring that such action is the result of the operation of an entirely physical mechanism and is transmitted at speeds no faster than that of light.

It was clear then that the photon is the quantum of the electromagnetic field, created and destroyed when charged particles interact. But it took very many years of extraordinary hard work to develop a

1. But Dirac's theory doesn't resolve the apparent problem of faster-than-light signalling in the collapse of the wave function.

2. For simplicity, I'm going to continue with the word 'particle' in what follows although, strictly speaking, we should always think of these as quantum wave-particles.

3. The archetypal way of thinking about force fields is to recall that experiment you did in science class when you were young. You know, the one where you sprinkle iron filings on a piece of paper held over a bar magnet. The filings quickly orient themselves along the 'lines of force' that stretch from the north to the south poles of the magnet, making visible the otherwise invisible magnetic force field.

theoretical description that could accommodate this kind of creation and destruction.

When it was finally developed, the theory known as *quantum electrodynamics* proved to be extremely accurate and precise. Witness the g-factor of the electron, a physical constant characteristic of the electron which governs its interaction with a magnetic field. Early quantum theories predicted a g-factor of exactly 2. But in quantum electrodynamics the interaction is perceived to be a little more complicated, involving the creation and destruction of so-called *virtual particles* representing an electron interacting with its own electromagnetic field.[4] Correcting for these interactions gives a g-factor for the electron of 2.00231930476, which should be compared with the experimental value of 2.00231930482. The American physicist Richard Feynman compared this level of accuracy to knowing the distance between Los Angeles and New York to within the thickness of a human hair. In essence, virtual photons that are created and destroyed in the interaction carry away some of the mass of the electron but leave its electric charge unchanged. This distortion in the ratio of the electron's charge to its mass increases its g-factor.

Electromagnetism is one of two very familiar physical forces of everyday life. The other is gravity. The first generation of particle accelerators revealed the existence of two further forces that work at the level of atomic nuclei, and are therefore not so familiar. These are the so-called strong and weak nuclear forces.

These four 'forces of nature' are characterized by their different strengths and their ranges. Gravity is by far the weakest, but extends over a vast range and helps keep your feet firmly on the ground. Electromagnetism is much stronger and works at the level of atoms. It holds atoms and molecules together and makes objects possible – you and everything around you. The weak nuclear force, revealed in a specific type of radioactivity known as beta-decay, operates inside atomic nuclei and is much weaker than the electromagnetic force but much stronger

---

4. The fact that these particles are called 'virtual' should not be taken to mean that they are not real, at least in the sense that they can't have real effects. The particles are virtual because they are very short-lived (see below), but their effects are very real, though they are also very subtle.

than gravity. Finally, the strong nuclear force is the strongest force of all. It holds atomic nuclei together and makes atoms possible.

These forces are now understood to operate between two types of fundamental particles, called *leptons*[5] and *quarks*, and are transmitted or carried by 'messenger' particles that are exchanged between them. The weak nuclear force operates between leptons and quarks and is transmitted by particles called *intermediate vector bosons*. The strong force operates between quarks and is transmitted by *gluons*.

Protons and neutrons are themselves no longer regarded as fundamental particles. They are in their turn composed of quarks. What does a quark look like? Nobody knows, for they are predicted to be permanently trapped (or 'confined') within their larger hosts. There are lots of different types of quark. A proton consists of two 'up' quarks and a 'down' quark. A neutron consists of two down quarks and an up quark. These properties up and down, and further properties called 'strange', 'charm', 'top' and 'bottom', are referred to as *flavours*.

Through the 1960s and early 1970s, the theoretical physicists Sheldon Glashow, Steven Weinberg and Abdus Salam developed a form of quantum theory which unifies the electromagnetic force and the weak nuclear force, in effect reducing these two forces to a single 'electro-weak' force. The mechanism of beta-decay involves the mutation of a down quark in a neutron into an up quark, turning a neutron into a proton. The down quark exchanges an intermediate vector boson (called a W-particle) with another particle called a neutrino, thereby turning the down quark into an up quark and the neutrino into a high-velocity electron (a beta-particle). This unified electro-weak theory is sometimes called *quantum flavourdynamics*.

Evidence for all the new particles predicted by quantum flavourdynamics was subsequently found in particle accelerator experiments. But the methods used to fuse together electromagnetism and the weak nuclear force were not without an element of sophisticated magic. Photons, the carriers of the electromagnetic force, have no mass, which is why photons are so abundant in the universe. In early

5. The family of leptons includes the familiar electron.

attempts to combine electromagnetism and the weak nuclear force, the intermediate vector bosons were also thought to have no mass, just like photons. But this implies that these particles should be as abundant as photons, whereas they clearly are not. Somehow, these intermediate vector bosons had to acquire mass from somewhere.

The theorists reached for a mechanism developed by the British physicist Peter Higgs. This mechanism envisages a universe filled with a veritable ocean of so-called Higgs particles (hinting at a modern-day aether theory). The intermediate vector bosons acquire mass by absorbing Higgs particles. Indeed, it has been suggested that all fundamental particles with mass acquire their mass this way. The essential symmetry between electromagnetism and the weak nuclear force is disguised by the fact that photons zip through the Higgs ocean as though it wasn't there, but the intermediate vector bosons wade through it as though through molasses, picking up mass on the way.

The use of this mechanism resolved the problems of quantum flavourdynamics, and made possible its triumphant predictions. But the ocean of Higgs particles remains purely hypothetical. The Large Hadron Collider is being built at CERN in Geneva in order specifically to look for evidence of Higgs particles, and should come on stream in 2007.

Quarks have a further property, called *colour*, with properties 'red', 'green' and 'blue'. The strong nuclear force is believed to be no more than a by-product of a much stronger 'colour force' that binds together different-coloured quarks and their messenger particles, called gluons. The quantum theory of coloured quarks and gluons is called *quantum chromodynamics*.

The theory of the particles and forces described by quantum chromodynamics and quantum flavourdynamics is collectively known as the 'standard model'. This theory has been enormously successful, bringing together as it does three of the four fundamental physical forces. But the standard model requires a very large number of 'fundamental' particles, totalling sixty if we include all the anti-particles as well. If we add the hypothetical Higgs particle, this makes sixty-one. The theory also requires a significant number of arbitrary constants to specify the masses of all these particles.

The standard model might have been enormously successful, but it is clearly not the end.

You will have noted that there is no room for gravity in the standard model. We might have expected to find the force of gravity operating between all particles[6] and carried by *gravitons*. We know what the properties of gravitons would have to be, but they are not found or predicted in any theoretical structure in the standard model. In order to attempt to understand the force of gravity, we have had so far to reach for a completely different theory which operates at the opposite end of the size scale.

General relativity is about the large-scale structure of planets, stars, galaxies and the universe sitting within a four-dimensional spacetime. It deals with the universe in all its vastness.[7] These structures are described by a set of complex mathematical equations known as Einstein's gravitational field equations. They are complex because the mass they consider distorts the geometry of spacetime around it and the geometry of the spacetime around it governs how the mass moves through spacetime. In fact, when Einstein first developed the field equations in 1915 he considered them too complex to solve. Yet only a year later Karl Schwarzchild had produced a solution (which he discovered whilst serving in the German army on the Russian front). Schwarzchild's solutions predicted that a particularly massive body would distort the spacetime around it so much that nothing, not even light, would escape its surface. The idea of the *black hole* was born.

The early predictions that Einstein made using general relativity are well known. The theory helped to account for a wobble in the orbit of the planet Mercury around the sun, a wobble that Newton's gravity had failed to explain. Einstein also predicted that light from a distant star passing by the sun would be bent in its path by the curvature of

---

6. Gravity would be expected to operate on all particles, not just those with mass, as mass and energy are known to be equivalent from Einstein's special theory of relativity.
7. 'Space,' as Douglas Adams wrote in *The Hitch Hiker's Guide to the Galaxy*, 'is big. Really big. You just won't believe how vastly, hugely, mindbogglingly big it is. I mean you may think it's a long way down the road to the chemist, but that's just peanuts to space.'

spacetime around the sun. Such bending of starlight was proved by observations made during a solar eclipse, and helped to make Einstein a cultural icon of the twentieth century.

Many thousands of solutions of the field equations are now known, describing many different types of hypothetical universe. Many of these solutions describe an expanding universe.[8] Einstein initially resisted the idea of an expanding universe and fudged his equations to produce static solutions. But the fact that our own universe is indeed expanding was supported by the astronomer Edwin Hubble's observations in 1929 that distant stars are all receding from us at rates that increase with their distance, much like two dots scribbled on a deflated balloon will move apart as the balloon is inflated.

If the universe is expanding today then this implies that it had an origin at some point in time in an infinitesimally small, immensely hot 'big bang'. Subsequent expansion and cooling would then give rise to the universe as we know it.

That our universe is expanding was put beyond all reasonable doubt by the accidental discovery in 1965 of the so-called *microwave background radiation*. This is literally radiation left over from the big bang, cooled by expansion to a temperature just a little under three degrees above absolute zero and appearing in the form of microwaves. More recent satellite observations of this background radiation have allowed the big-bang origin of the universe to be set about 13.7 billion years ago, give or take a couple of hundred million years.

So, we have two theories – general relativity and quantum theory in the form of the standard model of particle physics – both wonderfully productive in helping us to understand the large-scale structure of our universe and the small-scale structure of its fundamental constituents, but destined to explode whenever one is shoehorned into the other. Why is this?

One of the reasons for this difficulty concerns the uncertainty principle. From our previous discussion you might be tempted to think of the uncertainty principle in a somewhat negative light. It appears to

8. Note that in these models it is spacetime itself that is doing the expanding.

limit our perspective by preventing us from acquiring the kind of detailed knowledge of quantum objects that we might desire. There is another side to the principle, however. It became apparent during the development of quantum electrodynamics that the uncertainty principle actually allows an awful lot of things to happen that, on first sight, really shouldn't be possible.

Think of the uncertainty principle as a form of double-entry book-keeping. One version of the principle concerns uncertainty in energy and uncertainty in time interval. The less time we have to measure the energy of something the more uncertain the energy. Now turn this on its head. Energy can be created literally from nothing (credit), provided it is returned (debit) within a short time interval consistent with the uncertainty principle. The principle opens the door to chaos, to the literal creation of particles out of nothing using borrowed energy, provided these particles are destroyed and the energy given back within the time allowed. These particles are the virtual particles referred to above.

The uncertainty principle changes our perspective on 'empty' space. It is not empty at all. It is filled with virtual particles, flickering into and out of existence (the word 'seething' is often used in most descriptions of this effect). If you think this must be some kind of delusion, think again. Taking account of the interactions between an electron and a host of virtual particles is what makes quantum electrodynamics so precise in its predictions.

Furthermore, the effect of the creation and destruction of these virtual particles in empty space (the vacuum) can be demonstrated in the laboratory through something called the Casimir effect, named for the Dutch physicist Hendrik Casimir. Two closely spaced metal plates will actually be pushed closer together owing to the fact that the pressure from virtual photons in the gap between the plates no longer balances the pressure of virtual photons outside the gap. It is a small effect, to be sure, most recently measured using metal plates spaced no more than a thousandth of a millimetre apart, but it is measurable nonetheless.

General relativity is not a quantum theory. It therefore allows us to continue to think of spacetime as though this is certain, and not subject to quantum theory's characteristically probabilistic laws. In general relativity we can be certain that spacetime is 'here' or 'there' and curves this way or that way, at this rate or that rate. But what if we now apply the logic of quantum uncertainty to the very fabric of spacetime itself? We replace the perspective of a flat or gently curving spacetime with the chaos of uncertainty and quantum fluctuations. The topology of spacetime becomes twisted and tortured and riddled with bumps, lumps and tunnels – 'wormholes' connecting one part of spacetime with another. The American physicist John Wheeler, ever ready with an apt turn of phrase,[9] has referred to this as quantum or spacetime *foam*.

If this was to happen on a large scale then our lived reality would be a good deal odder than it is. There would be no guarantee that things would be found where I left them, no guarantee that tomorrow I will wake up in the early twenty-first century. The truth is that these fluctuations in spacetime occur only at extremely small distances, of the order of a millionth of a billionth of a billionth of a billionth of a centimetre (a distance called the Planck length) and in extremely small time intervals of the order of a tenth of a millionth of a trillionth of a trillionth of a trillionth of a second (called the Planck time). In fact, on these scales the very concept of distance and time interval lose their meaning. There is no distance smaller than the Planck length, no time shorter than the Planck time.

The essential 'graininess', uncertainty and indeterminism characteristic of quantum theory are completely at odds with the smooth continuity, certainty and determinism of general relativity. Put them together and all hell breaks loose.[10]

Nature, as I have said once before, is indifferent to any concerns we might have about our theories. Whilst we might find it very difficult to

9. Wheeler also coined the term 'black hole'.
10. This is only a mathematical hell, of course, reflected through the appearance of infinities where finite numbers would generally be more helpful. A modern calculator will respond to this hell by dumbly reporting the result of a calculation as 'E'. Microsoft's Excel spreadsheet software will report #DIV/o!

bring together all the forces of nature in a single theory, the simple fact is that nature manages this with ease. If we accept what general relativity has to say about the large-scale structure of our universe, then it is apparent that this universe was once very small indeed. Shortly after the big bang, the universe was of quantum dimensions and therefore subject to the vagaries of quantum dynamics, with all its graininess, uncertainty and indeterminism. Describing this early stage in the history of the universe is the task of *quantum cosmology*.

Strictly speaking, the big-bang origin of the universe was not an origin at all, since the use of this word implies a starting point at some time zero. There can be no time zero, as there is no sense in quantum theory in seeking to ascribe to something a time shorter than the Planck time. The current view is that the universe we inhabit is the result of a quantum fluctuation, literally some kind of cosmic burp, that allowed everything we see and everything we are to be created from nothing in an accident of uncertainty.

But if quantum fluctuations are happening in empty space all the time, what made this particular fluctuation so special that it led to the creation of the entire universe? Physics doesn't yet have the full answer to this question (and may never have it) but, incredible though it may seem, it has a significant part of the answer.

The fluctuation that gave rise to the universe was special in that it created conditions of high potential energy within a particular kind of quantum field called an inflaton field (a kind of Higgs field). Think of this like the poor sperm whale that is created spontaneously (and accidentally) as a result of the operation of the Infinite Improbability Drive in Douglas Adams' *The Hitch Hiker's Guide to the Galaxy*. Sadly, the whale is not created in a warm sea but at some height (and therefore with some potential energy) above the surface of the planet Magrathea. As it starts to come to terms with and ponder on the meaning of its existence, the whale's potential energy is rapidly converted to kinetic energy and it ends the only way it can, with a 'sudden wet thud'.

As the inflaton field gave up its potential energy this was converted into an incredibly powerful and *repulsive* form of gravity, pushing

A BEGINNER'S GUIDE TO REALITY

every part of space away from every other part, causing the universe to double in size every millionth of a billionth of a billionth of a billionth of a second.

Doubling always sounds a bit modest because we tend to think of everyday objects doubling in size and this seems no big deal – it doesn't stretch our imaginations sufficiently. To get a real sense of the power of doubling, think instead of a chessboard. Place two coins on the square to the top left, four coins on the square adjacent and eight coins next to that and so on and on until you have covered all sixty-four squares. How tall is the pile of coins on the sixty-fourth square? Taller than you might think. It will stretch almost to Alice on Proxima Centauri.

The inflaton field pumped so much energy into the inflation of the early universe that it mushroomed from the Planck scale to the size of a small grapefruit within an incredibly short space of time. We owe an awful lot to this field. A relatively small amount of seed energy, amplified enormously by the inflaton field, is all that is required to produce a grapefruit-sized fireball containing all the energy in the universe we see today. As the individual forces began to separate one from the other, the universe continued to expand under its own steam, moderated by the more familiar attractive force of gravity. This inflationary episode had the effect of ironing out most of the 'wrinkles' and leaving us with an essentially 'flat' spacetime.

Most, but not all. The imprint of quantum fluctuations occurring during the inflationary phase are now frozen in the microwave background radiation, resulting in tiny variations in the temperature of this radiation in different regions of space that can be predicted by inflationary cosmology and detected by satellite probes.

The agreement between theory and observation is truly astonishing. From their vantage points in earth orbit, these satellites have been able to detect the signature of quantum uncertainty in the birth of our universe, a signature written 13.7 billion years ago.

These very recent triumphs of inflationary cosmology have been derived through the application of quantum theory to the early stages of the big bang. This is the way it has worked out. Certain solutions of Einstein's gravitational field equations of general relativity allow for universes to expand. Our universe appears to be an expanding universe. This implies that at some time in the past our universe would have been hot and dense and about the size of a quantum object. General relativity can't cope with quantum objects, so theorists have borrowed concepts from the (quantum theoretical) standard model of particle physics. The results have been profoundly exciting.

But these results do not come from a fully formed theory of quantum gravity or a theory of everything. Having to deal with this patchwork quilt of theories that do not get along with each other has become intolerably frustrating. It's now time to grasp the nettle.

There are a number of different approaches to a theory of quantum gravity. Applying the rules of the quantization of energy to general relativity (an approach that Einstein himself always thought of as 'childish') leads straight into conflict, as already mentioned. But the conflict is, perhaps, deeper and more profound than the imposition of quantum 'graininess', uncertainty and indeterminism on the calm surface of the pond of general relativity. There are at least two other areas of confrontation. The first of these comes from the subject of the last chapter – quantum measurement and particularly the concept of the collapse of the wave function. The second of these is the status of *time*. Like Newton's classical physics, on scales greater than the Planck time, quantum theory itself demands a definite time in which quantum events can happen. General relativity denies this definite time.

The first area of conflict is quickly summarized. If quantum states are not determined until the quantum objects have undergone some kind of interaction, such as a measurement, then how is the quantum state of the universe determined? Just as quantum theory demands a definite time, so it also demands something 'outside' with which it can interact. But if everything there is, is in the universe, then there can be nothing outside the universe with which it can interact. There is nothing outside the universe that can collapse its wave function. Unless we want to get theological, there is no 'observer' outside the universe to make the universe real.

Quantum cosmologists have therefore felt that they have had no alternative but to reach for the many-worlds interpretation of quantum theory, as this does not require an outside agency to collapse the wave function. In fairness, this is a modified form of the many-worlds interpretation which avoids much of the schizophrenia. Instead of multiply existing versions of me, you and the rest of the world, the interpretation is reworked into one of multiple and mutually decoherent 'histories' each with a different probability.

However, whilst this interpretation resolves some of the problems associated with many worlds it brings new problems all of its own. In this interpretation there can be no 'correct' history that emerges as a result of some law of nature. The theory is obliged to treat all possible histories as equally real. Taken literally, the interpretation implies that we cannot take the existence of fossils today to conclude that dinosaurs ruled the earth a hundred million years ago. Our choice of different histories depends on what questions we want to ask.

This leaves us with a significant context-dependence, in which our ability to make sense of the theory depends on our ability to ask the 'right' questions. Rather like the vast computer Deep Thought, built to answer the ultimate question of 'life, the universe and everything' in *The Hitch Hiker's Guide to the Galaxy*, we are given the answer, but can only make sense of this if we can be more specific about the question.

Now we come to the problem of time. Quantizing gravity was found to be possible only by first unravelling the structure of the four-dimensional spacetime that had been so carefully constructed by Einstein and Minkowski. The infamous Wheeler–DeWitt equation, developed in the late 1960s, is an equation in three spatial dimensions only. Time has simply disappeared from this equation. Different solutions of the equation can be thought of as different configurations of a universe at different instants in time.

In this approach, which also goes by the name of *canonical quantum gravity*, time appears to be an illusion, the appearance of time the result of rearranging the furniture of the universe, a bit like rearranging the deckchairs on the *Titanic*. Time has become an emergent property of a spatial universe.

In a variant of this approach known as *loop quantum gravity*, both space and time are the result of weaving together fundamental quanta or 'atoms' of space itself. In this theory, the quantum states of geometry are conceptualized as 'loops', representing the solutions of the equations of quantum gravity. The theory is one of loops only, and how they 'knot, link and kink'. Space is the result of weaving together these loops to make a kind of fabric. The loops themselves are not loops in space (or in time), they are the precursors of space, forming fundamental units of area and volume the smallest of which has the dimensions of the square or cube of the Planck length. Think of these units as a kind of cosmic Lego. Every area or volume of space is constituted by an integral number of Lego bricks. Space is the relationship between loops. Time is the relationship between different configurations of the universe, different arrangements of the Lego bricks. We might even say that time is the result of our perception of change in a spatial universe.

Kant would have been impressed.

But there is more than one way to skin Schrödinger's cat. There is yet another way of looking at the fundamental incompatibility of quantum theory and general relativity. This has to do with the way that the standard model of particle physics treats particles. Even when thought of as quantum wave-particles, leptons and quarks – the fundamental particles of the standard model – appear in the quantum-theoretical equations as *point-particles*, with all their mass concentrated at a point with no dimensions. You might think that nothing would be so likely to create problems in the mathematics as infinitesimally small point-particles. You'd be right.

The 'work-around' for the point-particle problem is, however, not simply to give the particles some dimensions. It is to conceptualize the particles themselves as the result of different possible vibrational patterns in fundamental one-dimensional filaments of energy, called *string*. This would mean that there is nothing particularly 'fundamental' about the fundamental particles; they are simply the lowest-energy vibrational patterns constituting a few members of a potentially vast set. Needless to say, we can never see these strings. If they exist at all then they may exist only at the Planck scale. The strings have lengths of the order of the Planck length (but see later).

String theory may never have been more than an interesting footnote to modern physics were it not for one simple fact. Understanding the family of fundamental particles contained within the standard model as different types of vibrational pattern in pieces of string would have been simply adding a new way to catalogue them and, as such, relatively unimportant. But string theory holds the promise of predicting the masses of the particles from these vibrational patterns, something that the standard model cannot do. Most importantly, string theory predicts a particle with the properties characteristic of the graviton, the purported carrier of the gravitational force.

At the time of its discovery, this was nothing less than a revelation. Being able to reproduce the classification of known fundamental particles into families was one thing, but being able to fit gravity into the picture was something else entirely. Suddenly, string theory was both a theory of quantum gravity and a potential theory of everything.

But in physics, like in life, there is no such thing as a free lunch. String theory demands not just three dimensions of space and one of time. It demands a further six spatial dimensions, curled up so tight that we can never see them, but able to exert a strong influence on the vibrational patterns in the string and hence on the properties of the fundamental particles. And, perhaps somewhat embarrassingly, there emerged not just one variant of string theory but five, all requiring the six extra dimensions but all quite different in their treatment of the strings themselves.

Here, at least, we have a partly happy ending. The five variants of string theory have recently been subsumed into a single overarching version, called *M-theory*, which requires seven extra spatial dimensions, the seventh having been missed in the earlier versions of the theory because it is so much smaller than all the other extra dimensions. The meaning of the M in M-theory has not so far been specified.

A further revelation from M-theory is that it is not just a theory of one-dimensional strings in an eleven-dimensional spacetime. It accommodates higher-dimensional objects, called *membranes*. Two-dimensional membranes are referred to as two-branes, three-dimensional membranes as three-branes, and so on. The possible existence of three-branes had led to an intriguing way of looking at our own universe.

The strings themselves can take two forms. Open strings are strings with their ends left dangling. Closed strings are strings in which the ends are joined together to form a closed loop. Now, open strings have properties that cause them to 'stick' to a membrane. They can move quite freely anywhere on the membrane but they cannot leave it. Closed strings are not so constrained, they are free to roam anywhere at all.

The particles of the standard model that are involved in carrying forces – photons, intermediate vector bosons and gluons – are all described in M-theory by open strings. So, here's the scenario. If our universe is a gigantic three-brane, then all the particles responsible for transmitting the strong nuclear force and the electro-weak force are constrained to move within these three dimensions only.

Most importantly for the purposes of our own perceptions, light itself can only ever explore the three dimensions of the three-brane. The other seven spatial dimensions of M-theory are hidden in this scenario not necessarily because they are small, but because the particles responsible for transmitting force (for which we could read 'information') cannot explore them. For all we know, these extra dimensions are all around us, but we simply can never see them.[11]

There is an interesting exception. Gravitons are described in M-theory by closed loops. If they exist, these particles can explore all eleven dimensions. This opens up the possibility that we might one day find evidence for all the extra dimensions by careful studies of gravitation. To date, experimental studies have confirmed Newton's inverse-square law of gravitation to distances of the order of a tenth of a millimetre. The inverse-square law is the signature of three-dimensional space. So, we conclude from this that if gravity is to reveal the existence of the extra dimensions predicted by M-theory, these dimensions can be no larger than a tenth of a millimetre. This is small, for sure, but it is orders

11. Of course, there may be other three-branes involving other dimensions and hence other universes existing right alongside the one that constitutes our own universe. M-theory is not without its spooky elements.

upon orders of magnitude larger than the Planck scale. In his recent book *The Fabric of the Cosmos*, the physicist Brian Greene writes:

Only gravity can give insight into the nature of the extra dimensions, and, as of today, the extra dimensions could be as thick as a human hair and yet they'd be completely invisible to our most sophisticated instruments.

Dimensions larger than the Planck scale imply strings longer than the Planck length. This has many theoretical advantages, not least in bringing the energies (and hence the masses) of as yet unseen particles predicted by the theory within reach of the Large Hadron Collider.

M-theory is taking over as the most popular candidate for a quantum theory of gravity and a theory of everything. Many problems remain, however. For one thing, unlike loop quantum gravity, M-theory assumes the pre-existence of space and time. The strings have to be strings in space. They have to vibrate in time. The theory is said to be 'background'-dependent: space and time are assumed to be already sitting in the background and do not arise as some kind of fundamental property of the strings themselves.

As we saw, loop quantum gravity is believed to be background-independent. Space and time are the result of stitching together the quantum states of geometry. The theorists themselves are not downhearted, however. They feel confident that these theories will eventually come together in a single, fully background-independent theory.

So, where does all this leave us? Remember that we grew weary of the philosophers and turned to science for some answers concerning the reality of matter and light, of space and time. What have we got?

We have wave shadows and particle shadows. We have spooky action-at-a-distance between entangled quantum objects. We have space built from hypothetical loops in a universe without time. We have hypothetical vibrating strings in an eleven-dimensional space-time. We have a universe that might be a three-dimensional membrane in which there might be seven extra dimensions hidden in your hair. Some of these things are experimental or observational fact. Others are theoretical speculation.

So, what is real? We have to admit that we don't know.

We have reached the very bottom of the rabbit hole. But it seems we have no choice but to keep following the white rabbit:

Alice was not a bit hurt, and she jumped up on to her feet in a moment: she looked up, but it was all dark overhead: before her was another long passage, and the White Rabbit was still in sight, hurrying down it. There was not a moment to be lost: away went Alice like the wind, and was just in time to hear it say, as it turned a corner, 'Oh my ears and whiskers, how late it's getting!'

EPILOGUE

The Persistent Illusion

Reality is merely an illusion, albeit a very persistent one.
                                                    Albert Einstein

*Reality is that which, when you stop believing in it, doesn't
go away.*   Philip K. Dick

At this stage it is good to look back to where we started. We made some common-sense assumptions about what we felt reality should be like. We thought that reality should be independent of us, of our ability to conceive it and form theories about it. We also figured that reality must be logically consistent, conforming to natural laws underpinned by the concept of cause and effect. It made sense to ascribe the success of science to the simple fact that refinement of our scientific theories takes us progressively closer to the truth about reality as it really is. Finally, we acknowledged an element of trust. We accepted that reality is made up of things we can't see, such as molecules and atoms, but we also accepted that these unobservable objects really do exist and do have real effects.

We must now come to terms with the fact that there is no hard evidence for this common-sense reality to be gained from anywhere in the entire history of human thought. There is simply nothing we can point to, hang our hats on and say *this is real*.

We began by trying to make sense of the everyday reality of our social existence. We took the trouble to push beyond the hyperreality of modern consumer society, to see through the web of illusion created by our world of consumer gadgets, mega-brands and spin. According to Baudrillard, our perceived reality of existence in society is based on models, or maps, not the real world itself. We penetrated Baudrillard's postmodern critique to the institutions that underpin society itself, institutions like money, marriage, politics and war.

We learned of John Searle's theories of social reality, based on three fundamental building blocks. These are the use of physical objects to serve social functions, a system of rules that constitute social or institutional facts and the collective intentionality that makes the use of physical objects, the rules and the facts possible. Searle's theory gives us a perspective that allows us to make some sense of our social structures, and we came to the conclusion that these structures are imprinted on our minds from childhood. What makes social reality possible is the similarity of these mental impressions. Within my mind is the social reality with which I have learned to interact. Within your mind is the social reality with which you have learned to interact. My reality is not your reality. But these realities possess many common features, such that we perceive these separate realities as one.

Not surprisingly, social reality is not possible without humans with minds. We therefore turned our attention to our perceptions of the physical world. We learned of the eternal dichotomy of experience and reason. Experience tells us that all is flux. Reason tells us that change is an illusion. Perhaps what we experience is real enough but is merely a shadowy projection of the true form of reality, a reality that we can never perceive because we are chained in the prison-house of our senses. Perhaps we are really living in Descartes' dream world. If we trust only to our senses then reason tells us that our perception of colour, tastes, smells, the feel of an object and the hearing of sounds are creations of our minds and, as such, cannot be regarded to be real.

Berkeley challenged the differentiation between such secondary qualities and the primary qualities of objects, and declared that perception *is* reality. With the disappearance of this difference, we acknowledged that our perceptions might be derived from any one of a number of possible sources, such as God, an evil scientist, a belligerent machine intelligence, the operators of experience machines, a pharmacological dictatorship, the director of an elaborate reality TV show, or an ancestor simulation run by a posthuman civilization. Or, of course, our perceptions might still be derived from reality itself.

If perception and experience is really all we have to go on, then Hume says we must question the basis of our understanding of cause and effect. Kant concluded that space and time are no more than intuitions. Space becomes the mind's way of preventing everything from being in the same place. Time becomes the mind's way of preventing everything from happening at once. According to this view, without minds, space, time and cause-and-effect cease to exist.

This is a view that would appear to demand a clear boundary between mind and world and makes the world a product of our mental capacities and intuitions. There is, however, much evidence to suggest that the mind is very much a product of the world around it. Our mental backgrounds have been formed from all the experiences we have ever had, all the things we have ever been told or have ever read. The direction of our perceptual experience would appear to be firmly 'outside in', or world-to-mind, and we see that the mind cannot function without the world. That the mind is a product of the world helps in some respects but tells nothing of the relation between the product – our perceptions and experiences – and the reality that might (or might not) be responsible for it. It does not provide a defence against Descartes' demon or Kant's intuitions.

We turned, finally, to science in search of some answers. But the scientific answers look remarkably like philosophy. The Copenhagen interpretation of quantum theory tells us that we are forever imprisoned in Plato's cave, able to witness the shadowy wave-like or particle-like projections of a reality that might exist beyond our ability to perceive it, but nothing more. Like Kant's noumena, physical reality is simply beyond experience. Our measurements reveal not reality itself, but a reality exposed to our method of questioning. Quantum theory gives us a spooky action-at-a-distance between entangled quantum objects that we cannot even begin to understand.

More recent theories of quantum gravity and candidates for a theory of everything don't really help that much. They tell of a space that might be constructed from the quantum states of geometry in a universe without time. They tell of vibrating filaments of energy in an eleven-dimensional spacetime. We await the resolution of these stories with bated breath, perhaps more because there will always be some fresh insight to be gained about the nature of our universe, not necessarily because we expect our questions concerning the fundamental reality of matter, of light, of space and time to be finally answered.

We drew a blank.

Scientists tend to get uncomfortable when they are accused of philosophy. The hallmark of the young theorist in the late twentieth century was an unquestioning acceptance of the infallibility of science and the unshakeable belief that the solution, the one true theory of everything, lay just around the corner. In later life, theorists like Stephen Hawking have tended to adopt a little more humility, as the solution has remained perpetually around the corner and always just beyond reach. This is not to say that young theorists are wrong, as real breakthroughs are often made in an environment of unquestioning certainty and against the background of a dismissive attitude to everything that has gone before (I may be wrong, to quote McLuhan, but I'm never in doubt). But we have now to ask ourselves if we believe that science can ever have answers to what are basically philosophical questions.

Why do I say this? After all, the pronouncements of the physicists, whether written in research papers or popular science books, are all concerned with the fundamental nature of physical reality. Or so they say. What is often missing from these pronouncements is a statement of an assumed philosophical position. Hidden beneath their words is the *assumption* of just the kind of independent reality we have sought, and failed, to find. If it is always assumed, perhaps it is no wonder that science has been unable to prove the existence of such a reality.

I want to explain what I mean by reference to three distinctly different philosophical positions and what they have to say about reality. These are empiricism, social constructivism and scientific realism. Choosing a position will determine what you make of advances in our understanding of both social and physical reality. But, make no mistake, making no choice is to choose by default. What we choose to believe presupposes a choice of philosophical position. If we do not first make such a choice, we fall back on assumption, on intuition, on a default view of reality.

Let's start with empiricism. Remember that David Hume was a no-nonsense sceptic. As far as he was concerned, our perceptions and experiences are all we can ever know, and to speculate about things that we can never know is an exercise in pointlessness. In his book *An Inquiry Concerning Human Understanding*, published in 1748, Hume wrote:

When we run over libraries, persuaded of these principles, what havoc must we make? If we take in our hand any volume; of divinity or school metaphysics, for instance; let us ask, Does it contain any abstract reasoning concerning quantity or number? No. Does it contain any experimental reasoning concerning matter of fact and existence? No. Commit it then to the flames: for it can contain nothing but sophistry and illusion.

Hume's principal target was organized religion, but his writings are the well from which sprang the idea that there is no knowledge to be gained from metaphysics. It requires but a short step to conclude that science is the only sure way to knowledge and that science must be 'purified' by eliminating all possible metaphysical elements from it. This is not unlike eliminating the pagan elements from Aristotle's philosophy in order to make it an acceptable foundation for Catholic theology.

This road led to a philosophical position known as *positivism*. In the positivist tradition, serious scientific inquiry does not concern itself with a search for ultimate causes that might derive from outside the framework of science (such as reality, or God). These are questions that science clearly cannot find answers for. Science must confine itself instead to the study of relations existing between facts which are directly accessible to experiment or observation. Science must deal with the empirical facts, and not concern itself with meaningless metaphysics, with sophistry and illusion.

The late nineteenth-century Austrian physicist Ernst Mach was an early adopter. For Mach, the purpose of science is to find the most economical way of summarizing experience. Science is therefore about making a catalogue of experiences and finding relationships between these experiences, a bit like collecting and cataloguing stamps. Scientific laws are precisely these economical summaries, and have no meaning beyond their ability to relate the results of one kind of observation or experiment to another. There is simply no purpose to be served by seeking to describe a reality beyond our immediate senses. Instead, our judgement should be guided by our ability to verify the predictions of a scientific theory (does the theory agree with our experimental results or observations?) and the simplicity of the theory (is it the simplest theory that will agree with our experimental results or observations?).

The positivist doctrine is utilitarian. It can be crudely described as a doctrine of 'seeing is believing'. If we can't perceive it with our own senses (if we can't directly experience it), we have no reason to believe it. If our theories invoke concepts or objects that are not in themselves directly observable (and hence empirically verifiable), then we have no grounds whatsoever for investing belief in the existence of these concepts or objects.

This merciless attitude to the elimination of metaphysics from scientific thinking led Mach to reject the concepts of absolute space and absolute time, and to deny the reality of atoms.[1] The application of such a view today might lead us to reject as meaningless everything that has been said about fundamental particles such as leptons and quarks, the quantum states of geometry, strings and eleven-dimensional spacetime.

Mach's views were enormously influential in the development of a new school of thought that emerged among scientifically minded philosophers in Vienna in the early 1920s, under the guidance of the Austrian philosopher Moritz Schlick. The so-called Vienna Circle extended this positivist outlook through the use of mathematical logic. The foundations of their philosophy, which is sometimes known as *logical positivism*, was logical analysis, a strict criterion of verifiability and an unforgiving attitude to metaphysics. Scientific theories became

1. Remember that Mach's denial of the reality of atoms came at a time when atoms were purely hypothetical objects. Today we have far more evidence for the existence of atoms.

mere instruments for making connections between observations or the results of experiments in the most economical way possible. Reality became an entirely empirical reality – a reality manifested as effects that we can directly perceive, experience and so verify, with any attempt to push beyond this to some kind of independent reality dismissed as meaningless non-science.

Here, then, lies our first choice. We can rationalize reality as purely empirical and give up any attempt to look beyond this. What we see is very much what we get, and there's nothing more to it than that. We can recognize strong shades of positivism in the Copenhagen interpretation of quantum theory, in its pronouncement that what we see in terms of the wave shadows and the particle shadows is all there is, and it's pointless to speculate about what might cause these shadows to appear the way they do. Bohr and (particularly) Heisenberg were very well aware of the implications of the Copenhagen interpretation for philosophy. For two years Schlick corresponded with and sought direction from Heisenberg on the Copenhagen interpretation's implications for causality and the philosophy of knowledge.

Before you commit to a decision, it is important to finish this particular story. Logical positivism came to dominate the philosophy of science in the middle of the twentieth century, but it was eventually discredited. First, the criterion of verifiability was shown to be highly problematic and it became transparently obvious that it is virtually impossible to eliminate metaphysical statements from science. Even pure observations or experiments require a theoretical framework, not only to enable interpretation but in order for the observations or experiments to be carried out in the first place. These frameworks often carry the kinds of concepts or objects that positivists would wish to dismiss as meaningless. Without the idea of an electron, for example, it is virtually impossible to conceive and perform experiments in electricity.

The Vienna Circle had made much of the use of the mathematical structure of symbolic logic, but in 1931 the Austrian mathematician Kurt Gödel demonstrated that any formal system of logic allows the possibility of constructing propositions that cannot be proved by reference to the rules or axioms of the system. Such propositions are said to be formally undecidable. This is Gödel's famous 'incompleteness theorem', which demonstrates that it is impossible to establish the internal logical consistency of a large class of systems, including elementary arithmetic.

The failure of the logical positivist programme led to a more ameliorative attitude to metaphysics, leading the philosopher A. J. Ayer, the Vienna Circle's British spokesman, to observe that the metaphysician 'is treated no longer as a criminal but as a patient'.

Despite these failures, the empiricist tradition is still very much alive and well, albeit in a more dilute form. Modern empiricism retains the negative attitude towards metaphysics and denies that scientific theories develop towards a literally true representation of some independent reality. The purpose of science is rather to give us theories that are empirically adequate or acceptable for the task of relating facts one to another. We should accept as true what theories have to say about those things that we can see for ourselves. But we should not believe that unobservable objects are real and that the theories themselves are literally true.

Stephen Hawking is a self-declared positivist.

For as long as we as human beings have been able to communicate, we have told each other stories. Many of these stories have been concerned with where we have come from, the nature of the world around us and the purpose of our lives; some have attempted to help reconcile us with our own sense of mortality. Many of these stories have become myths, and tell of legends. These stories are clearly socio-cultural constructions, developed to fill a basic human emotional need by creating a sense of identity, belonging and morality as well as an explanation of origins and of purpose. From our Western scientific cultural perspective, we tend to regard these stories as quaint superstitions, not to be taken literally. So, the story of the three life-supporting plants that sprouted from the body of the Sky Woman's daughter reflects the importance of the gift of agriculture to the Iroquois Indians of Northeastern America, not the true origin of these plants in nature.

But what if the concepts and objects of our Western scientific theories are also just parts of one great socially constructed story? We might seek to avoid much discomfort (and angry debate) by acknowledging that a story that talks of genetics and evolution might provide a more reliable explanation of the origins of plants than the story of the Sky Woman's daughter, and so avoid the pitfalls of cultural relativism. But we would still be left with the challenge that says that our theoretical descriptions, their interpretation and their acceptance as 'the truth' may be no more than conventions, constructed by the community of people engaged in science in any particular generation.

This philosophical position generally goes by the name *social constructivism*. This is a position famously associated with the American historian and philosopher Thomas Kuhn, and his book *The Structure of Scientific Revolutions*.[2] In this book Kuhn differentiates between two types or modes of scientific activity. According to Kuhn, 'normal' science is the everyday puzzle-solving that scientists undertake within the framework of concepts, descriptions, meanings and interpretations that constitute the prevalent body of scientific knowledge. This is the body of knowledge that science students are taught. What's more, they are taught to accept this knowledge as the 'truth', usually without question.

I don't want to make this sound particularly conspiratorial or Machiavellian. Science makes progress only by building on foundations already laid, by scientists able to stand on the shoulders of giants. Science cannot progress if every generation of scientists has to start by re-inventing or proving again what supposedly already passes for a body of factual knowledge.

Kuhn called this framework a *paradigm*. He used this word in at least two different senses. One of these is sociological: the paradigm represents the entire approach to puzzle-solving and the belief and value-systems of the community of scientists, their 'world view'. The other sense is exemplary – the paradigm is *the* observation, experiment or model that defines the rules and shapes the scientists' approach to puzzle-solving within the boundaries of normal science.

2. Kuhn's book is also famous for its ability to be interpreted in many different ways, usually to suit the purposes of the reader. What follows is a cartoon simplification of a complex argument, and I don't wish to suggest that this is necessarily the interpretation Kuhn intended (though it is a common one).

In contrast to normal science, 'revolutionary' science occurs when an accumulation of data throws increasing doubt on the veracity of the existing paradigm. The result may be a crisis in science, precipitating the replacement of one paradigm with another. The existing paradigm is replaced not because it is necessarily falsified by the evidence, or indeed because the replacement paradigm is verified. A paradigm-shift occurs because a sufficient number within the community of scientists become persuaded that the new paradigm is so much better than the old. This process is no less than a socio-cultural revolution and, as such, is often characterized by bitter argument as the community breaks into rival factions.[3] Kuhn saw parallels with political revolution. He wrote:

In both political and scientific development the sense of malfunction that can lead to crisis is prerequisite to revolution. Furthermore, though it admittedly strains the metaphor, that parallelism [between political and scientific revolutions] holds not only for the major paradigm changes, like those attributable to Copernicus and Lavoisier, but also for the far smaller ones associated with the assimilation of a new sort of phenomenon . . .

We are still living in the aftermath of one of the most significant scientific revolutions, the one begun by Planck in 1900 which led to the development of quantum theory.

What of reality? According to the social constructivist position, physical reality is whatever we make of it at whatever moment we have reached in the historical development of scientific understanding. This should not be taken to imply that reality can be whatever we want it to be. Our scientific theories tell of concepts and objects that are as real as anything can be. Electrons and quarks and the quantum states of geometry and eleven-dimensional spacetime can be as real as money, or marriage, or politics, or war.

This doesn't mean that there is no difference between social reality

3. Kuhn wrote that when this happens, individuals in the communities behave as though they occupy different (social) worlds. Even though they may use the same language, many of the words in this language have taken on quite different meanings in these different worlds. The worlds are *incommensurable*. The worlds no longer have any common measures by which they can be unambiguously compared.

and physical reality. A large fraction of society may reject the social institution of marriage, or religion, or the legitimacy of a particular political party or its leadership. These individuals in society will point to reasons that they consider sufficient to justify their position. Marriage is an outdated concept, religion is incapable of adapting to the needs of people in modern society, the political party is fundamentally corrupt and self-serving.

However, no matter what individuals in society choose to believe about physical reality, certain aspects of that reality cannot be rejected in the same way. I might not believe in religion but it's pointless not believing in the force of gravity. What can change is the way scientists attempt to understand reality in terms of concepts lying beneath the physical appearances. Gravity is a brute empirical fact, but theories of gravity are social constructions. Provided I can develop suitable reasons, I am perfectly at liberty to reject any scientific theory.

As for science taking us progressively closer to some kind of ultimate truth about reality as it really is, Kuhn argued that paradigm-shifts do not promote any real evolution of theories towards some final truth. For example, he saw progression in the theories of Aristotle through Newton to Einstein, but only as instruments for puzzle-solving in normal science. In terms of what their theories actually had to say about reality, he found Einstein's general theory of relativity closer to Aristotle than either of them is to Newton.

This is our second choice.

We turn, now, to our third and final choice. This choice is, in fact, right back where we started.[4] Belief in a physical reality independent of the human mind, a reality independent of anybody's ability to conceive it or form theories about it, is a perfectly legitimate philosophical position called *scientific realism*. We can go further. It is perfectly legitimate to claim that reality is logically consistent, conforming to natural laws underpinned by the concept of cause and effect. It is legitimate to

4. You might be concerned that here, on p. 238, we appear to have come full circle. You shouldn't feel cheated, however. If you take reality for granted without understanding why you believe in it, then you are what philosophers call a 'naive realist'. Having made it this far, you are no longer naive.

claim that refinement of our scientific theories takes us progressively closer to the truth about reality as it really is, and that reality is made up of things we can't see, and that these unobservable objects really do exist and do have real effects.

Where is the justification for this position? There is none. At least, there is no justification that will satisfy a scientist demanding a body of hard evidence, though there may be arguments that might be convincing to a philosopher. You can either choose to believe in such an independent reality or you can reject it in favour of an empirical or socially constructed reality. The justification that can be given for realism demands an appeal to nothing less than an act of faith or, as Einstein put it, to a 'trust in the rational character of reality and in its being accessible, to some extent, to human reason'. Scientific realism is justified because it is the most natural position – the default assumption – of most working scientists.

The philosopher Ian Hacking tells the story of a friend who described to him the details of some experiments he was working on. The friend was trying to obtain evidence for the fractional electric charges characteristic of quarks. The experiment was a modern equivalent of the classic oil-drop experiment, in which the magnitude of the charge of an electron can be determined by trapping charged oil drops between balanced gravitational and electromagnetic fields. In this case the oil drops were replaced by balls of niobium cooled to extremely low temperatures. Hacking, in his book *Representing and Intervening*, asked how his friend changed the charge on the niobium ball:

'Well at that stage,' said my friend, 'we spray it with positrons to increase the charge or with electrons to decrease the charge.' From that day forth I've been a scientific realist. *So far as I'm concerned, if you can spray them then they are real.*

Scientific realism is justified as the position most likely to produce advances in scientific understanding. Is the Copenhagen interpretation really the last word on our ability to make sense of reality at the quantum level? Should we accept that in this interpretation we have reached the end of the road? Can we ever really expect to arrive at the one true theory of everything?

We may indeed have reached the end of the road, the one true theory of everything forever beyond our grasp. But how can we ever be sure? What if we've missed something? Can we really afford not to push science down apparently 'meaningless' paths in our search for an elusive reality? What if there is something more to discover about reality if only we have the wit to ask the right questions? Whatever our personal thoughts on this matter, we might be prepared to admit that it goes against the grain of human nature not to try.

I, for one, believe that we are a long, long way from the end of science. I believe that there is much more to be discovered about the nature of our reality and I believe that the best way to gain new knowledge is to assume that this reality exists independently of our minds and our measurements. Challenge me to defend this assumption and you may find me wanting, for I can do nothing more than declare my faith in the existence of an independently real world.

As Trinity tells Neo: '. . . you've been down there, Neo. You already know that road. You know exactly where it ends.'

We are at the end of our road, at the bottom of the rabbit hole. What you do next is up to you. If you look carefully you can just see the white rabbit turn a corner. You can resign yourself to the fact that you will never catch the elusive creature or, like Alice, you can set off like the wind in pursuit. You have a choice.

Where are you right now? What is real? How do you know? The answers are here, but to understand them you must first choose what to believe.

Bibliography and Filmography

BOOKS

Adams, Douglas, *The Hitch Hiker's Guide to the Galaxy*, Pan, 1979. Based on the original BBC radio play, this remains a marvellous comic novel and a refreshing antidote to an overindulgence of philosophy.

Baggott, Jim, *Beyond Measure: Modern Physics, Philosophy and the Meaning of Quantum Theory*, Oxford University Press, 2004. The definitive guide to the history and philosophy of quantum theory. Covers recent experiments and surveys alternative interpretations.

Barbour, Julian, *The End of Time*, Phoenix, 1999. Powerful arguments from a contemporary physicist that time is an illusion.

Baudrillard, Jean, *Simulacra and Simulation*, trans. Sheila Faria Glaser, University of Michigan Press, 1994. Baudrillard's original postmodern essays and the inspiration for one sub-text of the film *The Matrix*.

Beller, Mara, *Quantum Dialogue*, University of Chicago Press, 1999. An historical and philosophical exploration of the emergence of the Copenhagen interpretation. For science and philosophy students.

Butler, Rex, *Jean Baudrillard: The Defence of the Real*, Sage Publications, 1999. An interpretation of Baudrillard's work, in case you can't follow the original . . .

Chalmers, David J. (ed.), *The Philosophy of Mind*, Oxford University Press, 2002. An anthology of some of the most important original contributions to the philosophy of mind, from Descartes to Putnam. For philosophy students.

Clark, Michael, *Paradoxes from A to Z*, Routledge, 2002. An excellent little compendium of all the philosophical conundrums, including the prisoner's dilemma, Zeno's paradoxes, and much more.

Cushing, James T., *Quantum Mechanics: Historical Contingency and the Copenhagen Hegemony*, University of Chicago Press, 1994. Arguments about how things might have turned out differently for the de Broglie–Bohm pilot wave theory. For science and philosophy students.

Davies, Glyn, *A History of Money*, 3rd edition, University of Wales Press, 2002. It's a rich man's world.

Davies, P. C. W. and Brown, J. R. (eds.), *The Ghost in the Atom*, Cambridge University Press, 1986. Based on a series of radio interviews with leading quantum physicists, including Alain Aspect, John Bell, John Wheeler, Rudolf Peierls, David Deutsch, John Taylor, David Bohm and Basil Hiley.

Feynman, Richard P., *QED: The Strange Theory of Light and Matter*, Penguin, 1985. The development of quantum electrodynamics, told by one who was there at the time.

Fotion, Nick, *John Searle*, Acumen, 2000. An interpretation of John Searle's philosophy. Aimed at professional philosophers.

Gaarder, Jostein, *Sophie's World*, Phoenix, 1995. A history of Western philosophy dressed as fiction. A deserved bestseller.

Gamow, George, *Thirty Years That Shook Physics*, Dover, 1966. A highly entertaining and idiosyncratic telling of the historical development of quantum theory.

Gardner, Martin (ed.), *The Annotated Alice* by Lewis Carroll, Penguin, 1965. Follow the white rabbit. Not just a kid's story . . .

Gardner, Sebastian, *Kant and the Critique of Pure Reason*, Routledge, 1999. One of the few interpretations of Kant that makes his philosophy accessible to the uninitiated.

Gillies, Donald, *Philosophy of Science in the Twentieth Century*, Blackwell, 1993. One of my favourite guides to the philosophy of science.

Greene, Brian, *The Fabric of the Cosmos: Space, Time and the Texture of Reality*, Penguin, 2004. Virtually everything you might ever want to know about relativity, quantum theory, string theory, and more.

Gribbin, John, *Q is for Quantum: Particle Physics from A to Z*, Weidenfeld & Nicolson, 1998. A reference book from one of the best of the science popularizers. If it's not in here, it's probably not worth knowing.

Haber, Karen (ed.), *Exploring the Matrix*, Byron Preiss Visual Publications, 2003. More takes on the themes of the *Matrix* from science fiction writers.

Hacking, Ian, *Representing and Intervening*, Cambridge University Press, 1983. A defence of scientific realism. For students and professional scientists and philosophers.

Heil, John, *Philosophy of Mind*, Routledge, 1998. A comprehensive introduction to the philosophy of mind, for philosophy students.

Heisenberg, Werner, *Physics and Philosophy*, Penguin, 1989. A classic survey of the philosophical implications of quantum theory and relativity from one who passed through the eye of the storm.

Irwin, William (ed.), *The Matrix and Philosophy*, Open Court, 2002. One of a series of books in which contemporary philosophers use popular culture to explore philosophical issues. Previous titles include *Seinfeld and Philosophy* and *The Simpsons and Philosophy*. Future titles will explore *Buffy the Vampire Slayer*, *The Lord of the Rings* and *Woody Allen*. I can't wait.

Jammer, Max, *The Philosophy of Quantum Mechanics*, Wiley, 1974. A definitive study and the book that really got me started on this subject. Definitely for professional scientists and philosophers, however.

Kennedy, J. B., *Space, Time and Einstein*, Acumen, 2003. An excellent and very readable overview of the philosophical problems posed by space, time and Einstein's relativity.

Koepsell, David and Moss, Laurence S., *John Searle's Ideas about Social Reality*, Blackwell, 2003. An anthology of articles from the *American Journal of Economics and Sociology* full of challenges and embellishments to John Searle's theory of social reality. For professional philosophers.

Koestler, Arthur, *The Sleepwalkers*, Penguin, 1964. Still one of the best explorations of the historical development of classical cosmology.

Kuhn, Thomas S., *The Structure of Scientific Revolutions*. 2nd edition, University of Chicago Press, 1970. Rightly hailed as a landmark in intellectual history, Kuhn's book succeeded in overturning the view that science progresses by a series of small, inexorable and cumulative steps towards some objective truth. For philosophy professionals, although the book has been read widely outside this discipline.

Lane, Richard J., *Jean Baudrillard*, Routledge, 2000. Another interpretation of Baudrillard, should you need one . . .

Lawrence, Matt, *Like a Splinter in Your Mind*, Blackwell, 2004. Explores the philosophy behind the entire *Matrix* trilogy.

Lem, Stanislaw, *The Futurological Congress*, Harcourt Brace, English trans., 1974. Best known for another work of science fiction, *Solaris*, Lem here explores a pharmacologically created reality that is prescient of our modern Prozac culture.

Morgan, Michael, *The Space between Our Ears*, Weidenfeld & Nicolson, 2003. A popular presentation of current theories of cognitive science, explaining how our brains interpret what we see.

Nozick, Robert, *Anarchy, State and Utopia*, Blackwell Publishing, 1974. Arguments in favour of limiting the power of the State. The experience machine appears in Chapter 6.

Omnès, Roland, *Quantum Philosophy: Understanding and Interpreting Contemporary Science*, Princeton University Press, 1999. A fascinating survey for a more general audience.

Putnam, Hilary, *Reason, Truth and History*, Cambridge University Press, 1981. An exploration of the nature of truth, knowledge and rationality. Chapter 1 is entitled 'Brains in a vat'. For professional philosophers.

Rae, Alastair, *Quantum Physics: Illusion or Reality?*, Cambridge University Press, 1986. An excellent short summary of the implications for reality of the Copenhagen interpretation of quantum theory. Intermediate in level of exposition between this book and my other book *Beyond Measure*.

Rose, Stephen, *The Making of Memory*, Bantam, 1992. The chemical basis of memory and how memories are created.

—, *The 21st-Century Brain*, Jonathan Cape, 2005. A marvellous exploration of the evolution of our brains, from the beginnings of life to modern consumer society, and from a single fertilized egg to a mature adult.

Rowlands, Mark, *Externalism*, Acumen, 2003. A wonderfully clear defence of externalism. For students and professional philosophers.

—, *The Philosopher at the End of the Universe*, Random House, 2003. A delightful survey of the main themes of philosophy as explored by modern 'sci-phi' blockbuster movies, including *Aliens*, *Blade Runner*, *Frankenstein*, *Hollow Man*, *Independence Day*, *Minority Report*, *Star Wars*, *Terminator I* and *II*, *The Matrix*, *The Sixth Day*, and *Total Recall*.

Schacht, Richard, *Classical Modern Philosophers*, Routledge, 1984. An excellent overview of the philosophies of all the major figures from the classical period, from Descartes to Kant.

Searle, John R., *The Construction of Social Reality*, Penguin, 1995. Searle's original summary of his theory of social reality. Extremely clear and well argued.

—, *Intentionality*, Cambridge University Press, 1983. Searle's philosophy of mind and theories of intentionality. For professional philosophers.

Smolin, Lee, *Three Roads to Quantum Gravity*, Phoenix, 2000. An accessible overview of recent attempts to find a theory of quantum gravity.

Stroud, Barry, *The Quest for Reality: Subjectivism and the Metaphysics of Colour*, Oxford University Press, 2000. A contemporary account of the search for reality in the perception of colour. For professional philosophers.

Swain, Harriet (ed.), *Big Questions in Science*, Vintage, 2003. Contains brief but illuminating chapters on the origin of the universe, time, consciousness, thoughts and dreams.

Van Fraassen, Bas C., *The Scientific Image*, Oxford University Press, 1980. A contemporary defence of empiricism. For professional philosophers.

Wachowski, Larry and Andy, *The Matrix: The Shooting Script*. Newmarket Press, 2001. Includes bits that didn't make the final edit. With a foreword by William Gibson and scene notes by Phil Oosterhouse (associate producer for the sequels).

Weatherford, Jack, *The History of Money*, Three Rivers Press, 1997. But it still makes the world go round . . .

Yeffeth, Glenn (ed.), *Taking the Red Pill*, Summersdale, 2003. Highly readable survey of the themes of *The Matrix*, from a mix of science fiction writers, inventors, presidential advisers and professors of economics, English, media studies, philosophy, psychology and religion. Who said it was just a movie?

FILMS

Cube 2: Hypercube (2002). Directed by Andrzej Sekula, story by Sean Hood and screenplay by Sean Hood, Ernie Barbarash and Lauren McLaughlin. Welcome to the new dimension in fear. The first quantum physics horror movie, to my knowledge.

Dark City (1998). Directed by Alex Proyas, story by Alex Proyas, screenplay by Alex Proyas, Lem Dobbs and David S. Goyer. A world where the night never ends. Where man has no past. And humanity has no future. A dark tale of identity crisis in a reality controlled by mysterious 'strangers'.

eXistenZ (1999). Written and directed by David Cronenberg. Where does reality stop . . . and the game begin? A leading game designer tests her new virtual reality game.

Fight Club (1999). Directed by David Fincher, screenplay by Jim Uhls based on the book by Chuck Palahniuk. Mischief. Mayhem. Soap. Not about reality as such, but about the mind's ability to create false realities.

Ghost (1990). Directed by Jerry Zucker, written by Bruce Joel Rubin. Before Sam was murdered he told Molly he'd love and protect her forever. In part an interesting meditation on the mind–body problem.

Identity (2003). Directed by James Mangold, written by Michael Cooney. The secret lies within. Another one about mentally created reality.

Matrix, The (1999). Written and directed by Andy and Larry Wachowski. Reality is a thing of the past. The mother of all reality movies. Followed in 2003 by *The Matrix Reloaded* and *The Matrix Revolutions*. The sequels didn't quite manage to live up to the expectation generated by the original, but remain thought-provoking action movies in their own right.

Memento (2000). Directed by Christopher Nolan, written by Christopher and James Nolan. Some memories are best forgotten. A vivid illustration of externalism and the art of tattooing.

Minority Report (2002). Directed by Steven Spielberg, screenplay by Scott Frank and Jon Cohen based on a Philip K. Dick short story. What would you do if you were accused of a murder you had not committed . . . yet? Notable for its futurology, including experience machines.

One, The (2001). Directed by James Wong, written by Glen Morgan and James Wong. Stealing the power of the universes one by one. Or (alternatively) at home in the multiverse.

Sixth Sense, The (1999). Written and directed by M. Night Shyamalan. I see dead people. A false reality created by a mind that doesn't yet know its body is dead.

Strange Days (1995). Directed by Kathryn Bigelow, story by James Cameron, screenplay by James Cameron and Jay Cocks. An extreme taste of reality. Set in the last days of 1999, the film explores the illicit trade in recorded memories.

Terminator, The (1984). Directed by James Cameron, screenplay by James Cameron, Gale Anne Hurd, Harlan Ellison and William Wisher, Jr. Your future is in his hands. A different take on the mind–body problem. Further elaborated with a meditation on fate and free will in *Terminator 2: Judgment Day* (1991) and *Terminator 3: Rise of the Machines* (2003).

They Live (1988). Directed by John Carpenter, screenplay by John Carpenter based on a short story by Ray Nelson. You see them on the street. You watch them on TV. You think they're people just like you. You're wrong. Dead wrong. The opposite of rose-tinted spectacles reveals a reality in which the minds of humans are controlled by aliens through the medium of advertising.

Thirteenth Floor, The (1999). Directed by Josef Rusnak, adapted by Rusnak from the book *Simulacron-3* by Daniel Galouye. Question reality: you can go there even though it doesn't exist. An exploration of ancestor simulations (inside ancestor simulations).

Truman Show, The (1998). Directed by Peter Weir, written by Andrew Niccol. The story of a lifetime. The town of Seahaven is not what it seems.

Index

PENGUIN SCIENCE

THE BLANK SLATE STEVEN PINKER

'The best book on human nature that I or anyone else will ever read. Truly magnificent' Matt Ridley, *Sunday Telegraph*

'A passionate defence of the enduring power of human nature … both life-affirming and deeply satisfying' Tim Lott, *Daily Telegraph*

'Brilliant … enjoyable, informative, clear, humane' *New Scientist*

'If you think the nature/nurture debate has been resolved, you are wrong. It is about to be reignited with a vengeance … this book is required reading' *Literary Review*

'Startling … Pinker makes his main argument persuasively and with great verve … This is a breath of air for a topic that has been politicized for too long' *Economist*

HOW THE MIND WORKS STEVEN PINKER

'Why do memories fade? Why do we lose our tempers? Why do fools fall in love? Pinker's objective in this erudite account is to explore the nature and history of the human mind' *Sunday Times*

'Witty popular science that you enjoy reading for the writing as well as for the science' *The New York Review of Books*

THE LANGUAGE INSTINCT STEVEN PINKER

'A marvellously readable book…illuminates every facet of human language: its biological origin, its uniqueness to humanity, its acquisition by children, its grammatical structure, the production and perception of speech, the pathology of language disorders and its unstoppable evolution' *Nature*

'An extremely valuable book, informative and well written' Noam Chomsky

'Brilliant … Pinker describes every aspect of language, from the resolution of ambiguity to the way speech evolved … he expounds difficult ideas with clarity, wit and polish' Stuart Sutherland, *Observer*

PENGUIN SCIENCE

SCIENCE: A HISTORY JOHN GRIBBIN

'Brilliant … So many scientists here come alive!' Roy Porter

Filled with pioneers, visionaries, eccentrics and madmen – from Galileo to Marie Curie to Feynman and beyond, this book is an enthralling story of the men and women who changed the way we see the world.

'Essential reading' John Cornwell, *Sunday Times*, Books of the Year

'A magnificent history… enormously entertaining' *Daily Telegraph*

'We experience his subjects' triumphs and failures as if we knew them personally … I found myself whizzing through the pages' *Sunday Telegraph*

'Gripping and entertaining … Wonderfully and pleasurably accessible' *Independent on Sunday*

STARDUST JOHN GRIBBIN

Every one of us is made of stardust. Everything we see, touch, breathe and smell, is the by-product of stars as they live and then die in spectacular explosions, scattering material across the universe which is recycled to become part of us. Taking us on an enthralling journey, John Gribbin shows us the scientific breakthroughs in the quest for our origins among the stars.

'[An] incredible story … Gribbin takes us through the life history of the universe … gives a sense of the almost unbelievable coincidence of physical laws and circumstances that resulted in your being able to read these words today' *Literary Review*

'Gribbin is an expert science writer and this book is as good as any he has written. Beautifully conceived and highly readable' *Independent*

'The book's pace never slackens, and the quest for clues doesn't falter … Gribbin skilfully and engagingly traces the historical sequence … rather like Sherlock Holmes reading clues' David Hughes, *New Scientist*

PENGUIN SCIENCE

FREEDOM EVOLVES
DANIEL C. DENNETT

'If anyone can claim to be the Leonardo of the New Renaissance, Dennett can'
Sunday Times

'This is a serious book with a brilliant message' Matt Ridley, *Sunday Telegraph*

'Dennett has produced the most powerful and ingenious attempt at reconciling
Darwinism with the belief in human freedom to date' John Gray, *Independent*

'An outstandingly good book. There is no better philosophical exponent of what
evolutionary biology really means' *The Times*

DARWIN'S DANGEROUS IDEA
DANIEL C. DENNETT

In one of the finest explanations of the nature and implications of Darwinian
evolution ever written, Dennett moves skilfully from a firm foundation in biology
to possible applications for the theory in engineering and cultural evolution,
presenting an unsurpassed analysis of the objections to evolutionary theory along
the way. Extremely lucid, wonderfully written, and scientifically and
philosophically impeccable.

'Dennett's dangerous idea: to use his gift for lucid explanation and his twinkling
wit to cure the strange allergy to Darwin in modern intellectual life. It is essential
– and pleasurable – reading for any thinking person' Steven Pinker

'If you want an exciting, wide-ranging romp through great ideas, read this book.
Daniel Dennett proves fully worthy of Charles Darwin' Jared Diamond

PENGUIN SCIENCE

THE ORIGIN OF LIFE PAUL DAVIES

Paul Davies presents evidence that life began billions of years ago, arguing that it may well have started on Mars and spread to Earth in rocks blasted off the Red Planet by asteroid impacts. This solution to the riddle of life's origin has sweeping implications for the nature of the universe and our place within it, and opens the way to a radical rethinking of where we came from.

'The best science writer on either side of the Atlantic' *Washington Times*

THE BLIND WATCHMAKER RICHARD DAWKINS

Science is how we know what we are, where we are and why we are. The title of this work refers to the Rev. William Paley's 1802 work, *Natural Theology*, which argued that just as finding a watch would lead you to conclude that a watchmaker must exist, so the complexity of living organisms proves that a Creator exists. Not so, says Dawkins: 'The only watchmaker in nature is the blind forces of physics, deployed in a very special way…it is the blind watchmaker.'

'Mr. Dawkins succeeds admirably in showing how natural selection allows biologists to dispense with such notions as purpose and design, and he does so in a manner readily intelligible to the modern reader' *The New York Times*

UNWEAVING THE RAINBOW RICHARD DAWKINS

Why do poets and artists so often disparage science in their work? Why does so much scientific literature compare poorly with, say, the phone book? Richard Dawkins has taken a wide-ranging view of the subjects of meaning and beauty in this examination of science, mysticism and human nature.

'The product of a beguiling and fascinating mind and one generous enough to attempt to include all willing readers in its brilliantly informed enthusiasm' Melvyn Bragg, *Observer*

PENGUIN SCIENCE

SOME TIME WITH FEYNMAN
LEONARD MLODINOW

In Mlodinow's intimate portrait of Feynman we look into his unfolding thoughts on the nature of creativity, his rivalry with colleague Murray Gell-Mann, his love for the women in his life, and the cancer that would ultimately kill him.

The result is a fascinating picture of an irreverent, charismatic and startlingly honest man, who believed in taking risks and breaking rules and who did research not from ambition, but for the thrill of discovery.

'An accessible picture of a brilliant man' Stephen Hawking

'A warm, delightful glimpse into a fascinating world' *Scotland on Sunday*

SIX EASY PIECES
RICHARD P. FEYNMAN

Drawn from Richard Feynman's celebrated and landmark text 'Lecture on Physics', this collection of essays reveals Feynman's distinctive style while introducing the essentials of physics to the general reader.

'A delightful volume – it serves as both a primer on physics for non-scientists and as a primer on Feynman himself ' Paul Davies

THE ORIGINS OF VIRTUE
MATT RIDLEY

'Are we driven by a profoundly selfish, determinist impulse? Or is there an escape clause that enables us to be genuinely unselfish and good? In an era in which biological science is challenging traditional ethics, he has raised the debate to a new level of seriousness and importance' *Sunday Times*

'A brilliant, lucid insight into the profound implications of modern biological thinking' Bryan Appleyard